18.00

Dependency and
Poverty

Dependency and Poverty

Old Problems in a New World

June Axinn
University of Pennsylvania

Mark J. Stern
University of Pennsylvania

Lexington Books
D.C. Heath and Company/Lexington, Massachusetts/Toronto

Library of Congress Cataloging-in-Publication Data

Axinn, June.
    Dependency and poverty.

    Includes bibliographies and index.
    1. Poor—United States. 2. Social security—United
States. 3. Public welfare—United States. I. Stern,
Mark J.   II. Title.
HC110.P6A93   1988   362.5'0973   88-8966
ISBN 0-669-14630-7 (alk. paper)
ISBN 0-669-14631-5 (pbk. : alk. paper)

Published simultaneously in Canada
Printed in the United States of America
Casebound International Standard Book Number: 0-669-14630-7
Paperbound International Standard Book Number: 0-669-14631-5
Library of Congress Catalog Card Number: 88-8966

The paper used in this publication meets the minimum requirements of American National
Standard for Information Sciences—Permanence of Paper for Printed Library Materials, ANSI
Z39.48-1984. ∞™
88 89 90 91 92 8 7 6 5 4 3 2 1

For Sidney and Susan

Contents

Tables

Preface

T his book grew out of our concern about the growing split that has developed between the social problems that the United States is facing in the late twentieth century and the organization of social welfare provision that developed a half century ago. The spread of hunger, homelessness, and poverty that has been seen in the United States during the past decade is particularly disturbing in light of the growth of this nation's aggregate wealth and productive capacity and the apparent increase in the amount of its spending on social welfare.

Although many of the social problems of the 1980s can be attributed to shifts in the commitment of the federal government, we believe that their source is more fundamental. The basic organization of U.S. economic and social life has been transformed in the past several decades. We need to undertake a thorough examination of how social welfare programs can respond to the new needs and new problems that these changes have created. This book is a contribution to that effort.

Dean Michael Austin of the University of Pennsylvania School of Social Work stimulated our systematic interest in this topic and provided both advice and criticism at the beginning of the project. We want to express our thanks to him. Many colleagues at the University of Pennsylvania have provided useful insights and criticism of our work: Fred Block, Stanley Brody, Jerry Jacobs, Michael Katz, Janice Madden, Ira Rosenwaike, and Steve Taber. Theda Skocpol shared her comments of an early draft of chapter 4 with us and helped to sharpen the argument. We want to thank David Willis, editor of the *Milbank Memorial Fund Quarterly,* for his encouragement and for permission to use material from the journal. A portion of chapter 7 originally appeared in *Human Services at Risk* (Lexington Books, 1984), edited by Felice Perlmutter. We want to thank her for her suggestions and firm editorial hand.

This project was funded in part by grants from the University of Pennsylvania Research Foundation and the Philadelphia Corporation for Aging. The University's Program for the Advancement and Revitalization of the Social Sciences, funded by the Mellon Foundation, also provided support. The School of Social Work provided clerical assistance. The data used in this book were made available in part by the Inter-university Consortium for Political and Social Research. The data for the *Current Population Survey: Annual Demographic Files* for 1974, 1983, and 1986 were originally collected by the U.S. Department of Commerce, Bureau of the Census. Neither the Census Bureau or the Consortium, of course, bear any responsibility for the analyses or interpretations presented here.

We are particularly indebted to our students at the School of Social Work, who have listened to early versions of practically every argument in this book. Their questions, suggestions, and criticisms were of major assistance in the development of our thinking. In particular, Nancy Floom and Kevin Grigsby provided research assistance.

Most of all, we want to acknowledge Susan Seifert and Sidney Axinn who—when all is said and done—provided the real support for this project.

1
Introduction:
The Troubled Welfare State

T he 1980s have been a decade of crisis and concern for the welfare
state. In all the major Western nations, social and economic planning
have come under attack.[1] Battered by stagflation, declining economic
performance, and rising social conflict, a number of the western democracies
turned against social welfare spending as a strategy for improving the plight
of their citizens. Although the most dramatic example of this turn of events
was the rise of Thatcherism in the United Kingdom, the attack on the welfare
state was a broadly popular movement among many of the advanced
industrial economies.

In the United States this attack is less surprising than those in Western
Europe. The United States has always been viewed as an "incomplete"
welfare state." It developed its major national social insurance programs well
after those in many European nations, and some elements of the textbook
welfare state—most notably national health protection and children's
allowances—have totally escaped the United States. Finally, unlike Western
Europe and Canada, the United States never developed a social democratic
movement to serve as protector of the welfare state.[2]

As in other nations, the attacks on social welfare have come in many
forms. Some have claimed that the problem is fundamental to western
society, while others see it as a mere transitional problem brought on by the
overly rapid expansion of programs during the 1970s.[3] The critiques of
welfare have come from all areas of the political spectrum, with some
political bedfellows often proposing contradictory explanations of the problem. For example, Martin Anderson, President Reagan's first domestic policy
advisor, and David Stockman, former director of the Office of Management
and the Budget, declared that the War on Poverty had been won and that
poverty had become simply a statistical artifact.[4] At the same time, Charles
Murray, in a widely read (and widely criticized) study, declared that the
structure of welfare had rendered the poor worse off than they had been
before the Great Society.[5]

Given criticism of social welfare's range and depth during the early eighties, the situation in 1987 is surprising. Tax and government spending reductions still attract their share of political rhetoric, but social concerns are moving closer to center stage once more. In a recent poll, almost six times as many people thought the United States was spending too little on programs for the poor as thought it was spending too much; the ratio was even higher for Social Security.[6] Welfare reform has emerged as one of the major domestic policy priorities for the White House and the Congress. Finally, with the return of Democratic control of the Senate, Congress has taken the lead on a variety of social welfare issues, including public assistance, health protection, and the minimum wage.

Under the veneer of normality, however, the social politics of the late 1980s remain hard to predict. On the one hand, politics has moved back to the center in the past several years, but there remains little taste for substantial increases in social spending above the automatic increases brought by entitlement programs and cost-of-living adjustments. At the same time, yesterday's social problems are still with us and new ones have been added. Homelessness, hunger, and unemployment have brought increasing misery to millions and have gained public attention.

The Problem Defined

Dependency and poverty have once again been recognized as major problems in the United States; public concern about these social problems has increased at a time when politicians are demanding that a solution be found to the "welfare mess." The statistical reality of increased poverty is visible to all. In 1985, 14 percent of the population—more than 33 million people—were counted as poor by the official U.S. definition. Although this was lower than the recession high of 15.3 percent, it was undeniably higher than the 11 percent nadir that had been reached in the early 1970s.[7]

A nation that just two decades ago believed it was on the verge of winning a war against want is now faced with poverty and its consequences: hunger, malnutrition, ill health, homelessness, and illiteracy. Whereas earlier the United States faced these problems with confidence, today it no longer feels sure either of the inevitability of its economic success or that it possesses the knowledge and ability to combat these ills. Today, unlike in the 1960s, faith in the United States' inevitable international economic success has been shaken. Old economic responses to poverty, like old technology, are suspect.

The United States has a continuous series of official poverty data going back to 1959. Almost 40 million people—over 22 percent of the population—were estimated to fall below the poverty threshold in that and the next several years. With economic growth and the expansion of government social welfare programs, the number of needy people in U.S. society decreased throughout the 1960s, reached a plateau during the 1970s, and then began to climb in the 1980s.

Not all groups within the population had the same poverty experience. Some have fared much worse than the average would suggest. Poverty rates for children, for example, have increased during the 1980s at twice the rate for the entire population. The poverty rate for the aged as a group has decreased steadily, but women over the age of seventy-five remain highly vulnerable. The poverty risk of female-headed families—38 percent in 1985—has attracted much attention. It is worth noting, however, that while this is an extraordinarily high rate, it has not changed significantly over the past decade. By contrast, the rate among two-parent families actually has risen by 15 percent. Along similar lines, the poverty rate of black Americans remains almost three times that of whites, but has stayed fairly constant, while the white poverty rate rose 18 percent. And so it goes. Poverty has been and continues to be etched deeply into the age, race, and gender, and family structures of the United States.

Although public concern about poverty and dependency has increased, the revival of professional interest in these topics is only beginning. Recently, both public and professional attention has focused on the relationship of poverty to racial discrimination, to the growth of female-headed households, to lack of educational opportunity, and to technological changes.[8] These are all important, but the components of change in today's society that are reshaping the contours of affluence and need must be isolated.

Four major changes have rocked the welfare state: the population has aged; the stable two-parent family is no longer predominant; the postindustrial service economy has replaced the blue-collar work world; and the political foundation of the U.S. welfare state—the New Deal coalition—has been shaken. At the same time, the combination of inflation and economic stagnation have sapped Americans' traditional confidence in and support for social welfare programs.

Indeed, these profound changes have led to a paradox: although poverty has increased since the mid-1970s, social welfare spending also has increased. Because the welfare state has failed to adjust to changes in demography, family, and work, social expenditures appear not to work. It may very well be that the declining political support for social welfare of the 1970s was a reaction to this apparent "inefficiency" of social spending.

The growth of spending is undeniable. Government has spent what—by historical standards—are huge sums of money to alleviate want. In 1960 total expenditure—federal, state, and local—on social welfare was $52.3 billion. By 1984 government outlays exceeded $672 billion, a nominal increase of 1,100 percent. If inflation and population growth are taken into account, much of this increase disappears. Still, the real expenditure per person increased from $1,016 to $2,835 using 1984 dollars, an increase of 279 percent. Looked at another way, health, welfare, and education absorbed 10.3 percent of the gross national product in 1960; by 1984 over 18 percent of the GNP was devoted to social welfare.[9]

For the past half century, spending for social welfare has risen steadily in the United States. For the first thirty-five years, it was related to a steady and dramatic decline in poverty. Since 1970, however, the relationship between social spending and poverty has broken down. We are faced with a contradiction: the more we spend, the larger the poverty gap.

Table 1–1 highlights the situation. From 1975 to 1980 welfare spending increased by $144 billion, about 70 percent, while the poverty gap—the total income necessary to bring all poor people to the poverty threshold—increased by 20 percent. Correcting both figures for inflation, between 1960 and 1965, it cost about $2 to reduce the poverty gap by $1; during the next five years the rate jumped to $3.91 and then rose to $12.10 and $7.04 for 1970–74 and 1975–79. It became more expensive to reduce the poverty gap by a dollar.

During the 1980s the trend became even more worrisome. An increase of $180 billion in welfare expenditure was associated with a rise of almost $4 billion in the poverty gap. In the 1960s investing in social welfare appeared to be a shrewd investment; by the 1980s it appeared to be a slot machine; we kept feeding the one-armed bandit, but there never was a payoff.

This depressing fact has led some observers to press for a cut in social spending. The advocates of a reduced role for government joined hands politically with those who favored reduced taxes to stimulate the economy.

Table 1–1
Governmental Social Welfare Expenditures and the Poverty Gap
1960–1984
(billions of current and constant 1967 dollars)

Fiscal Year	Poverty Gap		Welfare Expenditures	
	Current	*Constant*	*Current*	*Constant*
1960	$35.3	$39.8	$ 52.3	$ 59.0
1965	26.8	28.4	77.2	81.7
1970	20.0	17.2	145.9	125.5
1975	20.4	12.7	290.1	180.0
1980	24.4	9.9	492.8	199.7
1981	27.4	10.1	550.3	202.0
1982	31.4	10.9	594.8	205.7
1983	33.2	11.1	642.1	215.2
1984	33.3	10.1	672.0	216.0

Source: Calculated from U.S. Department of Health and Human Services, Social Security Administration, *Social Security Bulletin* (Washington, D.C.: Government Printing Office), November, 1981, Vol. 44, Number 1; December 1984, Vol. 47, Number 12; *Orsip Note*, No. 1, January 1987.

The erosion of workers' (and taxpayers') income made budget cutting and especially budget cutting of social programs politically attractive. It provided at least a superficial plausibility to the belief that problems could not be solved by "throwing money at them."

By the late 1970s the War on Poverty had become the war on the poor. Some, among them Charles Murray, have argued that increased welfare expenditures were actually the cause of the increased poverty; not only did welfare do no good, but it did positive harm by hurting initiative, increasing helplessness, and encouraging laziness and dependence on the public purse.[10]

The changing political and economic winds of the past seven years have redirected the debate over welfare. Although the Reagan administration continued to enjoy widespread popularity, public opinion began to shift toward a concern for those excluded from the recent U.S. economic recovery. To counter this trend, the president proposed a new initiative on welfare reform in his 1986 State of the Union address. His internal study led to few recommendations, but it sparked a number of reports and studies by others concerned about Aid to Families with Dependent Children and other welfare programs.

In rapid succession the American Public Welfare Association (representing public administrators), a task force appointed by New York governor Mario Cuomo, and the bipartisan Project on the Welfare of Families, issued reports.[11] These were followed by a major report and lobbying effort by the National Governors' Association, with Bill Clinton of Arkansas and Michael Dukakis of Massachusetts taking the lead in publicizing the report. In the Senate, both Ted Kennedy, new chairman of the Labor and Human Resources Committee, and Daniel Moynihan, head of the Finance subcommittee on Social Security and Family Policy, began promoting welfare reform and family policy legislation. Although differences remained, in 1987 a new consensus had emerged. Welfare should be reformed with a simplified program structure. The "able-bodied" (including women with small children) should be required or encouraged to work. Training, educational, and transportation opportunities should be increased. Taken together, these in time would lead to the disappearance of need; welfare would "wither away."

Despite the enormous energy that has been expended on the issue, however, the analytical framework of welfare reformers has remained surprisingly unsophisticated. Welfare recipients have been seen—by both liberals and conservatives—as an "underclass" of poor women and men, who are either unwilling or unable to take advantage of the promise of American life. The new welfare reform movement shared with the War on Poverty the belief that "solving" the problem of poverty could be cut off from a larger examination of U.S. society. The number of poor, black female-headed households living in poverty may have increased, reformers seemed to be saying, but this had no connection to broader trends among whites and blacks, among men and women, and among those working, unemployed, or out of the workforce.

This book argues that this blindered view of welfare reform is fundamentally wrong. The recent increase in poverty and dependence is not tied to the growth of an underclass. Rather, the spread of poverty is a result of broad forces that are central to the organization of U.S. society: the work changed, the length of lives has increased, the number of children we have has decreased, and domestic arrangements have become more turbulent. These forces do not affect just a few million illiterate, unmotivated, young black women; they affect us all. Unless the nature of these changes and their implications for U.S. society are questioned, we will be unable to understand the depth of the problem and the difficulty of its solution.

The welfare state is not concerned simply with poverty but with the risks of dependency for the entire population. The current welfare debate is difficult to grasp because it isolates the poor from the rest of the population, an intellectual tendency with a long pedigree.[12] Much of the current growth in poverty, however, is the result of the narrowing split between the poor and the "normal" population. The "middle-class" mother of three who leaves her abusive husband is likely to be one of the poor, as is the blue-collar worker whose factory closes down and leaves him without job prospects, the young worker who is disabled in an accident and cannot find work, and the elderly woman who survives her husband and then must live on one-half of his Social Security check.

The reasons for the increase in poverty stem in part from the ways Americans live their lives in the 1980s. They also are related to the neglect that the social welfare system endured during the late 1970s and 1980s. Even if nothing had changed in U.S. society since 1976, it would be facing rising poverty. Women on welfare are a case in point. The earnings of female householders have risen sharply, thanks in part to their rising labor participation rate, yet this economic progress among low-income women has been wiped out by declines in public assistance. Female householders are doing more to help themselves, but government neglect has taken away more than they gain on their own.

Finally, the challenges of the new economy have not been met. The new industrial order—computerized, internationally interdependent, and constantly innovative—will no longer provide the lifetime jobs that many workers have come to expect. U.S. social welfare programs will have to adjust to new turbulence in the labor market, increased periods of unemployment, and training needs of those with redundant skills. These are all problems that the current welfare system has not addressed.

This book begins with a survey of the major social changes that the United States is experiencing: an aging population, changing families, and the transformation of work. Particular attention is paid to the contrasts between the risks of the old industrial social order and those of the new postindustrial world.

In a philosophical and historical examination of dependency, chapter 3 discusses changes in how dependency has been conceptualized and how different definitions lead to different conclusions about growth in the past and the future. This is followed by a historical study of the two largest dependent groups—children and the aged—and how the family and economic forces have created a striking paradox: the emergence of the child-centered family has been paralleled by the rise in child poverty.

From history and philosophy, we move to an examination of current trends in poverty and dependency. First, we examine trends in pretransfer and posttransfer income and its relationship to family and work. Then, in chapter 6, comes an examination of the new risks that blacks and women are encountering in American society and the problems that these risks pose for the welfare state. We argue that the gap between women and blacks, on the one hand, and white men, on the other, is closing. The decline is occurring not through a process of leveling up (bringing blacks and women up to the income and opportunity level of white men) but because the advantages formerly enjoyed by white men are eroding.

We next turn to the politics of social welfare. We examine the development of the welfare state from 1935 to the 1970s and assess those forces that led to its political troubles. The focus then shifts to the Social Security crisis of the 1970s and 1980s as a case study of how the reaction against the welfare state first gained steam and then played itself out. We conclude that the retreat of the past decade will be reversed; the question of where to cut social welfare budgets will be replaced during the 1990s by where to grow.

This leads, finally, to our conclusion, where we assess the fit between current social welfare programs and the emerging postindustrial social order. We recommend a direction for reforms in a number of program areas—Social Security, unemployment insurance, public assistance, and job training—and discuss some strategies that might be used to pursue these reforms.

Notes

1. See, for example, Ramesh Mishra, *The Welfare State in Crisis: Social Thought and Social Change* (New York: St. Martin's Press, 1984), xiii.

2. Harold L. Wilensky and Charles N. Lebeaux, *Industrial Society and Social Welfare* (New York: Russell Sage Foundation, 1958).

3. Albert O. Hirschman, "The Welfare State in Trouble: Systematic Crisis or Growing Pains?," *American Economic Review* (May 1980): 113–16.

4. Martin Anderson, *Welfare: The Political Economy of Welfare Reform in the United States* (Stanford, Calif.: Hoover Institution, 1978); David A. Stockman, *The*

Triumph of Politics: The Inside Story of the Reagan Revolution (New York: Harper & Row, 1985).

5. Charles Murray, *Losing Ground: American Social Policy 1950–1980* (New York: Basic Books, 1984).

6. *The Washington Post National Weekly Edition,* 8 June 1987, 38. According to the poll, 63 percent of the respondents thought we should spend more, 11 percent thought we should spend less, and 21 percent thought we were spending the right amount (5 percent had no opinion). For Social Security, the figures were 63 percent, 5 percent, and 27 percent, respectively. The programs that were most viewed as underfunded were taking care of the homeless (68 percent), education (66 percent), and Social Security, programs for the poor, and health (63 percent). The most commonly viewed as overfunded programs were foreign aid (71 percent), the military (48 percent), and space exploration (42 percent).

7. U.S. Bureau of the Census, *Money Income and Poverty Status of Families and Persons in the United States: 1985,* Current Population Reports, Series P-60, No. 152 (Washington, D.C.: Government Printing Office, 1986), and *Characteristics of the Population below the Poverty Level: 1984* (Washington, D.C.: Government Printing Office, 1986). All poverty data are derived from these sources unless noted otherwise.

8. National Urban League, *The State of Black America 1987* (New York: National Urban League, 1987); Harrell R. Rodgers, Jr. *Poor Women, Poor Families* (Armonk, N.Y.: M. E. Sharpe, 1986); Children's Defense Fund, *A Children's Defense Fund Budget* (Washington, D.C.: CDF, 1985); Ruth Sidel, *Women and Children Last* (New York: Viking Penguin, 1986).

9. U.S. Department of Health and Human Services, *ORSIP:* 2 (January 1987).

10. Murray, *Losing Ground.*

11. "Fixing Welfare," *Time* (16 February 1987): 10–13.

12. Michael Katz, *In the Shadow of the Poorhouse: A Social History of Welfare in America* (New York: Basic Books, 1986).

2
The Coming of Postindustrial Society

T he notion that there is a necessary tie between the welfare state and industrialization is an intellectual commonplace. In this view, the welfare state is one of a series of responses to the excesses of early capitalism. The spread of the franchise, rising standards of living, the development of the labor movement, and the spread of social welfare programs are all ways in which the forces of capitalism and democracy were brought into balance.[1]

Much of this story is political—the use of democratic politics to constrain the market economy—but economic and social developments also contribute to the emergence of social welfare. Later industrialization solves some earlier problems but at the same time creates new ones. Harold Wilensky and Charles Lebeaux, for example, note that

> In shifting from the "early" impact of industrialization to the more recent, much . . . [seems] contradictory of what has gone before. That is as it should be. Business domination and militantly ineffective labor protest, the polar ization of social classes (with poverty and insecurity at the bottom, where peasants make the painful adjustment to the machine and the new family system it imposes)—against this picture must be put another, perhaps more rosy one. . . .
>
> Along with the dilution and obsolescence of skills, which continue to present problems, go a massive development of new occupations and new skills and a general upgrading of the skill level of all. These changes in specialization are accompanied by a redistribution of income and important changes in stratification. Changing technology and increased specialization continue to push the big organizations to the center of the stage. Labor protest, if allowed to express itself, becomes regularized and ordered. All these developments . . . are reflected in family life.[2]

Wilensky and Lebeaux identify five elements of later industrialization that affect the structure of the welfare state: (1) the upgrading of the skills of the population; (2) the redistribution of income and the creation of a less polarized society; (3) the increasing organizational centralization; (4) the regularization of labor protest; and (5) the changing nature of family life. It is these developments that set the agenda of social welfare.

The last of these factors is particularly important. For Wilensky and Lebeaux, social change leads to the "emergence of new, perhaps more stable patterns of family life." Writing in 1958, they saw "new patterns . . . linked . . . to the rapid shift of population to the suburbs, which will in time bring greater stability to family life and may even lower the divorce rate."[3]

The purpose here is not to evaluate this interpretation but to argue that—from the perspective of 1987—the situation in society, work, and family is radically different. Most of the trends that Wilensky and Lebeaux saw in the 1950s are no longer present. Where they saw the upgrading of skills, many now see de-skilling. Where they saw income redistribution, there is now increased inequality. Where they viewed technology leading to increased centralization, today's more permissive technology allows greater decentralization of organization. Where they saw the spread of regularized labor-management relations, there is now a massive decline in unionization. Finally, where they saw increased stabilization of family form, today the family is experiencing increasing strain and breakup. It is these trends in postindustrial society that set the agenda for the postindustrial welfare state.

This chapter looks at the general shakeup of work and the family, beginning with a social trend that has remained the same since the 1950s—the increasing number of aged persons in U.S. society.

Population Shifts and the Graying of America

The United States is a society with a rising percentage of older people in its population—a "graying" society. In 1935 when the Social Security Act was enacted, those age sixty-five and over constituted just over 6 percent of the population. By 1950 this proportion had increased to 8.1 percent and then to 11 percent by 1980. In 1985 it was almost 12 percent—one in every nine persons. This is only the beginning: because of the baby boom generation, by 2030 23 percent of the population will be over age sixty-five. This pattern is the product of the declining birth rate of the past three decades and the declining death rate, particularly among those over age sixty-five.

The shifts in population aging that shape economic need, however, are even more complex. Life expectancy is not the same for men and women. A male born in 1930 could expect to live, on average, 58.0 years; a female, 61.3 years. By 1980, a male could look forward to a life of 69.9 years; a female, one of 77.5 years.[4] Looked at another way, male life expectancy increased by

21 percent during that half century, and female life expectancy increased by over 26 percent.

Moreover, the source of increasing life expectancy shifted during this period. During the early period a major contributor to increasing life expectancy was declining infant mortality. In recent years, the infant death rate has continued to edge downward, but the bulk of the increase has been the result of the aged living longer.

The overall predominance of women is not uniform throughout the life cycle. For the first thirty years of life, there are more men than women. There is a balance at age thirty and then slowly, in midlife the balance shifts. In older age, the greater life expectancy of women takes precedence. By age eighty-five, for example, there are about two and a half as many women in the population as men. These broad trends have a number of implications:

1. Not only does the United States have more elderly persons to support, but the old are older. Between 1930 and 1980 the population as a whole increased by 84 percent. The aged population meanwhile grew 280 percent. Within this category, the young old (age sixty-five to seventy-four) increased by 230 percent, the middle old (age seventy-five to eighty-four) by 370 percent, and the old old (over eighty-five) by 720 percent.

2. The gap between female and male life expectancy continues to grow. In 1930 it was only 3.3 years; in 1950 it was 5.5 years. In 1980, it was up to 7.6 years—that is, women, on average, live 7.6 years longer than men. Much of this gap maintains itself through adulthood. Thus, at age fifty, the average male could expect to live 25.7 more years, while the average female had a life expectancy of 31.2 years. Thus, whereas at birth the gap between men and women was about 10 percent, by age fifty it was over 20 percent.[5] Even if this gap gets no larger, we must look forward to an increasing number of single women at economic risk in old age.

3. The problem of familial care for the aging is no longer just a question of the support offered by children in midlife to their aging parents. Increasingly, the children of the old will also be well beyond their highest earning years. Because of physical and economic limitations, they will be less able to assume full caretaker responsibilities.

4. Older people now must plan for longer periods of retirement than ever before. This includes the potential for at least some years of disability.

The population shifts that have occurred since the Society Security Act became effective mean that, compared to 1930, we now have proportionately more elderly people—especially women—and fewer youths to support. The fertility rate began to fall in the United States by the mid–nineteenth century.[6]

As the percentage of population that was young declined, the percentage that was old increased. In 1900 there were 6.6 aged persons and 55.8 children and youths for every 100 adults between the ages of eighteen and sixty-four, leading to a *dependency ratio* of 62.4.[7] By 1933 this figure had fallen to 55.6—a combination of the aged dependency ratio of 9.1 and the youth ratio of 46.5. Because of the Depression the aged could not support themselves through employment, nor could midlife adults continue to support their parents.

Federal policy explicitly recognized that workers could not afford to continue to carry the major costs of supporting both the young and the old. By 1940, when the dependency ratio had reached its low of 50.7 per hundred the policy of governmental support for the aging and private familial support as the major support for children and youth had been clearly established.[8]

Since 1940 the number of aged drawing on public programs has risen steadily, reflecting the continued prolongation of life. The youth dependency ratio was more volatile during the period. The total dependency ratio moved up with the baby boom to a high of 71.6 in 1960, but by 1983 it was down again, close to 1940 levels.[9]

According to current estimates, the total dependency ratio should hold steady until the turn of the century, then rise through 2025 as the baby boom generation ages. The rise in the aging population will be partially offset by the regular decline in the youth dependency ratio. Thus, although the total dependency ratio will rise, it is not expected to reach its 1960 level unless an unforeseen baby boom occurs in the twenty-first century.[10]

More important, perhaps, the composition of that population will have changed significantly from past periods. The fastest-growing part—women over age seventy-five—is extremely vulnerable. They have fewer personal and familial resources, fewer public entitlements and private pensions, and greater demands for health and social services than the "young old."

On a macroeconomic level, it is likely that the society as a whole can look forward to a manageable age-dependent population, a point that will be explored in greater detail in the next two chapters. Although the aged consume more public resources than children, if private resources are considered, they may be less expensive to support. The shift in composition makes it hard to forecast the total costs of support for the dependent population.[11]

The demands on the U.S. retirement system and health insurance system for the aged—Old-Age Insurance, Supplemental Security Income, and Medicare—may be far more extensive in the future than was originally foreseen. It seems clear that the adequacy of the fit between current programs and demographic realities needs to be reviewed, yet the data suggests that although planning is needed, there is no inevitable crisis.

One element of planning uncertainty is how medical technology affects demography. Disability to some extent has replaced death at every age level, creating a larger class of medical dependents. Compared to the dependent populations of the past and present, that of the future will be composed of fewer children, more elderly, and more handicapped persons.

In the past social programs have been designed to be both individual support systems and effective market support mechanisms. Current programs must be evaluated from these perspectives, too, to keep pace with the demographic changes that have occurred in the past fifty years and with an eyes to those that are foreseen for the next twenty-five- or fifty-year period.

The Changing Family

The two-generation nuclear family has been the typical domestic structure throughout modern Western history. Over the past century, the centrality of the nuclear family and an elaborate ideology of parenting has, if anything, strengthened. Legal and political realities followed social practice in defining the two-generation family as the legal unit of economic responsibility.

When the Social Security Act was passed in 1935 and the public sector took on the role of ultimate support for the older generation, the moral and economic pressure of parental provision for minor children increased. Now, more than ever before, parents were expected to be able to provide for their minor children. The poorest families and their children were caught. Public financial aid became available to both groups, but from the inception of the Social Security Act, children with parents received dramatically lower grants than did the aging—with or without adult children.[12]

The age inequities of public programs were compounded by gender discrimination. The model family of social welfare programs had a wage-earning father and a homemaker mother. The further the family moved from this norm, the less equitable and adequate public programs have been as supplements to the market economy and family transfers.

The American family has experienced sharp changes since the 1930s. Three of the most critical of these are the change in women's work patterns, the impact of marital disruption, and the distribution of child responsibilities.

1. The Rise in Women's Labor Force Participation

The labor force participation rate for women has risen sharply in the past fifty years. Only 27 percent of American women worked outside their homes in 1940; 55 percent do today. All groups of women, however classified, have participated in this change: all races, all age groups, all varieties of marital status, women with all ages of children. Married women, living with their husbands, and with children under age six were responsible for most of the gain. Looked at another way, the number of children in the population is down by 1.2 million since 1980; nonetheless, the number of children with mothers in the labor force has risen by 2.5 million.[13] Most of these women are working full time, although many are employed in low-paying jobs with little in the way of fringe benefits either to help care for their young children or to provide adequate retirement income.

2. Changes in Family Forms

In the past thirty-five years the changes in the structure of the American family have become visible to all. Falling birthrates, rising divorce rates, separations, and desertions, as well as an increasing number of out-of-wedlock births are indicative of changing family norms. In 1950 almost 80 percent of American homes were headed by a married couple; in 1985 only 58 percent were. Furthermore, in 1950 less than 10 percent of families were headed by women; by 1985 more than 16 percent of families were female headed. Additionally, the number of nonfamily households—unmarried couples and other unrelated individuals living together—has risen, as has the number of people living alone.

By the late 1980s the typical American family—mom, dad, and the kids—was a misnomer; it applied to less than 40 percent of American families. The reasons for this shift are complex. Between 1970 and 1980 the number of elderly women living alone, for example, grew by 63 percent, while the number of young adults living alone nearly tripled, as did the number of unmarried couples. The two biggest causes of these shifts, however, were changes in marriage and divorce.

Over most of this century, the percentage of the population ever married rose, and the age at marriage fell. After 1970, however, both of these trends were reversed. For example, between 1970 and 1984, the proportion of thirty- to thirty-four-year-olds who had never married increased for men from 9 to 21 percent and for women from 6 to 13 percent, while the average age at first marriage rose by about two years for both men and women.[14] More adults were either waiting longer to marry or not marrying at all.

At the same time, divorce became more common. The divorce rate grew from 2.5 per thousand in 1965 to over 5 per thousand during the 1980s. Remarriage rates remained high, but this did not prevent the proportion of the population that was divorced from increasing to 6 and 8 percent, respectively, for men and women.

Finally, as the number of unmarried women increased, the number of children they bore also rose. In 1970 fewer than 400,000 children were born to unmarried women (one in thirteen births); by 1984 there were 770,411 (over one in five). This was not simply a matter of teenage pregnancies; the proportion of out-of-wedlock children born to women under nineteen years of age declined from 50 percent in 1970 to 35 percent in 1984. Although the raw number of teen pregnancies increased, it was part of a general trend among unmarried women of all ages to have children.

The result of fewer marriages, increasing unwed birthrates, and more divorces was the growth of female-headed families. Between 1970 and 1985, the proportion of families that were female-headed increased by 54 percent among blacks and by 42 percent among whites.

For children the impact of these changes has been particularly severe; the shifts have meant a startling increase in the number of children living with just one parent—23 percent in 1985. For the black and Hispanic populations, the trend belies the assumptions of a "normal family" even more obviously. In 1985 only 40 percent of black children and 68 percent of Hispanic children were living with both parents.[15]

Ninety percent of single parents are women, many of whom are the sole support of their children. It is estimated that after divorce fewer than half of all children receive support from their fathers. For children born out of wedlock the figures are even lower. Fathers are disappearing as economic supports for an ever-increasing proportion of children.[16]

The combination of the change in family structure and the change in family work roles has meant a decrease in the effectiveness of social programs, which are based on a market wages system. Absent parents do not pay child support. Female householders have worked more, but this has not led to adequate income. As single-parent families have become more numerous, financial responsibility for children has been distributed among fewer adults. Overall, the past several decades have seen the substitution of female earnings for male earnings in the support of children.

Neither the market economy nor the welfare system has been able to provide a "family wage" for these families. The result has been the pauperization of women and children. In 1985, among female-headed families, 45 percent of white children, 67 percent of black children, and 72 percent of Hispanic children lived below the poverty line.

3. The Distribution of Children in the Population

The responsibility for the raising of children is distributed unequally throughout the population. Over the years, the average size of the U.S. household has declined from 3.37 in 1950 to 3.14 in 1970, to 2.69 in 1985. This sharp drop, almost 15 percent in as many years, reflects in part, the increase in single households and the decision of many young people to postpone marriage. The decision to have children is often delayed and in some cases foregone. Thus, between 1960 and 1970 the percentage of families with no minor children remained stable at between 43 and 44 percent, but by 1985 half of American families had no current child-rearing responsibilities. In 1960, 80 percent of the population supported 60 percent of the children. By 1985, 80 percent of children were supported by only 30 percent of the population.[17]

These results are even more extreme if racial distribution is also considered. Although the birth rates of both blacks and whites have fallen since 1960, the rate among whites has fallen farther and is substantially lower than the black rate (14.5 and 20.8 per thousand population in 1985). Thirty-three percent of the black population was under age eighteen in 1985, compared to only 25 percent of the white population. Because black family incomes remain only 60 percent of the average for the entire population, a disproportionately large share of the responsibility for childrearing is being carried by a group with far fewer resources.

The three shifts in the family—women's work patterns, family structure, and the distribution of responsibility for children—have placed America's children at risk. This is clear from trends in official income and poverty data. The child poverty rate in 1985 was 22 percent. It was lower if one included as income the value of inkind transfers, higher if the formula for calculating the poverty threshold is adjusted to reflect the increased importance of nonfood items in the budget, or if a relative threshold is used.[18] By any definition, the poverty of children is up despite the increased labor force effort of mothers of children of all agres.

The Restructured Workplace

Although changes in demography and family life have been important, the most significant changes in postindustrial society have been in the workplace. Since 1970 the economy has failed to live up to expectations. The underlying problems became apparent during the 1970s when the U.S. economy, like those of most Western societies, labored under extraordinary conditions. Slow growth, recession, jolts in international commodity prices, and the upward drift of both inflation and unemployment characterized the decade. After the recession of the early 1980s, inflation was brought under control, but high budget deficits were added to continuing slow growth and stubbornly high unemployment. Taken together, these macroeconomic conditions contributed to the increasing inequality and poverty on which this study focuses.

The changes can be traced in part to a basic shift in the structure of the U.S. productive system. Whereas previously economic growth was synonymous with the expansion of manufacturing, today the service economy is the major source of growth. The changes in the job opportunity structure facing Americans—regardless of age, gender, or race—are changing the nature of economic need and the effectiveness of the welfare programs of the past. The existing welfare state—appropriate as it was for industrial society—needs to be evaluated in light of the new problems presented by the emerging service society.

The current U.S. welfare state is a response to industrial society. It had its origins in early industrialization when the growth of a wage-earning class caused widespread dislocation, and it matured during late industrialization when new technologies promised rising living standards and a new level of stability to the majority of the population. The threat to that promise posed by the Great Depression triggered the basic social welfare legislation of 1935 and the creation of the U.S. welfare system.

Five characteristics of the current economic situation are relevant to the revised welfare state. The most far-reaching and obvious is the displacement of manufacturing by service industries. In addition, technological change has affected the organization of the labor force, management philosophy has changed, unions have declined, and dislocation has affected unemployment, poverty, and inequality.

The Rise of the Service Sector

The hallmark of postindustrialization has been the shift from goods production to service production. In 1950 the ratio of goods to services in the United States' gross national product (GNP) was over two to one, by 1986 it was one to one. Within this, the fall in the relative position of manufacturing, a labor-intensive sector of goods production, was particularly notable. Twenty-nine percent of gross national product originated in manufacturing in 1950, but only 20 percent did so in 1985. It is hardly surprising that whereas 60 percent of the Harvard Business School class of 1956 started in manufacturing on graduation, thirty years later, almost 60 percent chose investment banking and consulting as their preferred fields.[19]

The maturation of basic U.S. industries was accompanied by increased foreign competition. Labor-intensive manufacturing has tended to move out of the United States, and the interdependence of the U.S. and world economies increased. Imports and exports now make up a greater share of GNP, and by the mid-1980s a foreign trade deficit and a declining dollar added to U.S. economic problems. U.S. capital and productivity growth have slowed compared to the rest of the developed world.

Although many jobs were exported to nations with lower wage rates, others were lost due to technological changes. Just as the United States once revolutionized agriculture by producing more food with fewer workers, now the rise of manufacturing productivity was eliminating millions of industrial jobs.

The labor force changes of the past thirty-five years have been sharp. First women and then the baby boom generation swelled the labor force. This was partially offset by the decline in male labor force participation and the steady rise of the unemployment rate. Changes in employment led as well to the regional shift of jobs from the Middle Atlantic and Midwest to the high-tech zones of the Sun Belt and New England. Finally, after a period of stability, the poverty rate as well as the degree of inequality of income began to increase.

One challenge for the policy analyst who attempts to disentangle these massive changes is to separate the transitional from the long-run employment problems to evaluate the main social welfare effects. Four issues of particular importance are (1) the amount of total employment and unemployment that the technological shift leaves in its wake; (2) the distribution of unemployment (are new jobs available for those who have been displaced?); (3) the balance of full-time and part-time jobs; and (4) the responsiveness of the economy to changing labor supplies.

Deindustrialization has resulted in a shift of jobs away from the manufacturing sector of the economy. In 1950, 34 percent of all nonagricultural workers were employed in manufacturing, and 12 percent in the services. Slowly, the percentage in manufacturing went down and the percentage in services went up. It was in the decade from 1960 to 1970 that the most dramatic changes occurred in manufacturing; nonagricultural employment dropped from 31 percent to 21 percent. Employment in the services picked up slightly that decade and even more in the next when, from 1970 to 1980, employment increased from 6 to 20 percent. By 1985 nearly three-fourths of all jobs in the economy were service producing.

Looked at another way, of the 23 million new jobs created in the U.S. economy between 1970 and 1984, fully 22 million were in service industries: over the same period, only 1.3 million new jobs were created in goods production. Of the 9.1 million jobs added to the economy between 1980 and 1985, 8.2 million—89 percent—were in retail trades and miscellaneous services.[20]

For many years, the growth of the service economy evoked the image of employment in computer programming. Recently, as the reality of service dominance has emerged, it has become clear that this picture is not accurate. The service sector is split between well-paying and poorly paying jobs. For example, by one estimate, of 56 million service-sector jobs in 1985, 9 million were in high-paying occupational categories (managers and professional workers) and 20 million in low-paying occupations (service workers, clerical workers), leaving less than half of the jobs in middle-income categories (technical, production, and sales workers). By contrast, nearly three-quarters of manufacturing jobs are in the middle-income categories. Thus, the shift to the service economy implies a shift from a middle-income society to one marked by class differences.[21]

The slow growth of manufacturing employment does not mean that this sector is stagnating—quite the opposite. Employment in manufacturing hardly increased, but the value of consumption goods increased by almost 50 percent in real terms between 1970 and 1985.[22] The declining importance of manufacturing employment was testimony to the rapid productivity increases in this sector.

The key to the rapid transformation of manufacturing over the past decade has been the impact of technological change. Since the 1950s Americans have been announcing the coming of automation; today its impact is finally being felt. The application of computers and robotics is changing the nature of manufacturing from design of goods to their delivery. The switch is changing the nature of employment throughout the economy.

The byword for this change is flexibility. The past industrial revolution was based on the assembly line and huge integrated production facilities that produced the mass-market goods that transformed American life: cars, appliances, and other consumer goods. The undifferentiated mass-market goods that once fueled the economy, however, have saturated the U.S. market.[23] As a result, the market for manufactured goods is now more specialized, directed at specific submarkets. As consumers became more selective, the production run for manufactured goods was reduced from six or seven years to one or two. The change in consumer demand forced U.S. industry to become more flexible so that they might switch from product to product at minimum expense.

The computer revolution met these requirements. The centerpiece of computerization is the industrial robot that actually replaces the production workers. This is only the most visible of the many ways in which technological innovation alters the modern factory. Computer-assisted design and manufacture (CAD/CAM) have reduced the time it takes to get an item from conception to production. The paperwork of middle managers is cut, inventory management is simplified, and waste is reduced. The new technologies have allowed manufacturing to become as flexible as the new consumer market demands.

These changes signal an era of more "flexible specialization": production based on flexible, multi-use equipment, skilled workers, and the decentralization of production facilities.[24]

The most complete example of a switch from large, mass-production to decentralized, flexible specialization is the U.S. steel industry. The expansion of the integrated steelworks based on open-hearth technology symbolized the industrialization of American society during the early twentieth century. As it has faltered, specialty steel, based on electrically powered minimills, expanded. Between 1970 and 1985 electric furnaces more than doubled their share of domestic steel production. Because of higher productivity, lower wages, product specialization, and geographical specialization, minimills were able to compete successfully with older integrated facilities and to stay ahead of foreign competition.[25]

The rise of flexible specialization has serious implications for the U.S.

labor force. Its biggest impact is to decrease the number of workers needed. The most affected group is the semi-skilled production workers of the old industrial giants. In their place, flexible specialization requires a smaller, more skilled, and more adaptable workforce. At the same time, the permanent revolution sparked by high technology means that just as product lives are reduced, so too is the career life of the production worker. In the future, workers will not enter a factory at age eighteen and leave at retirement age. Workers may well experience several career shifts—and the resulting life crises—during their working years.

White-collar jobs are also at risk with the new manufacturing technologies. Flexibility calls for a responsiveness that is inconsistent with the layers of middle managers that have swelled the white-collar workforce. Instead, computerization permits the flattening of management pyramids—which in time leads to a reduction in lower-skilled white-collar jobs as well. The greater job stability of white-collar workers is being eroded, increasing their vulnerability to unemployment, layoffs, and job dislocation.

The current technological revolution, then, is Janus-faced. On the one hand, it can appear as a disastrous combination of deindustrialization, dislocation, unemployment, and increasing poverty. On the other hand, it produces possibilities for job enrichment, increased skill and diversity, and more humanistic management styles. Both of these faces are present in the economy.

The Decline of Labor-Management Cooperation

There is little doubt any longer that the United States has entered a new economic epoch, one dominated by the service sector and high-tech manufacturing. As with previous economic revolutions, there are many losers in the current transformation. Although it is too early to fill in a scorecard, it is clear that literally millions of Americans have become the casualties of postindustrialization.

Some of those suffering are already in the advancing sector. For example, while technological innovation has led to record numbers of new businesses, it has led at the same time to an unprecedented number of business failures and bankruptcies.[26]

Still, the major losers in the current industrial revolution are the members of the old industrial workforce. The semiskilled workers in basic industries and a host of supporting sectors have been forced to undergo the painful dislocation, unemployment, and psychological damage that have accompanied postindustrialization. A combination of technological, economic, and political forces have worked to make this transition more painful than it might have been.

The U.S. industrial working class has had a unique history. Throughout the twentieth century, the "American standard of living" has been the envy of the world. Indeed, it was the success of the working class during the postwar period that was the base of the belief that the working class had become middle class. These claims were exaggerated, but they did reflect the rapid rise in the income of workers during and after World War II.[27]

The reasons for this success were complex. The improved standard of living derived from the productivity edge that the United States had over the rest of the world.[28] The prosperity of the working class was not simply the automatic benefit of technological advantage. It was a result as well of the U.S. labor relations system and the rise of the U.S. welfare state that provided workers with unprecedented security and opportunity.

The economic crisis of the 1970s and economic shifts of the 1980s have undercut this prosperity. Labor peace has been superseded by increasing conflict, with labor unions losing. Millions of workers have found themselves displaced and unemployed. As a result, economic inequality and poverty have both increased rapidly. The middle-class blue-collar worker has borne the brunt of these changes.

At the same time, management found ways to keep unions out of new enterprises and challenge them in existing businesses. In addition, government policies—particularly, tight money policies, the deregulation of transportation and communications, and a laissez-faire stance by the National Labor Relations Board—encouraged management to free itself of union

c:

p   S. economy has declined
th   half of the proportion of
m   some sectors, including
be   ications, the decline has

T

Tl   problems that economic
tra   kers in older smokestack
inc   secure jobs, while the
hig   re skill and possess less
sec   poses risks for both the
old

                                                           tion, and the decline of
uni   , In January 1986, for
exa   ...... Bureau found that over 5 million workers had lost their
jobs since 1981 after having been employed for over three years. Of this
number, only about a quarter had found jobs that paid as well as the ones

they lost. Nine hundred thousand of the 5 million displaced workers were still unemployed (18 percent), another 800,000 had left the labor force (16 percent), and another 1.1 million were now working at lower-paying jobs (22 percent). These figures compared favorably to a similar study in 1984, but they suggest that massive job displacement has become a significant element of the current economy.[31]

In addition, poverty and unemployment have increased significantly over previous decades. During the recession of 1981–82, unemployment rose to 11 percent, the highest rate since the Great Depression. Although the civilian unemployment rate fell to 6.3 percent in the spring of 1987, it remained significantly higher than it had been at comparable points in past recoveries. Similarly, poverty, which had fallen to 11 percent during the early 1970s, rose above 15 percent in 1983 and has remained in the 14 percent range. The rising poverty of black female-householders has attracted much attention, but the poverty rate of white male-householders has increased even more rapidly.

The fall in the unemployment rate since 1983 itself gives an incomplete picture of the reality of the current recovery. The number of unemployed at any specified time is down, yet the unemployment experience of individuals across the entire year has improved much less. Overall, the proportion of the labor force who experienced at least one spell of unemployment declined from 19.6 to 16.7 percent between 1983 and 1985. Although official unemployment declined by a quarter, the extent of unemployment dropped by only 15 percent. Indeed, the number of workers experiencing three or more spells of unemployment during the year hardly fell at all over those two years—from 3.1 million to 3.0 million.

The rise of unemployment is even more troubling because it raises questions about the compatibility of the twin goals of the economy—low unemployment and rapid economic growth. Increasingly, economists are claiming that the "natural" (noninflationary) unemployment rate has risen to the 6 to 7 percent range; many believe that economic health will be built on the economic redundancy of 8 million Americans. Leontief, based on an analysis of the Austrian economy, concluded that to maximize economic growth in advanced industrial economies, higher dislocation and unemployment had to be tolerated: to maintain employment, one has to sacrifice growth. The old adage that "a rising tide lifts all boats" is being proved wrong.[32]

The kind of new jobs available in the postindustrial economy presents a problem. The size of the labor force has expanded rapidly, adding over 9 million jobs between 1979 and 1985. According to a study by the Joint Economic Committee of Congress, however, most of these have been low-paying jobs. Bluestone and Harrison estimate that whereas in previous expansions only about one in five new jobs was low-wage, in the current recovery 44 percent of the new jobs are in this range. The new economy is producing more jobs, but a larger share of them are either low-wage or part-time. The middle-income jobs that once dominated the economy are no longer there.[33]

The "job miracle" of the early 1980s is also called into question by the increase in part-time and temporary work. Almost a third of all new jobs created since 1980 are part-time. Three-quarters of these have been filled by people who would have preferred full-time employment. Indeed, the evidence suggests that underemployment continues to be a major problem for Americans. A Bureau of Labor Statistics study, for example, suggests that four times as many Americans would like their work hours lengthened than would like them cut. Moonlighting, or the holding of more than one job, is at its highest level in over twenty years as many workers try to put together several part-time jobs. Given the differences between full- and part-time wages and benefits, in this case the whole is considerably less than the sum of its parts.[34]

Temporary work has also increased. Employers seeking flexibility in the workplace and an escape from the restraints and employee protections of union contracts have increasingly turned to leasing and subcontracting. The services are both the fastest-growing sector of the economy and the sector most involved in the hiring of contingency labor.[35] Fewer workers are now in unionized companies with the job protections and fringe benefits that unions provide. From a worker's viewpoint, these jobs provide few long-lasting ties to their firms and few social welfare entitlements. In the immediate present, health insurance, Disability Insurance, and Unemployment Insurance payments are affected. For old age, pension issues are a major concern.[36]

As a result of these conditions, there has been a significant increase in inequality during the 1980s. In 1985 the top fifth of families in the United States held 43.5 percent of aggregate income, while the share of the lowest fifth was 4.6 percent. In 1979 the top fifth held eight times as much income as the bottom fifth: by 1984 it held over nine times as much. The index of income concentration—a summary measure of income inequality—rose to the highest figure recorded since data were first collected in 1947.[37]

American society is in danger of polarization. In the past twenty years, poverty, unemployment, low-wage jobs, and inequality have increased. The middle class has hardly disappeared, but it has been significantly threatened. In place of large numbers of middle-income white- and blue-collar jobs, the 1980s are witnessing significant increases in both high- and low-wage jobs. These trends have continued even as the economy has recovered from the recession. They threaten to become a permanent structural feature of the economy.[38]

The impact of displacement and disruption in the workplace affects as well the racial and sexual division of labor. Although the blue-collar, unionized workforce—a sector dominated by white men—has been hardest hit by deindustrialization, blacks and Hispanics have suffered greatly as a result of job displacement. In the 1986 study, their proportion of the displaced was approximately the same as that in the labor force (11.3 percent for blacks, 6.1 percent for Hispanics). The reemployment experience, however, was much worse. Although two-thirds of all displaced workers (employed three years or more) were reemployed by January 1986, only 58 percent of black workers and 57 percent of Hispanic workers were. Hispanic women in particular had difficulty; only 42 percent were reemployed, and nearly a third had dropped out of the labor market.[39]

Ironically, the growth area of the economy—the services—is one in which black and female workers have historically predominated. In the past, it was assumed that a convergence of the economic status of blacks and whites, men and women, would come about through "leveling up"— bringing disenfranchised groups up to the white male standard. If women and blacks are in fact in the workplace vanguard, however, what may be occurring is a process of "leveling down." As is shown in chapters 6 and 7, the low wages and benefits, high turnover, and low security that women and blacks have long experienced in the workforce may become increasingly common among white men in the years ahead.

The Erosion of Benefits

The trends in age structure, family, and work provide new problems that social welfare programs will be called on to address. Far from considering new problems, however, during the 1980s the U.S. welfare system has sought to restrict its growth. Not only have these new problems gone unanswered, but the core programs of the old welfare state have been cut. We have neglected the present and failed to plan for the future.

Welfare benefits have eroded for needy populations in two ways during the past fifteen years. For the social insurances—the most desirable and expensive programs—eligibility has declined because of the social and economic changes already discussed. The means-tested public assistance programs have fallen victim to restrictions in eligibility standards and an inflation that has decreased the real value of these benefits.

Eligibility and payment levels of existing U.S. social insurance programs are tied to an individual's work status and work history. Therefore, the completeness of coverage under Old-Age, Disability, and Unemployment Insurance depends on the consistency of one's career. The income disruptions being experienced by today's workers will further weaken their position when they need the benefits of these programs.

Unemployment Insurance offers the most striking example of this process. The standard program, which provides twenty-six weeks of coverage at about 40 percent of previous wages, was designed to meet the cyclical unemployment problems of industrial society. It appears less suited, however, to the long-term unemployment that is endemic to a postindustrial economy. Between 1975 and 1985 the percentage of the unemployed eligible for unemployment compensation declined from 50 percent to under 30 percent. At the same time, the benefits exhaustion rate—the percentage of recipients who do not find a job before their benefits run out—rose to 34 percent.[40]

Although unemployment compensation has already been affected, the effect on retirement and disability benefits will take longer to surface. Retirement benefits are computed on an indexed average of monthly earnings (AIME) with the five lowest years of earnings disregarded. Work history disruptions that lead to lower annual earnings will lead to reduced benefits at retirement when they are needed. For families, this effect is multiplied because benefits for survivors and dependents are a multiple of the worker's basic insurance benefit.

Older workers who experience job disruption and forced retirement suffer from serious benefit loss. Since 1970 this has been an increasing problem. Between 1970 and 1983, for example, the proportion of men age sixty to sixty-one who were out of the labor force rose from 17 to 30 percent, while the increase for those aged fifty-five to fifty-nine was from 10 to 20 percent.[41] Workers in their fifties who lose their jobs and cannot find others not only face a decline in their monthly payments, but because they must take early retirement, their monthly benefits are reduced by 20 percent. Consider a worker who becomes displaced at age fifty-nine. For twenty-six weeks there is Unemployment Insurance, then nothing until age sixty-two, when early retirement income starts, but permanently set at a level 20 percent below what the worker was expecting to receive at a normal sixty-five-year-old retirement age.

Calculations of Social Security benefits are based on the assumption of a steady work history, lasting until normal retirement. This is a poor assumption for married women who may experience five years or more out of the labor force for child rearing and whose subsequent years of employment are often substandard. For these women, the Social Security system is inappropriately designed for their work and family situations. As a result, many married women, even though they have worked and contributed, never in fact collect their own Social Security benefits. Ninety-two percent of men receive Social Security or railroad retirement benefits in old age; only 22 percent of women do because so many would find their benefits so low that they elect instead to receive dependent or survivor payments.[42]

The public assistance programs have done an even poorer job than the insurance programs in keeping pace with the requirements of the needy. The Supplemental Security Income program (SSI), the safety net for the old, disabled, and blind, has a maximum federal payment set at only 75 percent of the poverty line and has seen the administrative tightening of eligibility during the 1980s. SSI has fared well, however, compared with Aid to Families with Dependent Children.

AFDC—the main anti-poverty program for women and children—has become steadily less effective since 1970. As a percentage of the federal budget, AFDC peaked at 1.6 percent in 1973 and has been going down since then. In part this has been because, with the changing U.S. demographic and political picture, AFDC has not grown as fast as OASI. The proportion of the aged in the population has grown rapidly in these years. Additionally, it has become increasingly difficult for poor families to become beneficiaries of public assistance, in spite of the creation of optional two-parent programs (AFDC-U) in many states. Although the number of poor families has increased by almost 2 million since 1970, the number of families receiving payments has risen only 1.2 million. Furthermore, those receiving benefits are receiving much less in real terms. OASDI and SSI have been indexed since the early 1970s, but AFDC has not. As a result the average payment's real value has dropped 34 percent.[43]

The Problem Restated

The social welfare system in the United States was built on the distinction between the worthy and unworthy poor. The worthy—hard-working, thrifty, and responsible—were to be protected through a system of contributory social insurance and public assistance for specific categories (what in the past were called the "impotent poor"), including the aged and disabled. For those able to work, social insurance was premised on the model of a male worker with a continuous work history. He had a stable marriage and family and was assumed to support them. Old-Age and Survivors' Insurance benefits were tied to his lifetime earnings. Unemployment Insurance was protection for short periods of cyclical unemployment. Disability Insurance was the family refuge against the physical risks of industrial work.

Given the changes in the age distribution of the U.S. population, the shifts in family norms and behavior, and the transformation of the workplace, this system operated in unforeseen ways. The pension system solved some problems but created greater inequality as women's work histories and marriage patterns changed. Unemployment compensation aided those for whom it was originally targeted but reached fewer and fewer and, because it was not universal, encouraged workers to stay in declining industries with no incentive to prepare for a new vocation. For older displaced workers, Disability Insurance became a program of last resort. Mothers and their children were particularly hard hit: their labor force participation increased, but the loss of male support and the erosion of government aid more than balanced their own efforts at economic improvement.

The current U.S. welfare system was designed for a particular age mix of dependents, a particular combination of family and public support, and an economy in which cyclical unemployment was the major problem. The reality behind those assumptions has changed, however, and we need now to examine the current nature of poverty and the effect of these changes on different at-risk groups.

To a limited extent this is occurring. The attention of policy makers and of a concerned public seems focused almost exclusively on the high poverty rates associated with nonwhites and women. The welfare debate is dominated by concerns about the "underclass" and its family stability, individual morality and pathology, and culture of poverty. The "feminization of poverty" debate, although possessing its own urgency, has led to discussions of child care, illegitimacy, and desertion but has failed to examine these in their full economic and social context. Many debate work motivation, but few examine work availability; much is heard about black teenagers' sexual values, but little about their life chances.

Although changes in family have monopolized the poverty debate of the 1980s, the link between poverty and work experience has been less frequently examined. Where the issue has been raised, the disincentives that welfare payments create for work effort have dominated the discussion. The policy debate has failed to keep up with the socioeconomic changes of the past twenty years.

The separate trends that are creating the "new poverty" of the 1980s must be untangled and evaluated. Before this can be done, the philosophical and historical roots of the current debate over dependency and public responsibility must be charted.

Notes

1. Harold Wilensky and Charles Lebeaux, *Industrial Society and Social Welfare* (New York: Russell Sage, 1958), provide a clear statement of this interpretation. See also Stephen Hill, *Competition and Control at Work: The New Industrial Sociology* (Cambridge, Mass.: MIT Press, 1981), and Herbert McClosky and John Zaller, *The American Ethos* (Cambridge, Mass.: Harvard University Press, 1984). Hugh Heclo, *Modern Social Politics in Britain and Sweden* (New Haven and London: Yale University Press, 1974), 1–17, takes a skeptical view of this interpretation.

2. Wilensky and Lebeaux, *Industrial Society and Social Welfare*, 90.

3. Ibid., 125

4. Charles A. Murray, *Losing Ground: American Social Policy, 1950–1980* (New York: Basic Books, 1984).

5. U.S. National Center for Health Statistics, *Vital Statistics of the United States, 1983* (Washington, D.C.: Government Printing Office, 1984). To be found in U.S.

Bureau of the Census, *Statistical Abstract of the United States, 1987* (Washington, D.C.: Government Printing Office, 1987) 70.

6. Ansley J. Coale and Melvin Zelnick, *New Estimates of Fertility and Population in the United States* (Princeton: Princeton University Press, 1963), 21–31.

7. For a full discussion of the definition and conceptualization of age dependency, see chapter 3.

8. Paul Douglas, "Introduction," in *The Care of the Aged,* edited by Isaac Rubinow (Chicago: University of Chicago Press, 1931); Isaac Rubinow, *Quest for Security* (New York: Holt, 1934); U.S. Advisory Council on Economic Security, *Report of the Committee on Economic Security* (Washington, D.C.: Government Printing Office, 1935).

9. June Axinn and Mark Stern, "Age and Dependency: Children and the Aged in American Social Policy," *Milbank Memorial Fund Quarterly/Health and Society* 63 (4) (1985), 648–69.

10. Wilbur Crown, "Some Thoughts on Reformulating the Dependency Ratio," *The Gerontologist* (1985), 166–71. See also Richard Easterlin, *Birth and Fortune: The Impact of Numbers on Personal Welfare* (New York: Basic Books, 1980), on the prospects of another baby boom in this century. It is worth noting that a rise in fertility during the 1990s would somewhat worsen the prediction for the next several decades but improve the prospects for the possible crisis period after 2010.

11. R. Clark and J. Spengler, "The Implications of Future Dependency Ratios and Their Composition," in *Aging and Income* edited by B. Herzog (New York: Human Sciences Press, 1978); Hilda Wander, "Zero Population Growth Now: The Lessons from Europe," in *The Economic Consequences of Declining Population Growth,* edited by E. Espenshad and W. Seron (New York: Academic Press, 1978).

12. June Axinn and Herman Levin, *Social Welfare: A History of the American Response to Need* (New York: Longman, 1982); V. J. Burke and V. Burke, *Nixon's Good Deed* (New York: Columbia University Press, 1974).

13. U.S. Bureau of Labor Statistics, *Special Labor Force Reports,* Nos. 13, 130, 134, Bulletin 2163 and published data; available in U.S. Bureau of the Census, *Statistical Abstract of the United States: 1986* (Washington, D.C.: Government Printing Office, 1986); Rosemary Sarri, "Federal Policy Changes and the Feminization of Poverty," *Child Welfare* 64 (3) (1985), 235–47.

14. In 1982 the average age of first marriage was twenty-four years of age for men and twenty-two years of age for women.

15. U.S. Bureau of Labor Statistics, *News* 86–345 (Washington, D.C.: Government Printing Office, 20 August 1986); U.S. Bureau of the Census, *Current Population Reports,* Series P-20, No. 411, to be found in U.S. Bureau of the Census, *Statistical Abstract of the United States* (Washington, D.C.: Government Printing Office, 1987), 48.

16. U.S. Department of the Census, *Child Support and Alimony,* Special Studies Series P-23 (Washington, D.C.: Government Printing Office, 1978, 1983); Frank Furstenberg and C. Nord, "Parenting Apart: Patterns of Childrearing after Marital Disruption," paper presented before a meeting of the American Sociological Association, San Francisco, 1982; S. Hoffman and J. Holmes, "Husbands, Wives, and Divorce," in *Five Thousand American Families: Patterns of Economic Progress,* vol. IV, edited by J. J. Duncan and J. N. Morgan (Ann Arbor: Institute for Social Research,

University of Michigan, 1976), 333–56; Daniel Moynihan, "Family and Nation," Harvard University, The Godkin Lectures, 1985; June O'Neill, "Determinants of Child Support," Research Report (Washington, D.C.: Urban Institute, 1986); Samuel Preston, "Children and the Elderly: Divergent Paths for America's Dependents," *Demography* 21 (4) (1984), 435–57.

17. June Axinn and Herman Levin, "The Family Life Cycle and Economic Security," *Social Work* 24 (6) (1979) 540–46; Paul Ryscavage, "Income Trends of the Young and the Elderly," *Family Economics Review* 2 (1987) 1–8.

18. A relative concept of poverty defines poverty as a percentage of median family income.

19. Floyd A. Oliver, "Harvard M.B.A.s Have Better Things to Think about Than Manufacturing," *The Japan Times*, 9 November 1986 p. 9; reprinted from *The Los Angeles Times*.

20. U.S. Bureau of the Census, *1980 Census of Population*, Supplementary Reports (PC80-S1-15). To be found in U.S. Bureau of the Census, *Statistical Abstract of the United States, 1986* (Washington, D.C.: Government Printing Office, 1986), 400, and U.S. Congress, Office of Technology Assessment, *Technology and Structural Unemployment: Reemploying Displaced Adults* (Washington, D.C.: Government Printing Office, 1986), 154.

21. Ibid., 157.

22. *Economic Report of the President, January 1987* (Washington, D.C.: Government Printing Office, 1987), 26–29, 45–50.

23. By 1980 there was one car for every two Americans: 99 percent of households had television sets, refrigerators, and radios; and 90 percent had washing machines, toasters, and vacuum cleaners. Michael J. Piore and Charles F. Sabel, *The Second Industrial Divide: Possibilities for Prosperity* (New York: Basic Books, 1984), 184.

24. Piore and Sabel, *Second Industrial Divide*, 17, passim.

25. D. F. Barnett and Robert W. Crandall, *Up from the Ashes: The Rise of the Steel Minimill* (Washington, D.C.: Brookings Institution, 1986), 6–16.

26. Between 1978 and 1985 the annual rate of businesses incorporated increased from 478,000 to 669,000, a rise of 40 percent. During this same period, the number of business failures rose from 6,600 to 57,100, an increase of 765 percent. *Economic Report of the President, January 1987*, Table B-92, 351.

27. Godfrey Hodgson, *America in Our Time* (New York: Random House, 1976).

28. For example, in 1960 U.S. gross domestic product per worker was 70 percent higher than that of any other nation. "Survey: High Technology," *The Economist* (23 August 1986): 1.

29. See, for example, Sam Rosenberg, "Reagan Social Policy and Labor Force Restructuring," *Cambridge Journal of Economics* 7 (1983): 179–96.

30. The decline in the rate among nonagricultural workers has been from 35 percent in the mid-1950s to approximately 18 percent in 1984. For specific industries' declines, see Thomas A. Kochan, Harry C. Katz, and Robert B. McKersie, *The Transformation of American Industrial Relations* (New York: Basic Books, 1986), 48–50.

31. U.S. Department of Labor, *News,* 14 October 1986.

32. Lester Thurow, *Zero-Sum Solutions: An Economic and Political Agenda for the 1980s* (New York: Simon and Schuster, 1985).

33. Barry Bluestone and Bennett Harrison, "The Grim Truth about the Job Miracle," *New York Times,* 1 February 1987. In response, Janet Norwood, "The Job Machine Has Not Broken Down," *New York Times,* 22 February 1987, argues that the upsurge in low-wage work is simply a cyclical phenomenon.

34. U.S. Bureau of Labor Statistics, *News,* 7 August 1986, and John F. Stinson, Jr., "Moonlighting by Women Jumped to Record Highs," *Monthly Labor Review* 109 (11) (November 1986): 22–25. The percentage wishing more hours is 27.5 percent; those wishing fewer hours 7.6 percent. The percentage of moonlighters in 1985 was 5.4 percent of the labor force.

35. *The New York Times,* 9 July 1986.

36. Wayne Howe, "Temporary Help Workers: Who They Are, What Jobs They Hold," *Monthly Labor Review* (November 1986): 45–47.

37. U.S. Bureau of the Census, Current Population Reports, Series P-60, No. 154, *Money Income and Poverty Status of Families and Persons in the United States: 1985* (Washington, D.C.: Government Printing Office, 1986), 11.

38. Lester Thurow, "A Surge in Inequality," *Scientific American* 256 (5) (May 1987): 30–37.

39. U.S. Bureau of Labor Statistics, "Reemployment Increases among Displaced Workers," *News,* 14 October 1986.

40. U.S. Employment and Training Administration, *Unemployment Insurance Statistics* (Washington, D.C.: Government Printing Office, monthly), and U.S. Department of Labor, *Annual Report of the Secretary of Labor* (Washington, D.C.: Government Printing Office, annual). Data available in U.S. Bureau of the Census, *Statistical Abstract of the United States: 1986* (Washington, D.C.: Government Printing Office, 1986), 377.

41. Virginia P. Reno and Daniel N. Price, "Relationship between Retirement, Disability, and Unemployment Insurance Programs: The U.S. Experience," *Social Security Bulletin* 48 (5) (May 1985): 34–35.

42. U.S. Social Security Administration, *Social Security Bulletin: Annual Statistical Supplement, 1986* (Washington, D.C.: Government Printing Office, 1986); Barbara A. Lingg, "Women Social Security Beneficiaries Aged 62 or Older, 1960–1983," U.S. Social Security Administration, *Social Security Bulletin* (February 1985): 27–31; Christine Irick, "An Overview of OASDI Revenue, Expenditures, and Beneficiaries, 1974–1985," U.S. Social Security Administration, *Social Security Bulletin* (June 1986): 21–28.

43. U.S. Social Security Administration, *Social Security Bulletin* (monthly).

3
A New Look at the Concept of Dependency

The aging of the population of the United States has brought with it a new anxiety over the economic consequences of demographic change. The fear of overpopulation that gripped the national imagination not more than twenty years ago has been replaced by the threat of a mature economy dominated by an enfeebled mass of elderly, dependent people, consuming an increasing share of the resources produced by active workers. The prospect of further declines in the birth rate is seen as a cause of even more alarm—an even bleaker future.

A great deal of attention has been given to the measurement and projection of dependency, but relatively few scholars have examined the conceptualization of dependency and productivity as they relate to social welfare. This is a serious omission if one considers the relationship of dependence—or independence—to the changes in the last fifty years in the U.S. market economy, family structure, legal system, educational system, and employment and retirement laws. Even a cursory examination of the most obvious aspects immediately unmasks the complexity of this issue. Dependency and productivity are both dynamic concepts. Rather than being self-evident economic categories, they must be understood in their historical, social, and cultural milieux.

The point is not simply that social factors contribute to dependency—for example, through a rise in the birthrate—but that dependency itself is socially defined. Historically, its social definition has often been confused with its biological and physiological aspects. Even those authors who note the changing definitions of dependency often view these changes as the automatic process of history. For example, the exclusion of children from the labor force, a crucial element in their transition to full dependent status, has often been viewed as a functional response to industrial society. As Viviana Zelizer has demonstrated, however, the process of reclassifying children was anything but automatic. It required a protracted effort to alter the actual behavior and beliefs of a significant portion of the population.[1]

Rather than being a straightforward functional response to social change, dependency is socially constructed through a process of collective definition. At any particular time, there are competing and conflicting definitions of dependency; the "true" definition is a result of collective behavior—politics, intellectual battles, and social movements. In the 1930s, today, and in the twenty-first century, the terms of this conflict and its outcome have been and will be fluid.

The task of sorting out definitions is particularly difficult in the present case because whatever its definition, dependency is an ambiguous concept. Its complexity is immediately apparent in a simple dictionary definition. On the one hand, *to depend* is to rely or place trust in someone, as in the phrase, "I depend on my friends." At the same time, the definition entails a relationship of subordination and inferiority ("My entire career depends on you"). Indeed, one of the catch phrases of the 1980s—the increased "interdependency" of various regions of the world—is an attempt to finesse the cross-cutting relationships of subordination and domination that characterize the world order.

This chapter takes on four tasks. First, it examines the recent "dependency crisis" in historical context. How does today's public debate compare with that of the 1930s? Second, it reviews the current conceptualization of the problem of dependency and the various definitions of the dependency ratio that have been proposed in the literature. Third, it offers a reconceptualization of dependency and productivity based on the classification of individuals by their social contributions and their source of economic support. We propose a matrix based on the nature of individuals' work status and income sources that allows us to look at the current dependency ratio definitions and highlight the values and judgments that are often implicit in them. The final section uses the matrix analysis to clarify the contextual and political nature of today's dependency debate and to refocus the question of productivity and dependency on the issue of resource distribution rather than on market production.

The Historical Context

This is not the first time in the twentieth century that there has been a major debate over the question of the increasing number of dependent elderly and its economic implications. During the 1930s the debate over the establishment of Social Security focused on the same problem. Even before the coming of the New Deal, scholars confronted the impact of population aging on public welfare. The Research Committee on Social Trends appointed by President Hoover concluded in 1933 that the "increase of the aged will certainly result in an increase of the dependent aged." But the Committee found little reason for concern. "It should be remembered," the report continued, "that the decline in the number of children will decrease the group of young dependents. The net result should be no change in the total amount of dependency if older people can remain longer at suitable work or can accumulate reserves while younger."[2]

In 1935 President Roosevelt's Advisory Council on Economic Security considered the means for the support of the elderly:

> The number of the aged without means of self support is much larger than the number receiving pensions or public assistance in any form. . . . At this time a conservative estimate is that at least one half of [those] . . . over 65 years now living are dependent. . . . Children, friends, and relatives have borne and still carry the major cost of supporting the aged. . . . During the present depression, this burden has become unbearable for many of the children. . . . Many children who previously supported their parents have been compelled to cease doing so, and the great majority will probably never resume this load. . . . The depression has . . . deprived millions of workers past middle life of their jobs, with but uncertain prospects of again returning to steady employment. . . . Regardless of what may be done to improve their condition, this cost of supporting the aged will continue to increase. In another generation it will be at least double the present total.[3]

The Advisory Council, writing in a period of severe economic depression, when aging meant forced retirement and poverty, examined the alternatives for income support. It concluded that the aged could not support themselves through market employment and that families were equally impotent. The report recommended the contributory annuities and means-tested pensions that became the foundation of the U.S. social welfare system.

In contrast to the 1930s, the current controversy over dependency is occurring during a period of relative economic well-being. Personal incomes have risen, the number of Americans employed has never been higher, and poverty among the aged is down. The United States now has a Social Security system with expanded eligibility and benefit levels that has made it possible to provide most of the aged with a steady source of retirement income.

The debate of the 1930s focused on a discussion of life cycle impacts on poverty and how best to provide income support. The 1980s' debate has reversed these priorities; there is less concern with the condition of the aged and more worry about the well-being of the transfer mechanism itself.

The concern over the dependency burden emerged with incredible speed during the second half of the 1970s. As late as the 1960s population concerns had focused on the problem of overpopulation caused by the baby boom and the assumption that the high fertility of the 1940s and 1950s would continue. As the boom turned into a bust, the demographic projections of the future U.S. population began to change drastically.

The two recessions of the early 1970s combined with the expansion of social welfare benefits to rekindle interest in old-age dependency. A spate of studies appeared in the years just before the large set of Social Security tax increases were passed in 1978. Although a number of the papers were first presented at conferences, one of the first appearances in print of the new concern was Harold Sheppard and Sara Rix's 1977 monograph, *The Graying of Working America.*[4]

In their examination of the future of retirement-age policy, Sheppard and Rix invoked the term *crisis* to attract attention to their position. Taking what they described as a "worst-case" approach, the authors marshaled a wide range of data on biomedical technology, demography, resource availability, and economics to argue in favor of a rise in the retirement age. A crisis atmosphere was necessary because "changing the typical retirement age has not been given the priority it should." The purpose of the monograph was to promote "social learning" and to raise the issue in order to speed society's willingness to come to terms with it.[5]

Sheppard and Rix's belief in the urgency of the dependency crisis assumed that the data supporting this belief were clear and unambiguous. Therefore, the pivotal chapter in the book was devoted to the measurement of the dependency burden. Using a variety of definitions for the dependency ratio (which will be examined in more detail below), the authors found that in four of the five series of calculations the dependency ratio actually *dropped* between 1975 and 2050.

Although these calculations seemed to work against their case, the authors went on to consider confounding factors in the index, including labor force participation rates, unemployment, and work effort. Nevertheless, none of their data demonstrated an impending disaster. Some of their computations showed that there could be a rise in dependency, but the preponderance of their evidence did not support this case.

Despite the weakness of its evidence, the Sheppard and Rix monograph had a tremendous impact on the debate over dependency. Coming out as it did on the eve of the Social Security funding problems, it attracted popular attention, and a number of studies supported its conclusion despite the lack of compelling evidence.

The Social Security funding crisis confused the dependency debate by equating the short-term financing issues of the retirement trust fund with the longer-term question of demographic balance. Some experts attempted to separate the issue of Social Security funding from the larger worry over support of the dependent, but in the policy debate and the popular press, finances and demography became hopelessly confused.[6]

The work of Robert Clark and J. J. Spengler was perhaps the most influential in the development of the scholarly debate. Beginning in 1978 the authors produced a stream of papers that concluded that because children cost much less to support than the elderly, the shift in the composition of the dependent population would greatly increase the cost of support. When these calculations were challenged, they shifted ground, claiming that the support of children was an "investment" but that of the aged was merely consumption. Based on this distinction, but without data, Clark and Spengler raised the possibility that "a reallocation of resources toward older dependents *may* lower the future rate of economic growth."[7]

This line of thought achieved official status in 1980 with the release of a report by President Carter's Commission on Pension Policy. Barbara Torrey, a member of the staff, succinctly summarized the commission's position.

> Historically, there has been an implicit social contract that the working generations will help support the retired and disabled generations either privately or publicly. But the contract may have to be renegotiated if the future size of the retired and disabled more than doubles relative to the size of the working age generation. Therefore, the basic challenge that the demographic statistics discussed in this paper pose is how the society will prepare for the future retirement of increasingly large generations and how soon the preparations for their retirement will begin.[8]

The drumbeat of the dependency crisis did not go unchallenged. Donald Cowgill, for example, attacked the warnings of doom; "the analysis on which they are based is one-sided and misleading."[9] He concluded that the "question is not ability, but will." Still, the demographer Judith Treas captured the mood of the times more accurately: "If, half a century from now, one in five Americans is old, the costs of meeting their needs may outstrip the societal carrying capacity for social welfare programs."[10]

The contrast between the reports of Roosevelt's and Carter's commissions and their academic supporters is ironic. The Great Depression saw the federal government willing to assume public responsibility for the support of the older population, even if it doubled in size. In the late 1970s in spite of rather shaky evidence and the relative prosperity of the period, government doubted its ability to sustain such support. Were people naively optimistic in the depths of the Depression or are they peculiarly pessimistic today?

Current Conceptualizations of Dependency

The strange history of dependency stems in part from the changing view of its meaning. The definition of social problems and concepts is tied to particular cultures, societies, and historical periods. The expected age of retirement and age of labor force entry depend on technological factors, social organization, political forces, and social norms. At any one time whether a sixty-five-year-old woman or a nineteen-year-old male is an expected member of the productive population, an actual member of the productive population, or an expected member of the dependent population is a function of a host of factors.

In 1935 Congress settled on age sixty-five as the "normal" retirement age, but this was not intended to be unalterable. Sixty, sixty-two, seventy, and seventy-five were all viable alternatives; the triumph of sixty-five was the result of political compromise, not social convention. If seventy or sixty had been chosen, the count of dependents would have been far different in the subsequent half century.[11]

From the earliest days of the nation, government social policy has played a major role in determining who would become part of the dependent class and who would be considered independent. For example, the laws regulating labor force participation for the young and old have changed substantially during the twentieth century. In 1900 there was virtually no legislation limiting when young people could start work or when the elderly should stop working. By the last quarter of the century, U.S. laws limit youths and keep them in school through early adolescence, while at the same time mandatory retirement regulations have been limited by law since the 1960s.

Government policy on the responsibility of family members for each other has changed over the years as well. In the early nineteenth century family members were held to a broad range of legal responsibilities. Legislation and the courts have moved slowly to limit these obligations. At one time, both state and federal courts enforced a three-generation definition of family responsibility, while social custom included cousins and siblings. Over time, the scope of responsibilities has narrowed; today the responsibility of parents for their children and spouses for one another are the only unchallenged obligations. One major result of the release of relatives from financial obligation for members of their extended families, it should be clear, is a large increase in the number of potential public dependents.[12]

Government spending for social programs has also helped to shape dependency. Free public education, free land for homesteading, free land-grant colleges—all advanced the economic opportunity of specific groups and affected their work status. In the twentieth century the GI Bill of Rights of 1944 provided tuition payments and stipends for veterans attending universities, agricultural colleges, and vocational and technical schools. Close to 8 million veterans attended school during the twelve years of the original bill, increasing their value as "human capital" and decreasing their probability of dependency. Indeed, this connection was explicit in the intent of the legislation, motivated as it was by the fear of mass unemployment after the war.[13]

In summary, although the ebb and flow of social custom and cultural belief may seem "natural," government has played a crucial role in the definition of dependency.

The major tool that analysts have developed to examine dependency is based on age and labor force balances within the population. This measure—the dependency ratio—estimates the economic implications of changing demographic relationships. The many definitions of dependency all serve as an index of the relationship between dependent and productive groups in the population. Like any index, the dependency ratio simplifies and loses detail in the process of aggregating and weighting. Indexes are imperfect mirrors of reality. Their usefulness derives from the clarity and consistency of their conceptualization and the choices of logical categories. The dependency ratio has suffered on both counts.

At first glance, the dependency ratio appears to be a straightforward concept: the number of dependent people divided by the number of productive people. The literature reveals, however, wide variations in the interpretation of dependency and productivity.

In 1981, for example, *Newsweek* defined the ratio as the number of Social Security recipients divided by the number of workers.[14] A dependent was anyone receiving Social Security benefits. Barbara Torrey in 1980 used a similar age-segmented ratio but broadened the numerator to include everyone over age sixty-five and the denominator to include the entire working-age population.

Any definition of dependency that looks only at the ratio of the population of working and retirement age will conclude that dependency is rising because the proportion of the population over age sixty-five is growing. The conclusion is built into the assumptions behind the definition. Other sets of assumptions (for example, using age seventy instead of sixty-five) will lead us to different conclusions about the rate of change.

More sophisticated models include children in the definition of dependency. Here the number of younger and older persons are added together and then divided by the rest of the population. This conceptualization has the strength of acknowledging that the aged are not the only dependent group. Different authors again have used different cut-off ages for both children and the aged. For example, Sheppard and Rix used two different age cut-offs for children (fifteen and nineteen years of age) and three different ones for the aged (sixty-two, sixty-five, and seventy-five).[15]

In their research, Donald Adamchak and Eugene Friedmann have proposed a refined dependency ratio that includes nonmarket aspects of productivity as well as market work. Their model extends the denominator to include not only all who are of *working* age but those who are of *productive* age as well. They generated an array of estimates varying the cut-off for children from fourteen to seventeen years of age and for the aged from sixty-five to seventy-four years of age, which recognizes the contribution that nonworkers make to society. They estimate that using the most restrictive definition of productivity, dependency will increase by 19.5 percent between

1980 and 2050; using the least restrictive definition resulted in a figure of only 6.7 percent.[16]

A much different conceptualization has been proposed by William Crown: a labor market definition in which labor force participation, not age, defines one's dependency status. Those in the labor force form the denominator; those not in the labor force, the numerator. Regardless of one's age, by this definition one would be dependent if not engaged in market activity. Conversely, it includes as productive anyone who is working or seeking work, no matter how young or old. Crown estimated, using the labor force definition, that dependency would probably rise between 1979 and 2050, but not by an alarming amount. Using the moderate projections for growth in labor force participation, he estimated that dependency would rise by 13 percent.[17]

Both the age and the labor force definitions present methodological and conceptual difficulties. Age is far from a perfect definer of labor force activity. For example, using age as the sole indicator of dependency obscures the 25 percent of all males and 15 percent of all females between the ages of sixty-five and sixty-nine who are in the labor force. The situation is further complicated because the labor force participation rate of those sixty-five and over is not constant; there are cyclical movements as well as a long-term decline. At the other end of the age spectrum, whatever the cut-off age, not all children below it will be out of the labor force (that is, dependent) and not all above it will be productive (that is, in the labor force). Consider sixteen- and seventeen-year-old boys. The proportion in the labor force rose from 47 to over 50 percent between 1970 and 1980 and then fell back to 43.5 percent in 1984. It is projected to rise again during the next decade.[18] Whether these young men are dependent or productive members of society depends not on their age but on a host of social, educational, political, and economic factors that vary over time.

Disability rates also change over time. As medical science progresses and mortality rates decline, morbidity rates rise. Thus, the percentage of midlife adults who are out of the labor market for health and medical reasons has increased over time. It is also sensitive to the availability of public support programs, particularly Disability Insurance.

The age definition of dependency includes in the productive sector many who are not in the labor market. Clearly they are not all independent. Furthermore, it is insensitive to changes in the labor force behavior of the population and to changes in the participation and nonparticipation of different age groups or sexes. For long-term projections, this is a serious problem.

The labor force dependency ratio, while sensitive to these changes, has its own problems. Its inclusion in the denominator of all those in the labor market carries the implicit assumption that labor market participation and productivity are identical. The most obvious objection to this are the unemployed who are in the labor force but are not doing any work. In addition, those involved in illegal activity, because they are excluded from the national accounts, are also ignored. For example, reinstituting Prohibition would decrease the number of productive workers, while legalizing marijuana would increase it. Given the increased national awareness of the magnitude of the underground economy, this problem is far from trivial.

Conversely, can it really be assumed that all who are not in the labor force are dependent? Again using the national accounts analogy, does a cook's productivity decrease if she marries her employer and is no longer paid even though she continues the same job? In addition, this standard of dependency seems to miss those who are supported by private transfers like personal savings, investments, or inherited wealth.

The crux of this issue, then, is the question of productivity and the market. On the one hand, many productive events occur outside the marketplace. The unpaid work of family members—dependent care and domestic labor—is one example. The contributions of community service workers and volunteer workers on many levels is another. On the other hand, a growing share of market transactions appear to be socially dysfunctional and therefore of questionable productivity.

Although the labor market definition at first glance appears more attractive than the age definition of dependency, it has its share of conceptual drawbacks. Both definitions draw on a weak parallel between their definition and that of actual dependency. Some groups—like the working poor—suffer in both definitions because work and dependency are seen as mutually exclusive. Given the size of this population—over 9 million in 1985—it poses an inconvenient reminder of just how crude conceptualizations have been up until now.

Each of the two common definitions of the dependency ratio are open to question. In spite of their differences, they each give a consistent view of the future of dependency. Using the age dependency ratio, for example, the total support ratio has fallen from 83.7 to 64.4 per 100 working-age Americans between 1900 and 1980. The future projections of age dependency suggest a rise of about 20 percent between 1980 and 2050. Although this is a substantial rise, it is smaller than the one that occurred between 1940 and 1960 when the baby boom bloated the youth dependency ratio (see table 3–1).

The rise in age dependency has its precedents, but future changes in its composition do not. Historically, children have been the majority of the dependent population. In 1900 the support ratio for children was more than ten times that of the aged. By 1980 there were two and a half times as many children as aged in the age-dependent population. If current projections hold, by the middle of the next century, the two groups will be about equal in size.

Table 3–1

Age Dependency Ratios, Youth, Aged, and Total Components, 1900–2050
(*number of dependents per 100 persons, aged eighteen to sixty-four years*)

Year	Aged Support Ratio (Over 65)	Youth Support Ratio (Under 18)	Total Support Ratio (Under 18 & Over 65)
1900	7.4	76.3	83.7
1920	8.0	67.7	76.7
1940	10.9	51.9	62.8
1960	16.8	65.1	82.0
1980	18.6	45.8	64.4
1990	20.7	41.9	62.6
2000	21.2	40.7	61.9
2025	33.3	37.7	71.0
2050	37.9	36.6	74.5

Source: U.S. Bureau of the Census, *Projections of the Population of the United States, 1982–2050*, Current Population Survey, Series P-25, No. 922 (Washington, D.C.: Government Printing Office, October 1982), and *Estimates of the Population of the United States, by Single Years, of Age, Color, and Sex: 1900 to 1959*, Current Population Survey, Series P-25, No. 310 and No. 311 (Washington, D.C.: Government Printing Office, June and July 1965).

The general contours of the labor force dependency ratio are similar to those of the age measure, but the decline in dependency in the past has been greater and the rise in the future is smaller. The massive entry of women into the labor force almost cut in half the proportion of midlife dependents between 1950 and 1980. In the future, the labor force dependency ratio will rise, but at a much slower rate than the age dependency ratio. Declining birth rates should lead to even further increases in female labor force participation as women experience a longer period of their life cycle after their children have left home. Although dependency will rise in the future, it will not come close to the peak it reached in 1960.

These estimates underscore the inadequacies of both the theory of the dependency crisis and the quality of these measures. If demographic or labor force dependency were in itself such a problem for society, the historical correspondence appears peculiar; 1960 is hardly remembered as the year in which a massive dependent population swallowed up society's resources or stood in the path of economic growth.

The drive to generate concrete estimates of future support ratios has led analysts to accept flawed definitions. Practical necessities have overruled clear theoretical and analytical difficulties. In the remainder of this chapter, an alternative conceptualization of dependency is proposed—one more consistent with the multidimensionality of the phenomenon and the complex social process through which it is constructed.

The Reconceptualization of Dependency

At least four distinct dimensions have been used by various authors in their discussions of dependency and productivity. The first two focus on the work status of the individual and infer dependency from definitions of productivity. The second pair use income source as the criterion for defining dependency.

1. The most simple approach to dependency and productivity is to define them in terms of labor market participation, as Crown has done. As has been shown, by this definition anyone who works for wages or a salary or is self-employed is productive; anyone else is dependent.

2. The second definition uses the concept of "socially useful participation" as the standard of productivity. It includes, in addition to labor force members, anyone performing socially useful nonmarket work. This definition includes homemakers, caretakers, volunteers, and unpaid family workers in the ranks of the productive. A group harder to define— labor force participants who do not do social useful work—would be excluded from the ranks of the productive by this standard.

3. The third definition equates dependency with the use of public money. It therefore conforms with conceptions of dependents as the "impotent poor"—those unable to fend for themselves who become wards of government.

4. The final distinction takes a finer look at public money. This definition distinguishes support through contributory programs—the social insurances—from reliance on means-tested and noncontributory programs such as Aid to Families with Dependent Children, Supplemental Security Income, and general assistance. This standard incorporates a major ideological element of the welfare state: the strong belief among recipients of social insurance that they are not on "welfare" because they have paid into the fund from which they receive their checks. Payments from contributory funds are seen instead as deferred compensation for productive labor. By contrast, the means-tested programs that draw on general revenue are not considered by most of the public as related to one's prior social contribution.

This list of categories is by no means exhaustive. It does not include, for example, the recipients of farm subsidies, protected industries, or a host of other beneficiaries of social policy interventions. It is presented to illustrate the size and diversity of the groups that may fall on either one side or the other of the dependency divide.

These four standards are arranged to produce a matrix with twelve cells in table 3–2. Within each cell, examples illustrate some of the social groups

Table 3–2
Definitions of Dependency

	No Public Money	Public Money	
		Contributory	Noncontributory
Employed:			
Socially useful	1. Working nonpoor	2. Double dippers (retired federal employees/veterans)	3. Working poor
Not socially useful	4. Working nonpoor employed in illegal occupations	5. Double dippers (retired and federal employees/ veterans) employed in illegal occupations	6. Working poor employed in illegal occupations
Not employed:			
Socially useful	7. Volunteers, homemakers, caretakers	8. Mothers on SI, Caretakers on OASDI or UI	9. Mothers on AFDC, home-makers/caretakers on SSI or GA
Not socially useful	10. Street people, "idle rich," students/children, recipients of alimony	11. Children on SI, disabled on DI, aged on OASDI, unemployed on UI	12. Other SSI recipients, children on AFDC, individuals on GA

Notes:

[a] Public/nonpublic: *Public* moneys refers to direct government income transfers; *nonpublic* money refers to nongovernmental income transfers.

[b] Contributory/noncontributory: *Contributory* refers to programs to which either the recipient, a defined relative, or the employer paid taxes to the benefit fund; benefits for noncontributory programs come completely from government revenues.

[c] Working/not working: *Working* is defined as being an employed member of the labor force; the unemployed and those not in the labor force are defined as *not working*.

[d] Socially useful/not socially useful: *Socially useful* work refers to legal paid work and nonmarket labor that supports at least another person, such as housework or volunteer work; *not socially useful* refers to illegal or criminal activities, such as drug smuggling or embezzlement.

[e] OASDI:Old Age, Survivors', and Disability Insurance
AFDC: Aid to Families with Dependent Children
SSI: Supplemental Security Income
UD: Unemployment Insurance
GA: General Assistance

that could be considered dependent or productive by these competing definitions. Only one of the cells—cell 1—includes groups that are unambiguously productive by all of these definitions. These individuals who work, do socially productive labor, and receive no public support (tax expenditures are also excluded from this consideration) are clearly members of the productive population and have not been considered dependent. This group would include most of the working nonpoor population, approximately 115 million

Americans in 1985, or about 48 percent of the 239 million people in the nation that year.

At the other end of the spectrum are those in cell 12: the unequivocal dependents. This includes those who are not in paid employment, do no socially useful labor, and who receive noncontributory public assistance. The most visible group in this cell is child beneficiaries of Aid to Families with Dependent Children, approximately 7.3 million. To a lesser extent, 4.3 million aged, blind, and disabled who collect SSI are considered part of this stratum. Note however that this does not take into account those who either receive social insurance (about 2 million in 1985) or do socially useful work—homemakers, caretakers, or active volunteers. In addition, included in this cell are general assistance recipients who are usually single individuals living on their own—about 1.3 million persons.[19] Cell 12 includes about 13 million people—about 5 percent of the population.

If a dependency ratio were computed in line with this conceptualization, the position of these groups would be unambiguous. All 115 million of those in cell 1 would be in the denominator, and all 13 million of those in cell 12 would be in the numerator. The rest of the population—approximately 111 million persons or 46 percent of the population—fall in between. By some standards they are independent or productive; by others they are dependent. Thus, at one extreme, the dependency ratio might include all of the remainder as independent leading to a dependency ratio of 6 percent. At the other extreme, the ratio might consider the remainder as dependent, leading to a dependency ratio of 108 percent.

The point of these extreme and rough calculations is not that there is no dependency problem or that the problem is an overwhelming one. It is simply that the dependency status of roughly half the population is debatable. Depending on one's economic, social, and cultural assumptions, the members of these groups could be placed in either part of the dependency ratio. A closer examination of who is included in each cell clarifies this point.

The most difficult group to estimate and the most ticklish to define are those individuals in cells 4, 5, and 6: individuals who are employed but do no socially useful labor. Included in this group are persons involved in criminal activity as their primary occupation: drug smugglers, toxic-waste dumpers, and embezzlers. In addition, some well-paid activities of questionable value, like corporate raiders, might also be included here. Although this approach is conceptually interesting, it presents a number of methodological difficulties.

Two groups are included among those who are not employed but receiving no public aid—those in the paid labor force but not doing socially useful work (cell 7) and those doing neither paid labor nor socially useful work (cell 10). Homemakers who do household labor for at least one other person, caretakers, and volunteers are in cell 7. In 1984 the 62 million U.S. families included 26.6 million women with either husbands or children who worked in the home without pay. By one estimate, about one-third of the population over the age of sixteen who did not work during the year were involved in keeping house.[20] In addition, this cell would include some of the 55 percent of the population involved in volunteer efforts, including 53 percent of those between the ages of eighteen and twenty-four and 32 percent of the aged.[21] Finally, included here would be some 600,000 unpaid workers in family businesses.[22]

The occupants of cell 10—those neither in the paid labor force nor doing socially useful work nor receiving any public funds—are a heterogeneous group. They would include those supported by "unearned" income—Veblen's leisure class. Joining them are children and students as well as others receiving family income transfers. Recipients of alimony or palimony who have no children would also be in this group as would those who depend on individual income transfers, including beggars, members of some religious sects, and many of the homeless.

Cells 2 and 3 are for paid workers who are in socially useful employment but who nonetheless receive public support. Cell 2 is not large but would include veterans receiving pensions while working at civilian jobs and retired government employees drawing a pension from a first career and still actively engaged in their second nongovernmental job.

The stringency of eligibility for public assistance programs means that people who are employed rarely qualify for these programs. Nonetheless, the working poor are sometimes eligible for food stamps, low-income energy assistance, the earned-income tax credit, and some other means-tested programs. Given the growth of low-wage jobs that were discussed in chapter 2, it is likely that the size of this cell could grow over the next several decades. There were an estimated 9 million working poor in 1985; those who received support from these programs would be placed in cell 3.

Those not employed but performing socially useful tasks and receiving public funds are in cells 8 and 9. Mothers in need would be in cell 8 if they receive Survivors' Insurance (300,000) but in cell 9 if they received AFDC (4.8 million).[23] Similarly, the aged or disabled who receive Supplemental Security Income would be in cell 9, while Old-Age Survivors', and Disability Insurance recipients would be placed in cell 8 if they were caretakers, homemakers, or volunteers—that is, doing socially useful work.

Last, in cell 11 are those who are doing no work, either paid or social useful, but who receive contributory public aid. This includes most of the following groups: children receiving survivors' insurance, beneficiaries of government retirement, survivors', and disability programs, veterans on pensions, and those unemployed who are recipients of unemployment compensation. These are the groups that before the advent of the welfare state were considered part of the "dependency problem." The philosophy of social insurance—based on a combination of individual and social responsibility—was designed to distance these groups from the problem and to define them as independent. The recent dependency debate suggests that at least among some writers there is a wish to again see them as part of the dependent population.

This conceptual exercise produces few empirical surprises, but it orders perceptions of dependency in a different way. In particular, the heterogeneity of some of the cells and the similarity of individuals in different cells suggests how structured dependency is by social, cultural, and ideological values. In many ways, drawing comparisons between millionaire playboys and people who sleep on the sidewalk, drug pushers and inside traders may seem farfetched, but by at least some standards their position on the dependency-/productivity continuum is similar.

At the same time, social policy makes a series of distinctions between individuals who in most respects are quite similar. Compare, for example, the treatment of two families each composed of a widow and two children. One family finds itself in cells 8 and 11 and the other in cells 9 and 12. The differentiation is not based on the family's own characteristics or work history but on that of the deceased husband and father. A simple comparison of the average benefit levels—$12,144 per year for survivors' insurance versus $4,032 per year for AFDC—and eligibility—universal for Survivors', selective for AFDC—underscores that the issue is more than semantic.[24]

Note too that current conceptualizations are static; they do not reflect changes over time. One could argue that education and job training are a necessary basis for increased output in the long run. As the economy moves toward a postindustrial workplace with the demands that were outlined earlier, the supposedly clear line now placed between productive work and dependent education is likely to become fuzzy.

In summary, dependency is used in complex and sometimes contradictory ways by experts and the general public. When it is conceptualized in all of its dimensions, it yields a portrait that is neither clear nor decisive. If a dependency crisis emerges in the coming decades, it derives not from simple demographic imperatives but from a set of economic, social, and cultural factors that can be controlled.

The Future of Dependency

Is the United States facing a dependency crisis? As has been shown, much of the professional literature and the popular press suggest that it is, in spite of the slim evidence to support this case. Although there is little reason for alarm, the data do suggest that dependency—defined by age or labor force— willl rise in the next sixty years.

Taking a multidimensional approach questions the clarity of this image, but it does not allow projections because the number of assumptions needed to forecast increase geometrically with the number of variables considered. Nevertheless, even the one-dimensional definitions that allow easier predictions raise a number of issues worth considering.

The most important factor passed over by the advocates of the dependency crisis is the expansion of productivity. The hallmark of the agricultural and industrial revolutions has been the increased productivity of human labor. Two centuries ago it would have been unimaginable that a small percentage of the population would be sufficient to raise all the food for a nation or that the labor needed to make a family's clothes would take hours instead of weeks. Increasing output per hour of work is the central imperative and achievement of modern capitalist economic development.

This simple fact has barely figured in the dependency debate. Although historically it is impossible to discuss social welfare without considering productivity, somehow it has seemed possible to look to the future without doing so. The dependency ratio has declined since 1900, but this explains only a fraction of the growth in the per capita gross national product during this century. Productivity, not dependency, has been the key to U.S. economic and social well-being.

Should it be assumed that productivity increases have come to an end? Measured productivity growth has declined over the past several decades, but it is dangerous to project these trends into the future. It also must be kept in mind that most of the data on productivity are based on goods production. Other sectors of the economy have had greater productivity growth, but their output changes have not been adequately measured. If services and the rapid decline in the cost of high-tech production are included in the calculations, productivity has increased more rapidly than is currently believed.[25]

Even if the most pessimistic position is taken on the future of productivity growth, in the future as in the past, the impact of dependency will be buried below a rising tide of productivity. If the dependency ratio is adjusted for a 1 percent annual increase in productivity (half the annual rate during the slow growth 1970s), the age dependency ratio (the most pessimistic index) would actually be 26 percent lower in 2025 than it was in 1982. A growth in dependency would not result in an intense struggle over dwindling resources but rather a decision over how quickly various groups in the population would see their standards of living increased.

In addition to productivity, dependency will be affected by the relative cost of supporting dependent groups. As noted above, during the next century the aging will replace children as the largest dependent group. Clearly, the needs of each of these groups are quite different. We can readily imagine nursing homes replacing day care centers and wheelchairs outselling tricycles. The crucial issue is how the total resource demands of the two groups compare.

Public expenditures for the aged in the United States have been about three times the amount spent on children.[26] This has led to justifiable concerns over how population aging will affect public finance.

A distinction needs to be made between public expenditures and total social expenditures. Dependent groups are supported by more than public transfers; intrafamily transfers, usually across generations, also play a crucial role. For the most part, midlife adults support their minor children. There are some exceptions—free public education is the most visible—but in general, children are supported by private funds. To compare the costs of dependency, estimates are needed of the total costs of support of children and the aged, including both public and private expenditures.[27] The evidence on the relative social costs of the old and the young is inconclusive. As noted, Clark and Spengler have produced estimates that support the view that the aged absorb more public resources than children.[28] Wander, however, using national income data for West Germany, discovered that because of children's large private costs they absorb 25 to 33 percent more resources per capita than the aged.[29]

Although the data are inconclusive, they do suggest that at the level of total social support there is no clear case that the elderly cost more than children. They do suggest, however, that a progressive shift of resources will need to be made from the private to the public sector. This fact—so at odds with the current political mood—is the real challenge of the dependency debate.

Projecting future costs is an even more difficult task. Much of the concern about the costs of the aged population has to do with an increased demand for health and hospital services. Aggregate demand for these goods depends not only on demographic factors but on diet, exercise, the quality of air, and medical technology. Lincoln Day has noted, for example, that *"when* aging begins and *how* it manifests itself would seem to be explained far less by consideration of birthdays than of conditions of life."[30] Workforce entry and exit ages are also factors that affect the size of the group to be supported and its age distribution. Will a longer period of education and training be required as the postindustrial economy matures? If so, youths who are dependent will increase beyond current projections. Will people retire from the labor force at a later age? Legislation makes this possible, but tax laws and custom both work against this possibility.

What is obvious is that the resources are available to handle the situation. Families will have fewer—although it is not clear how many fewer—young dependents. There will be more—again it is not clear how many more—older people who will not be in the labor force. Working adults therefore will have to pay more in taxes to support the aged but will use less of their income to support children. At the same time, that income will have grown.

Since the early 1970s economists have been predicting the dependency crisis, although the scope of the crisis has been downgraded. When support of the young is included, the severity of the problem decreases. When expansion of the labor force is included, the crisis is reduced further. If the cost of support is included, it shrinks again. Finally, if productivity is accounted for, the crisis vanishes. If the past is a guide, the future will yield a social surplus that can be distributed among various groups in the population.

The Real Dependency Crisis

The Social Security Act addressed the dependency crisis of the 1930s as members of that generation understood it. In the twenty-first century, the United States will face a new set of challenges about the character of dependency and poverty and effective responses to them.

New responses must be examined in light of the legacy of the past. The foundation of the original Social Security system—contributory pensions based on a pay-as-you-go payroll tax—has expanded over the last half century to cover some of the new risks and new populations. The noncontributory public assistance system that was developed initially as a temporary measure has not "withered away." It too has grown but with results that win no cheers from administrators, recipients, politicians, or the general public.

Reform of both social insurance and public assistance are inevitable. Many avenues for reform are available, and the economic and political challenges posed by each must be examined. The debate promises to be heated and acrimonious, but the smoke from this debate should not obscure the fact that the United States has sufficient resources to support its dependent population of the next century. The problem involved in allocating resources cannot be confused with the lack of resources. The real dependency crisis, then, is to find the means by which to distribute the costs and benefits of reform equitably and effectively.

Although many individuals in U.S. society are at risk, the young and the old continue to be the groups that are most crucial to past, present, and future debates over dependency. An appreciation of the conceptual complexity of the issue can be heightened by turning to history to clarify how the social construction of dependency has changed over time and how the responses to the past continue to influence the present.

Notes

1. Viviana Zelizer, *Pricing the Priceless Child: The Changing Social Value of Children* (New York: Basic Books, 1985).
2. Warren S. Thompson and P. K. Whelpton, "The Population of the Nation,"

in President's Research Committee on Social Trends, *Recent Social Trends in the United States* (New York: McGraw Hill, 1933), 35.

3. Advisory Council on Economic Security, *Report of the Committee on Economic Security* (Washington, D.C.: Government Printing Office, 1935), 24–25.

4. Harold L. Sheppard and Sara E. Rix, *The Graying of Working America: The Coming Crisis in Retirement-Age Policy* (New York: Free Press, 1977); Marc Rosenblum, "The Future Path of Labor Force Participation and Its Impact on Retirement Policy," and Robert Clark, "The Influence of Low Fertility Rates and Retirement Policy on Dependency Costs," papers presented at the Future of Retirement Age Policy Conference, American Institutes for Research, 29 September–1 October, 1976.

5. Ibid., xvi.

6. Yung-Ping Chen and Kwang-wen Chu, "Total Depedency Burden and Social Security Solvency" (Los Angeles: University of California, 1977), present one of the few attempts to separate the two sets of concerns.

7. Robert Clark, Juanita Kreps, and Joseph Spengler, "Economics of Aging: A Survey," *Journal of Economic Literature* 16 (September 1978): 919–62; quotation appears on page 922, italics added.

8. President's Commission on Pension Policy, *Technical Report* (Washington, D.C.: Government Printing Office, 1980), 111.

9. Donald O. Cowgill, "Can We Afford Our Aging Populations?," paper presented at the Conference on Economics of Aging, 3–5 April 1981, 2.

10. Judith Treas, "The Great American Fertility Debate: Generational Balance and Support of the Aged," *The Gerontologist* 21 (1) (1981): 100.

11. W. Andrew Achenbaum, "The Elderly's Social Social Security Entitlements as a Measure of Modern American Life," in *Old Age in a Bureaucratic Society,* edited by David Van Tassel and Peter N. Stearns (New York: Greenwood Press, 1986), 188.

12. Alvin Schorr, ". . . *Thy Father and Thy Mother . . .": A Second Look at Filial Responsibility and Family Policy* (Washington, D.C.: Government Printing Office, 1980).

13. Robert Kuttner, "A Great American Tradition: Government Opening Opportunity," *Challenge* (March/April 1986): 18–25.

14. "Baby Boomers Come of Age," *Newsweek* (30 March 1981): 34–37.

15. Sheppard and Rix, *The Graying of Working America,* 13–35.

16. D. Adamchak and E. Friedmann, "Societal Aging and Generational Dependency Relationships: Problems of Measurement and Conceptualization," *Research on Aging* 5 (September 1983): 319–38.

17. William Crown, "Some Thoughts on Reformulating the Dependency Ratio," *The Gerontologist* 25 (2) (April 1985): 166–72.

18. U.S. Bureau of the Census, *Statistical Abstract of the United States, 1986* (Washington, D.C.: Government Printing Office, 1986), 392.

19. U.S. Social Security Administration, *Monthly Benefit Statistics* No. 2 (Washington, D.C.: Government Printing Office, 1986).

20. U.S. Census Bureau, Current Population Reports, Series P-60, No. 154, *Money Income and Poverty Status of Families and Persons in the United States, 1985* (Washington, D.C.: Government Printing Office, 1986).

21. *Voluntary Action Leadership* (Arlington, Va.: Volunteer: The National Center for Citizen Involvement, Spring 1984); cited in the U.S. Census, *Statistical Abstract 1985,* 383.

22. "Unpaid Family Workers," *Family Economic Review* (October 1983): 21–22.

23. U.S. Social Security Administration, *Monthly Benefits* (December 1986).

24. Ibid.

25. "A Puzzlingly Poorly Productive America," *The Economist* (29 March 1986): 55; Fred Block, "Rethinking the Political Economy of the Welfare State," unpublished manuscript, December 1986.

26. Robert L. Clark and J. J. Spengler, "Changing Demography and Dependent Costs: The Implications of Future Dependency Ratios," in *Income and Aging: Essays on Policy Prospects,* edited by B. R. Herzog (New York: Human Sciences Press, 1977).

27. John Myles, "Citizenship at the Crossroads: The Future of Old Age Security," in *Old Age in a Bureaucratic Society,* edited by Van Tassel and Stearns 193–216.

28. Clark and Spengler, "Changing Demography."

29. H. Wander, "Zero Population Growth Now: The Lesson from Europe," in *The Economic Consequences of Slowing Population Growth,* edited by T. Espenshad and W. Serow (New York: Academic Press, 1978), 41–69.

30. Lincoln H. Day, "The Social Consequences of a Zero Population Growth Rate in the United States," in Commission on Population Growth and the American Future, *Demographic and Social Aspects of Population Growth* (Washington, D.C.: Government Printing Office, 1972), 665.

4
Age and Dependency: Children and the Aged in U.S. Social Policy

T he nature of dependency is not clearcut. It is a multidimensional concept that must be placed in a political, philosophical, and historical context.

Of all the groups that in one way or another have been considered dependent, the age dependent groups—the very old and the very young—have been most durable. At the limit, the newborn and the aged approaching death are dependent on others. With the exception of these biological limits, the definition of age dependency has been extremely fluid over the course of American history. This chapter examines this history and the effect that social definitions of dependency and responsibility have had on public policy.

The Reagan presidency has seen major trend reversals in many social welfare programs. Legal services for the poor, housing and health care for the poor, school lunches, student aid, food and nutritional programs have been targeted by the administration since 1981, and even today, the president and his advisors continue to push for elimination or reduction of programs in these areas.

Notably absent from this list were programs for the aged, especially Social Security and veterans' programs. Although the president advanced some proposals to cut back Social Security during 1981—a story told in more detail in chapter 7—he has since avoided any proposal that did not already have bipartisan support.

How did the special public concern for the aging come about and how pervasive has it been as a matter of public policy? The political privilege of the elderly is marked both by change and continuity. On the one hand, aged, native white men secured substantial benefits from the Civil War pensions of the late nineteenth century, programs whose historical importance has only recently been appreciated. On the other hand, these pensions did not cover women or nonwhites, and when the Civil War veterans and their dependents died, the extended coverage ceased. By 1910 there was virtually no national protection of the aged from poverty.

At the time the Social Security system was developed in 1935, the aging were one of the poorest groups in American society. It is only in the relatively recent past that the aged have been able to gain public programs that put them at a relative advantage within the official social welfare system.

This chapter traces the history of this theme in the United States from the emergence of industrialization during the nineteenth century to the present. It examines the interplay of several factors: demography, politics, culture, and the economy. It explores the ways in which policy implications are reflected over time in income maintenance legislation and administration for dependent children and their caretakers and for the aging. Finally, it examines changes in state pensions and shifts in the provisions of the Social Security Act with respect to levels of support and terms of entitlements and explores evolving concepts of public and private responsibilities for young and old dependents.

Trends in Family Structure

In the past decade and a half, understanding of the nature of family life has improved as scholars using a variety of sources—land records, censuses, personal narratives, and folksongs—have investigated the family in history. Whereas sociologists and historians used to believe that the family had changed simply from an extended to a nuclear form as industrialization and urbanization progressed, they now know that the family processes of the past were far more complex.[1]

Peter Laslett's investigation of three centuries of records has demonstrated that the extended family was uncommon in Britain after the sixteenth century, but research on the European continent suggests that extended households, including either three generations or a number of married siblings, were quite common in some regions as late as the early twentieth century.

Given the importance of inheritance rules in these cultures, the relationship between the aged and their adult children has often been very tense. During the past three centuries, the conflict between the generations in rural settings has centered on the disposal of land. Almost universally, landownership and the power it entailed dominated the relationship between the aging and their children.

In Austria, according to Lutz Berkner's study, the family farm was passed to only one child, after elaborate negotiations between father and son. As a result, children often had to wait until middle age before they could marry. One benefit of this arrangement for society as a whole was to restrict fertility and thereby avoid runaway population growth. For individuals, the benefit was less obvious. Young men, frustrated in their economic and romantic ambitions, often expressed this frustration in songs such as following:

Father, when ya gonna gimme the farm,
Father, when ya gonna sign it away?
My girl's been growin' every day,
And single no longer wants to stay.

Father, when ya gonna gimme the farm,
Father, when ya gonna gimme the house,
When ya gonna retire to your room out of the way
And dig up your potatoes all day?[2]

As late as the 1940s, Arensburg and Kimball found a similar conflict in rural Ireland. There land was the key to passage to adult status (it was common for unlanded men in their thirties to still be called "boys"). Fathers retained control over the farm until they were physically infirm. When they did "retire," they did so only after specifying in detail what the younger generation would have to provide them, including separate lodging in the "west room" of the family's homestead.[3]

Although the situation in the United States was different in many ways, here too there is evidence of parent-child tension over land. In Colonial New England, for example, Phillip Greven found that generational conflict over land was the primary source of the move toward the frontier. In his detailed examination of Andover, Massachusetts, he found that the founding fathers sought to control the marriage and occupational choices of their children by refusing to deed land to the second generation. Ultimately, this led to outmigration and the settling of the frontier. The availability of unsettled land served ultimately to break the traditional power of the elderly:

A fundamental characteristic of most families . . . was the prolonged exercise of paternal authority and influence over sons. Long after the ostensible achievement of maturity, indicated by marriages which often were delayed until men were in their late twenties, sons remained economically dependent upon fathers, who usually continued to own and to control the land upon which their sons had settled.[4]

The ready availability of land served to weaken paternal authority. Although the choice to abandon one's family and status to travel to the frontier was not without cost, it provided an alternative for those who did not have an inheritance. Richard Easterlin speculates that as late as 1860 the fertility patterns of rural northern families were a response to fathers' desires to settle their sons on land near them.[5]

The patriarchal authority of landowning fathers had a clear impact on cultural beliefs about the elderly. In colonial America, according to David Hackett Fischer, the aged had high social status characterized by "veneration": a feeling of religious awe for the aged. Unlike today, when lying about one's age implies claiming to be younger than one is, the evidence suggests that the colonial aged actually claimed to be older than they really were.[6] Patriarchy had two sides, however: the veneration displayed toward the aged did not lead to love. Fischer found that the aged "received respect without affection, honor without devotion, veneration without love." In early America these two aspects of the social condition of the aged "were combined in a system of age relations which grew steadily stronger through time. As time passed, old age became more exalted rather than less so—more honored, and yet less loved."[7]

The dominance of the rural family declined as America urbanized and capitalism took hold, yet certain elements of family processes did not change. During early industrialization, the urban working-class family was characterized by high fertility, low educational achievement, and the early entrance of children into the labor force. The work experience of these families was different from that of earlier generations, but family life remained stable.

The family system of early industrialization depended on the labor of all of its members; parents benefitted from the labor of their children, while husbands relied on their wives and children to supply the domestic necessities. A family morality that stressed obedience to authority and the veneration of age provided the rationale for these arrangements. According to John Caldwell,

> The familial system in the West depended on a sharp division of labor: the husband worked outside the home for wages or profits . . . while a wide range of activities (clothing, feeding, providing a clear and comfortable environment, child rearing) was undertaken by the wife with the help of the children.

Thus, while early industrial families were caught up in a new market society, "the husband ran his own highly efficient family-based subsistence system for providing services."[8] The foundation of this family morality, however, was undercut by the changing opportunity structure of the industrial city. During the third quarter of the nineteenth century, the business class—particularly professionals and business employees—began to adopt a family strategy that put more emphasis on children.

The mid–nineteenth-century business-class family had high fertility, was likely to include other relatives or boarders, and usually sent its children into the labor force by age fifteen. By the end of the century, all of these elements had changed. Using Buffalo, New York, as a case study, the fertility of professionals and business employees dropped by a third between 1855 to 1900. At the same time, the proportion of boys aged fifteen to nineteen who were in school rose from a mere 27 percent in 1870 to 69 percent in 1900.[9]

These patterns soon spread through the rest of society. Families in other business occupations—merchants, manufacturers, and the like—slowly adopted the smaller, more intensive nuclear family. By the turn of the century, the patriarchal family system of the working class also gave way. The rising standard of living of the average working-class family improved the current and future life chances of the family members. Paralleling these changes, the expansion of clerical occupations and the increased importance of formal education altered the opportunity structure of the twentieth-century city.

Under these new conditions, the family's success called for a strategy that stressed lower fertility, greater consumption, and most important, increased attention to children. As business-class families had, the working class adopted lower fertility and higher school attendance. In Buffalo the school attendance of older teenage boys whose fathers were laborers doubled during the first fifteen years of the century, while fertility fell precipitously.[10]

Earlier in American history the family was structured around the economic benefit of the parents; the flow of resources was upward—from children to parents. By the turn of the twentieth century, this had been reversed among almost all social classes. The flow of resources was now downward—from parents to children. The child-centered family had arrived.

Although the origins of child-centeredness are complex, one precondition was the possibility that parents could provide adequately for their children. Among nineteenth-century workers, according to Steven Dubnoff, economic crisis and unemployment were predictable aspects of the family life cycle. Only with the rise of real incomes in the late nineteenth century could parents realistically hope to support their children through adulthood.[11]

The rise of standards of living changed the strategy of the extended kin network as well. When economic crisis was an expected part of the life cycle, the logic of family life favored the maintenance of these networks as a hedge against hard times. However, as the threat of deprivation faded, an alternative logic took hold: the nuclear family could insulate itself from the demands of other kin—including elderly parents—so that it could use its resources to advance the prospects of children.

This change in family strategy was not universal. Among the poorest social strata, a different attitude toward children was common. For example, during the Great Depression, Glen Elder found that among deprived families, parents pulled their children out of school and sent them to work. Among poor black families, according to Carol Stack, the use of extended kin networks for economic and social support continued to be common during the postwar period.[12]

These changes in American family life had a negative impact on the aged. Fischer found that "expressions of hostility to old age grew steadily stronger" during the nineteenth century. "Consciously omitted from the list of [the] worthy" poor by the New York Association for the Improvement of the Condition of the Poor, the aged found themselves subjected to discrimination by some charity organizations. By the turn of the century, the neglect of the aged by private charities transformed U.S. almshouses into little more than old-age homes.[13]

The movement to the new definition of family came about in a halting manner. In their study of Muncie, Indiana, during the 1920s, Robert and Helen Lynd noted that "old age is not generally considered a 'social problem.' " However, they did find signs of social strain, in particular "the apparently diminishing tendency of married children to take elderly parents into their homes." The Lynds believed that the problem of the aging was only beginning to be understood publicly: "Provision for old age is just reaching the stage of occasional questioning of the adequacy . . . of the traditionally assumed benefits of the threat of old age as an incentive to saving, and also of the adequacy of the poorhouse as the widest instrument for caring for the aged needy."[14]

Although public opinion showed little interest in the problem of the aged before the Great Depression, labor economists and social reformers behind the scenes had been advocating for social insurance and public pensions since the turn of the century. Beginning in 1921, for example, the Fraternal Order of Eagles directed its organization to secure old-age pensions. The stage was set for acceptance of public responsibility for the financial support of the elderly.[15]

The Depression brought the issue to light, but many social reformers viewed the changing status of the aged from a longer perspective. "The problem of old age is steadily becoming more important," Paul Douglas noted, "as the public health movement and the reduction of immigration increase the relative proportion of the total population which is formed by those past the ages of fifty and sixty-five." He continued:

> Not only are the relative numbers of the aged increasing, however, but they are also finding it more difficult to obtain gainful employment. This is largely due to the decline of agriculture and the rise of urban industry, since this means a transition from a society where an old man can work on his home farm to the limit of his powers to a society where men who fall below given levels of efficiency tend not to be permitted to exercise such efficiency as they possess. There is some evidence, moreover, that within the last decade, it has become more difficult for old men to find employment within the field of urban industry itself.[16]

As the aged became more needy, their numbers increased. The fall of the white fertility rate, which continued until the 1940s, combined with the rise in life expectancy, increased the share of the population that was elderly. Social investigators did not worry about the ability of society to support the aged. "This increased burden of caring for the increasing number of aged is more than compensated by the greater decline in the number of the young through the falling birth rate," one contemporary noted.

> The proportion of children under fifteen is falling at a very much greater rate than the proportion of old people is increasing. Thus, that part of society which must carry the economic burden of productive activity really has no right to complain. The total burden of the two extremes of the span of life the young and old—is not increasing. And the care of the young is a much more costly task than the modest provision for the physical needs and health and comfort of the aged. It is because this burden of caring for the young has been so rapidly declining that we are enabled to extend that care over a very much longer period. Hence, our child labor laws, almost universal high school training for the majority of the children, and the increasing thousands of youths in colleges.[17]

As children assumed the spotlight, the aged were increasingly marginalized. In 1935 the President's Advisory Council on Economic Security, for example, noted that although children, friends, and relatives were still the major sources of support for the elderly, many children could no longer support their parents. The Council's report recognized the difficulties of both self-support for the aged and family financial assistance. It recommended instead a major government role in contributory old-age insurance and means-tested pensions, and the inability of many children to support their parents, which would have been a cause for ostracism in earlier societies, gained overt social sanction. As Americans embraced this position, the care of support for the dependent elderly shifted to the public sector.[18]

The change in family ideology had a double-edged meaning for the parent-child relationship. As the child moved to center stage, an extra burden was placed on poor parents. Not only were they culpable for their own poverty, but they could not even fulfill the minimal demand of parenthood: the support of their children. At midcentury, Charles Loring Brace could laud the pluck and independence of the street urchin. By the early twentieth century, the child was no longer a candidate for independence. As Viviana Zelizer has noted:

> the expulsion of children from the "cash nexus" at the turn of the past century, although shaped by profound changes in the economic, occupational, and family structures, was also part of a cultural process of "sacralization" of children's lives [i.e. they were] . . . invested with sentimental or religious meaning. While in the nineteenth century, the market value of children was culturally acceptable, later the new normative ideal of

the child as an exclusively emotional and affective asset precluded instrumental or fiscal considerations.

As the child moved from "useful" to "priceless," the stigma associated with being a poor parent deepened.[19]

Finally, the shift in the status of the aged and children had a political dimension. During the past forty years the aged have become an increasingly effective political lobby in support of Social Security. Children do not vote, and their (largely women) political advocates have not been able to wield effective political power on their behalf. Additionally, an air of moral virtue surrounds benefits for retirees from the labor force, while the children's cause has continued to carry some stigma connected with the public's view of the behavior of the needy children's parents.

Thus, the improvement in the public condition of the elderly during the child-centered era is only an apparent paradox. The rise in public responsibility for the aged had a base in the economic and cultural forces that eased the traditional private responsibility of adult children for the support of their parents. How did these forces actually play themselves out in social welfare legislation during the past century?

Public Policy before the Great Depression

The twentieth century has witnessed a growth in government responsibility for dependents at both ends of the life cycle. The increase in governmental responsibility for children is seen most clearly in education, but many areas including income support, traditional child welfare services, recreational programs for adolescents, and health and nutrition programs have widened in scope and extended in reach. Similarly for the aging, financial aid, social services, transportation, and medical and nursing services have all expanded in this century at a rate that would have been hard to predict in the nineteenth century.

There are, however, some interesting differences in the nature of the changes in social welfare programs for the aging and children in the last century. For children, these years have been marked by a shift in emphasis from mass care to individualization in services. The history of child care in the nineteenth century begins with the general institution, the almshouse, then moves to the specialized institution, the orphanage, which often had educational goals and particular religious auspices. Finally, at the end of the nineteenth century, individualized foster care emerged. This shift to personal care for each child was paralleled in the legal system by the juvenile justice movement, beginning in 1899, which established special courtrooms for children.[20]

The movement away from large institutions and toward family care was much less true for those aged who could not manage independent living. There was certainly some development of specialized institutions for aged groups during the late nineteenth century, based on religious or past military affiliation, a trend that accelerated somewhat early in the twentieth century. In general, however, the foster care movement that placed dependent children in substitute families has not been paralleled by a similar system for the elderly. In its place institutions—boarding and nursing homes—have replaced the almshouse as the warehouses of the aged. Social insurance has enabled the well elderly to live independently, but those in need of care, for the most part, continue to receive mass care.

The impact of the interaction of changing economic needs, changing family forms, and public social policy can be seen in the evolution of financial assistance policy for the aging and for children in the United States. From its earliest period as a nation, the United States has maintained an ideology of self-sufficiency, a preference for market-oriented solutions to poverty and, except for veterans, for public aid tied to the lowest possible unit of government. For both groups the United States has undergone a series of income-maintenance policies ranging from almshouse relief to means-tested pensions to contributory entitlement programs. All demonstrate the historical development of public responsibility for the ultimate welfare of dependent people in the United States. Government—whether county, state, or federal—has been the provider of last resort for the aged and for children. An examination of the history of support legislation, levels of benefits, and the details of entitlement demonstrates that the aged and children have consistently been treated differently.[21]

Age-categorized pensions for nonveterans were first introduced in some states in the second decade of the twentieth century. These years were characterized by rapid population growth due to European immigration and the shift from agricultural to urban society that led to a stream of rural migrants as well. The cities swelled with those in need. The movement for income assistance was one of a host of reform efforts during the period.[22]

For children the reform drive had many new aspects, but a major thrust was a continuation of efforts to maintain them in individual homes. One part of the reform effort of the era was legal protection for children. By 1914 most states had laws covering hours and conditions of child labor in factories, mills, and mines. Coincidentally, as children were removed from the labor force, new state laws set minimum ages for leaving school. To help support poor children in their own homes, Missouri passed the first mother's pension law in April 1911. Two months later, Illinois enacted the first statewide mandatory law, the Funds to Parents Act. Within two years, twenty states had provided cash relief programs for single women with children. By 1950 forty states had such programs.

The adoption of mothers' pension laws was accomplished in spite of opposition from social work agencies. The basis for their opposition was their distrust of public money that would be given without "service"—that is, casework. Just as important, the right to aid made explicit in these laws removed a degree of discretion in the granting of aid that had been a touchstone for the antipauperization ideology of the charity organization movement. "The crux of my opposition to public pensions today," according to Frederic Almy, secretary of Buffalo's Charity Organization Society, "is that the public does not stand for fit salaries for relief." He continued:

> I am an advocate of more adequate relief, but I am an advocate first of more adequate brains and work for the poor. Relief without brains is as bad as medicine without doctors. I would much rather see doctors without medicine, or salaries without relief, as is the practice of some of the best of our charity organization societies. Like undoctored drugs, untrained relief is poisonous to the poor. Good charity is expensive, and poor charity is worse than none, yet what city would support adequate case work for its public aid?[23]

Eventually, in many states social workers were able to shape the legislation and its administration to permit case investigation and behavioral conditions for the receipt of the grant. Financial aid to children was removed from the almshouse, but not from the scrutiny and discretion of investigators.

Conflicting goals for the mother's pension program appeared early in its history. The policy intent that single mothers not be expected to work when their children were young suggested an adequate level of support, which was in conflict with a "spirit of self confidence, initiative, and generally a desire for economic independence at as early a date as possible."[24] The programs called simultaneously for full-time mothering and a rapid movement into the labor force. The result of this conflict came partly through law and partly through administrative practice. Mothers' grants were always too low to support a caretaker and children. Furthermore, they were subject to wide variability in rules of eligibility and consequently suffered from inadequate coverage.

The movement to provide aged pensions derived from several sources. As the proportion of the aged in the population rose, the unemployment rate of elderly men became more visible. For example, Alexander Keyssar estimates that in Boston the unemployment frequency in 1900 was 62 percent for those in their fifties and 53 percent for those over sixty.[25]

At the same time, the percentage of men covered by Civil War pensions declined rapidly by the second decade of the twentieth century. By 1913 Australia, Belgium, Britain, Denmark, France, Germany, New Zealand, and Sweden had all enacted old-age support systems. The National Conference of

Charities and Corrections, the major social work organization of the period, endorsed the principle of social insurance, although it failed to support public pensions. As with mothers' pensions, the belief in self-reliance and the role of investigation and discretion kept social work professionals from advocating for greater public responsibility.

It was not until the 1920s that the old-age movement recorded any political victories. Ironically, the first public pensions laws passed not in the industrial East but in the West, where there were large numbers of single men. Miners, cowboys, lumbermen— individualists in the public mind, but individuals alone in old age—were among the neediest of the aged. The first old-age pension laws were passed in Arizona in 1914 (declared unconstitutional in 1915) and Alaska in 1915. Three states—Montana, Nevada, and Pennsylvania (the first in the East)—passed voluntary pensions laws in 1923, and many states followed suit shortly after.[26]

The 1920s, then, saw a number of elements of the movement come together. Demographic trends made the issue more visible, particularly in California, which was to become the center of old-age pension pressure. The willingness of children to support their parents was declining. Economically, in spite of overall prosperity, the aged were suffering higher rates of dependency. Politically, the stage was being set by a combination of the work of professional analysts and grass-roots organization. It was 1929, however, before a mandated and partially state-funded program was enacted in California. In 1930 less than 5 percent of elderly Americans were receiving pensions. Most states had means-tested programs by 1935, but they all shared low benefits and inadequate coverage.

During the early years of the Depression, a great many other schemes were developed for the support of the elderly. Their names suggest the populist character of these programs: the Old Folks Picnic Association, EPIC (End Poverty in California), and the Ham and Eggs Movement. The plans included a wide variety of benefits: free fishing licenses, dated money, support ranging from $50 to $400 a month, and age limits from fifty on up. Most popular of all was the Townsend pension movement, which originated in California and quickly spread across the nation through a network of Townsend Clubs. Through rallies, marches, advertising, and political campaigns, the Townsend movement made its influence felt at the national and state level. Nationally, it is credited with influencing the speed with which the Social Security Act was formulated and passed. At the state level, particularly in California, it is credited with liberalizing pensions during the late 1930s, so that by 1940 they were the most generous in the nation ($417 per month).[27]

Prior to the New Deal, then, a comparison of income-transfer programs for children and the aged would show that for both groups the principle of public aid had been established, but on average the aged were maintained somewhat better. The principle of pensions—an entitlement without stigma—

had failed to be established for either group. What had been achieved was a compromise: a set of categorical public assistance programs that varied from state to state both in funding and in eligibility. Here, the young and old found themselves in similar positions.

Public Policy since the Great Depression

With the passage of the Social Security Act in August 1935, the United States entered a new period of income-transfer programming. The act established a tripartite approach to income maintenance: (1) a group of federally administered insurance programs; (2) a group of federally funded, state-administered assistance programs; and (3) a group of programs funded only by states and localities. Children and the aged were affected by the first two of these.

Social insurance originally covered the unemployed and the aged. Widows and children were included when Survivors' Insurance was added in 1939. The Old-Age, Survivors', and Disability (added in 1956) Insurance are funded by a joint employee-employer contributory tax scheme that assures an income to those who have worked but cannot necessarily be expected to maintain the burden of self-support in retirement. During the 1950s, as is discussed in more detail in a later chapter, the social insurance program was expanded and liberalized; it evolved from a limited individual retirement program for a small proportion of the aging population into a major protection system covering a majority of older Americans. The program lost ground to economic growth and inflation during the 1960s and early 1970s, but the increase in benefits and their indexation in 1972 made the program a major antipoverty measure for eligible children and the aged and the cornerstone for the retirement planning of middle-income Americans.

The categorical programs that composed the second tier of the post-1935 income maintenance system evolved from the means-tested state programs that had previously existed, including old-age and mothers' pensions. In 1935 aid to the blind was available in twenty-four states, aid to the aged in thirty-four states, and aid to mothers and children in all states and jurisdictions except Alabama, Georgia, and South Carolina. The Social Security Act added federal funds and some federal guidelines to these programs. The roots of the differential treatment of the aged and children lay both in differential coverage of the two tiers and in the lower payments provided by the federal government to children in the second tier—that is, public assistance.

Aid for the aging had achieved wide popular support during the early years of the Depression. The public viewed the aged as a worthy group in urgent need. One immediate testimony to the priority given to the aged was the designation of Old-Age Assistance as Title I of the Social Security Act; the insurance program for the aged was Title II. Indeed, because insurance payments did not begin until the 1940s, it was the means-tested assistance program that had the greatest visibility and impact during the Depression.

"Poverty in old age," according to Franklin Roosevelt, "should not be regarded either as a disgrace or necessarily as a result of lack of thrift or energy." For Roosevelt, it was "a mere byproduct of modern industrial life." The president underlined the worthiness of the poor elderly by noting, "No greater tragedy exists in modern civilization than the aged, worn-out worker who after a life of ceaseless effort and useful productivity must look forward for his declining years to a poorhouse."[28]

The priority shown the aged was expressed very concretely in the benefit levels of the various means-tested programs. The grant-in-aid formula limited federal payments for Aid to Dependent Children to one-third of a maximum of $18 per month per family for a single child and one-third of a maximum of $12 for each additional child. In other words, the program provided $6 of federal funding a month for a one-child family and $10 for a two-child family. Indeed, the federal government did not provide any funds for the mother of the children until 1950. By contrast, states received $30 a month in federal funds to support a poor aged couple. Furthermore, while the federal government paid some of the administrative cost of aid to the aged and blind, it made no such provision for ADC.

These federal leads affected states' commitment to the groups. The lower rate of federal reimbursement meant that it cost much more for a state and county to support a child at a specific level than an aged individual, and by and large, the states did not make up the difference. In addition, the states were slower at the outset to institute public assistance programs for children than to pick up the other programs, suggesting that they shared the federal government's preference for support for the aged.

The approach to health care also varied for the two groups. For both children and the aged, the public provision of hospital, nursing, and health care service had been related to ability to pay until the mid 1960s. Medicare and Medicaid, added to the Social Security Act in 1965, had the effect of sharply distinguishing the distribution of health services on the basis of age. Medicare (Title XVIII) provided hospital and medical insurance for those over the age of sixty-five (and later for the disabled). Medicaid (Title XIX) provided hospital and medical care for the poor and medically indigent. Thus, while all of the aged were eligible for federally funded health care, children qualified only if they were poor.

The issue of differential treatment of the aged and children came sharply to public attention during the welfare reform efforts of 1972. Although rejecting President Nixon's Family Assistance Program as a replacement for Aid to Families with Dependent Children, Congress enacted an expansion of federal responsibility for the aged and disabled—Supplemental Security

Income. "America rejected a federal income guarantee for its children on October 17, 1972," according to Vincent and Vee Burke, "but enacted one for its aged." From their perspective, "Better treatment of the needy aged than of needy children is customary in American welfare."[29] We may question how old this "custom" was, but by 1972 the contrast between the public treatment of the two groups seemed clear.

The combined effect of market factors and public income-transfer policy can be seen in data on the incidence of poverty in the United States for the two groups (see tables 4–1, 4–2, and 4–3). Three distinct trends are clear in these data:

1. The overall poverty rate fell from 1959 (the first year for which this series is available) until 1969, remained fairly constant through the 1970s, and rose through 1983, dropping slightly since then.
2. The rate for children followed the same general pattern. It fell the first decade, stabilized the second, and rose sharply during the 1980s.
3. The rate for the aged has fallen fairly consistently.

Note that in 1959 the aged had a poverty incidence of 35.2 percent, compared with 26.9 percent for children and 22.4 percent for the population as a whole. A combination of high employment and low inflation brought poverty down for all in the early 1970s, but as inflation and unemployment grew worse, only the aged were relatively protected. They were for the most part out of the labor market and did not suffer from unemployment, while the indexation of Old-Age Insurance and Supplemental Security Income protected their benefits from erosion due to inflation. Not only were more of the aged receiving aid, but for many (though not the very old) it was keeping them above the poverty line.

For children, meanwhile, the situation has grown much worse. Their income has been adversely effected by the rise in the unemployment of their parents and the increase in marital disruption, while their primary aid program—Aid to Families with Dependent Children—has failed to keep pace with the cost of living. The increase in nonmarital births, desertion, and divorce all mean that fathers in the United States are taking less financial responsibility for the upbringing of children. Thus, both public decisions and private lives have contributed to the sharp increase in the number of children in poverty.

The different treatment of the aged and children by federal programs is put into even sharper focus if specific programs are examined. If there had been no income-transfer programs, the poverty rate of the aged in 1981 would have been 63.7 percent and that of children, 24.2 percent. The net impact of federal and state programs was to cut the aged poverty rate by

Table 4–1
Number of Persons in Poverty, 1959–1985
(in thousands)

Year	Total Number	Total Poverty Rate	White Number	White Poverty Rate	Black Number	Black Poverty Rate	Spanish Origin Number	Spanish Origin Poverty Rate
1959	39,490	22.4%	28,484	18.1%	NA	NA	NA	NA
1960	39,851	22.2	28,309	17.8	NA	NA	NA	NA
1961	39,628	21.9	27,890	17.4	NA	NA	NA	NA
1962	38,625	21.0	26,672	16.4	NA	NA	NA	NA
1963	36,436	19.5	25,328	15.3	NA	NA	NA	NA
1964	36,055	19.0	24,957	14.9	NA	NA	NA	NA
1965	33,185	17.3	22,495	13.3	NA	NA	NA	NA
1966	28,510	14.7	19,290	11.3	8,867	41.8%	NA	NA
1967	27,769	14.2	18,983	11.0	8,486	39.3	NA	NA
1968	25,389	12.8	17,335	10.0	7,616	34.7	NA	NA
1969	24,147	12.1	16,659	9.5	7,095	32.2	NA	NA
1970	25,420	12.6	17,484	9.9	7,548	33.5	NA	NA
1971	25,559	12.5	17,780	9.9	7,396	32.5	NA	NA
1972	24,460	11.9	16,203	9.0	7,710	33.3	NA	NA
1973	22,973	11.1	15,142	8.4	7,388	31.4	2,366	21.9%
1974	23,370	11.2	15,736	8.6	7,182	30.3	2,575	23.0
1975	25,877	12.3	17,770	9.7	7,545	31.3	2,991	26.9
1976	24,975	11.8	16,713	9.1	7,595	31.1	2,783	24.7
1977	24,720	11.6	16,416	8.9	7,726	31.3	2,700	22.4
1978	24,497	11.4	16,259	8.7	7,625	30.6	2,607	21.6
1979	26,072	11.7	17,214	9.0	8,050	31.0	2,921	21.8
1980	29,272	13.0	19,699	10.2	8,579	32.5	3,491	25.7
1981	31,822	14.0	21,553	11.1	9,173	34.2	3,713	26.5
1982	34,398	15.0	23,517	12.0	9,697	35.6	4,301	29.9
1983	35,303	15.2	23,984	12.1	9,882	35.7	4,633	28.0
1984	33,700	14.4	22,955	11.5	9,490	33.8	4,806	28.4
1985	33,064	14.0	22,360	11.4	8,926	31.3	5,236	29.0

Source: U.S. Bureau of the Census, *Characteristics of the Population below the Poverty Level*, Current Population Reports, (Washington, D.C.: Government Printing Office, selected years).

Table 4–2
Persons Sixty-Five Years and Over in Poverty, by Race and Spanish Origins, Selected Years
(number in thousands)

Year	Total Number	Total Rate	White Number	White Rate	Black Number	Black Rate	Spanish Origin Number	Spanish Origin Rate
1959	5,481	35.2%	4,744	33.1%	711	62.5%	NA	NA
1966	5,144	28.5	4,357	26.4	722	55.1	NA	NA
1967	5,388	29.5	4,646	27.7	715	53.3	NA	NA
1968	4,632	25.0	3,939	23.1	655	47.7	NA	NA
1969	4,787	25.3	4,052	23.3	689	50.2	NA	NA
1970	4,709	24.5	3,984	22.5	683	48.0	NA	NA
1971	4,273	21.6	3,605	19.9	623	39.3	NA	NA
1972	3,738	18.6	3,072	16.8	640	39.9	NA	NA
1973	3,354	16.3	2,698	14.4	620	37.1	95	24.9%
1974	3,085	14.6	2,460	12.8	591	34.3	117	28.9
1975	3,317	15.3	2,634	13.4	652	36.3	137	32.6
1976	3,313	15.0	2,633	13.2	644	34.8	128	27.7
1977	3,177	14.1	2,426	11.9	701	36.3	113	21.9
1978	3,233	14.0	2,530	12.1	662	33.9	125	20.9
1979	3,682	15.2	2,911	13.3	740	36.2	154	26.8
1980	3,871	15.7	3,042	13.6	783	38.1	179	30.8
1981	3,853	15.3	2,978	13.1	820	39.0	146	25.7
1982	3,751	14.6	2,870	12.4	811	38.2	159	26.6
1983	3,625	13.8	2,776	11.7	791	36.0	173	22.1
1984	3,330	12.4	2,579	10.7	710	31.7	176	21.5
1985	3,456	12.6	2,698	11.0	717	31.5	219	23.9

Source: U.S. Bureau of the Census, *Money Income and Poverty Status of Families and Persons in the United States*, Current Population Reports, Series P-60 (Washington, D.C.: Government Printing Office, selected years).

Table 4–3
Related Children under Eighteen, in Poverty, by Race and Spanish Origin, Selected Years
(number in thousands)

Year	Total		White		Black		Spanish Origin	
	Number	Rate	Number	Rate	Number	Rate	Number	Rate
1960	17,288	26.5%	11,229	20.0%	NA	NA	NA	NA
1965	14,388	20.7	8,595	14.4	NA	NA	NA	NA
1966	12,146	17.4	7,204	12.1	4,774	50.6%	NA	NA
1967	11,427	16.3	6,729	11.3	4,558	47.4	NA	NA
1968	10,739	15.3	6,373	10.7	4,188	43.1	NA	NA
1969	9,501	13.8	5,667	9.7	3,677	39.6	NA	NA
1970	10,235	14.9	6,138	10.5	3,922	41.5	NA	NA
1971	10,344	15.1	6,341	10.9	3,836	40.7	NA	NA
1972	10,082	14.9	5,784	10.1	4,025	42.7	NA	NA
1973	9,453	14.2	5,462	9.7	3,822	40.6	1,364	27.8%
1974	9,967	15.1	6,079	11.0	3,713	39.6	1,414	28.6
1975	10,882	16.8	6,748	12.5	3,884	41.4	1,619	33.1
1976	10,081	15.8	6,034	11.3	3,758	40.4	1,424	30.1
1977	10,028	16.0	5,943	11.4	3,850	41.6	1,402	28.0
1978	9,772	15.7	5,674	11.0	3,781	41.2	1,354	27.2
1979a	9,993	16.0	5,909	11.4	3,745	40.8	1,505	27.7
1980	11,114	17.9	5,817	13.4	3,906	42.1	1,718	33.0
1981a	12,068	19.5	7,429	14.7	4,170	44.9	1,874	35.4
1982	13,139	21.3	8,282	16.5	4,388	47.3	2,117	38.9
1983	13,427	21.8	8,534	17.0	4,273	46.2	2,251	37.7
1984	12,929	21.0	8,086	16.1	4,320	46.2	2,317	38.7
1985	12,483	20.1	7,838	15.6	4,057	43.1	2,512	39.6

Source: U.S. Bureau of the Census, Money Income and Poverty Status of Families and Persons in the United States, Current Population Reports, Series P-60 (Washington, D.C., Government Printing Office, selected years).
a Revised.

three-fourths, while public action reduced the number of children in poverty by only 20 percent.[30]

Conclusion

Prior to the depression of the 1930s and the enactment of the Social Security Act, public financial aid—outdoor relief—was available both for the aging and for children in most states. Benefit payments were low, and terms of entitlement were highly restrictive. Not until 1935 did the different economic treatment of the two groups begin to emerge.

Part of this difference resulted from the evolution of the development of family responsibility, including the mutual obligations of husband and wife, parent and child, and grandparents and grandchildren to each other. Over the years, the concept of relative responsibility has narrowed. By the 1960s only a few states still viewed grandparents, grandchildren, or siblings as responsible for the support of a dependent individual. All states, however, continued to enforce the responsibility of husbands and wives for one another and of parents for minor children. The issue of the responsibility of adult children for older parents remained in question. Although the expansion of social insurance provided hope that the issue would disappear, the enforcement of children's obligation to parents varied from state to state. Some states actually dropped this responsibility, but more commonly states eased the contribution schedules until, over time, the obligation was practically circumscribed. The situation had finally become clear: parents were responsible for their children, but adult children were no longer legally obligated to support their parents in old age.[31]

The history of the emergence of the preferential treatment received by the aged over children in American social policy gives rise to the temptation to develop sweeping explanations of this phenomenon. In his 1984 presidential address to the Population Association, for example, Samuel Preston reviewed evidence of the increasing gap between the well-being of the elderly and children. Interpreting these trends, Preston noted that the declining base of family support for children and then, turning to politics, noted:

> In a modern democracy, public decisions are obviously influenced by the power of special interest groups, and that power is in turn a function of the size of the groups, the wealth of the groups, and the degree to which that size and wealth can be mobilized for concerted action. In all of these areas, interests of the elderly have gained relative to those of children.[32]

The shift in the legal definition of *relative responsibility* suggested a more massive change in the division of public and private responsibility. The aged, reaping the benefits of a vast array of public programs, improved their economic and social circumstances, while children, increasingly the responsibility of fewer and fewer parents, reaped a bitter harvest of poverty and lost opportunities.

The explanation of these trends lies in the complex interaction of culture, demography, and politics. As the child became the center of family life—both economically and emotionally—the aged were pushed from the stage. With the Great Depression, this movement gained public sanction in the assumption of public responsibility for the aged. Supported by a political coalition—including those who hoped to use the aged to set precedents for other groups—the aged have been able to maintain their public support in the face of cutbacks in other areas of social welfare.

The losers have been children—in particular, poor children. The discrimination they faced was intertwined with racism and sexism. The victims of public neglect are, indeed, "other people's children," in Marvin Lazerson and Norton Grubb's striking phrase.[33] If other people are women and in particular black women, the lack of public interest is more understandable. Indeed, from 1935 when caretakers were excluded from Aid to Dependent Children until today's debate over welfare reform, the worthiness of mothers and their willingness and ability to work have become the central issues of public assistance. If the price of punishing "unworthy" mothers is widespread poverty among America's children, society has been willing to pay the price.

Sociological and economic forces have played a role as well. The nineteenth-century separation of children into specialized institutions reflected several influences. There was the Catholic concern for the religious upbringing of Catholic children in a predominantly Protestant nation. A wish to provide role models to inculcate the correct work-oriented values has also persisted. When work and apprenticeship opportunities for children declined, the westward foster care movement exemplified by the New York Children's Aid Society provided an opportunity to provide the child with a "work model family" while meeting a labor shortage for farm laborers. The child was a worker—present and future. The dependent older person was just that—a dependent. Thus, although the early difference in the treatment of the elderly and children was not dominated by economic imperatives, at least it did not contradict them.

The slow and steady decision of the last thirty years to define the nuclear two-generation family as the unit of legal responsibility appears more clearly dictated by economic concerns. The nature of an expanding, industrial economy with its premium on mobility for the wage earner inspired greater emphasis on the nuclear family, even though wider kin networks remained important.

Although the public sector has accepted responsibility for a great portion of the support of the aged, it has resisted assuming the same obligation for children. One speculative question to be asked, however, is whether at some stage it might be desirable to consider an increased public financial role for the upbringing of children. Labor force requirements have led in the past to clear public policy for the aging but to ambivalence toward women and their children. The U.S. economy and demography have shifted dramatically since then; in the face of the clear and present threat to the nation's children, perhaps it is at a point of reevaluation.

Such a shift may well be underway already. Viviana Zelizer, in her history of childhood, detects a decline in the sacredness of the "useless" and "priceless" child:

> Once again, as at the turn of the century, two views of childhood are being disputed, but this time, the reform group proposes to selectively increase children's useful adultlike participation in productive activities, while traditionalists cling to the Progressive ideal of a separate, domestic domain for children. It is no coincidence that this re-evaluation of a child's place is taking place just as the world of their mothers is being dramatically transformed.[34]

We may have an urge to mourn the passage of the "sacred" child, but the reemergence of the child as a useful member of society may have positive effects. The ideal of the sacred child gave rise to a juvenile justice system that was suppose to protect the young offender but worked just as often to dispense rough justice without the protection of constitutional rights. It created a foster care system that was to individualize care but that now suffers from chronic underfunding. As shown, it has dealt out increasing poverty for children over the past decade. Perhaps as the child is viewed as more useful, more action will be taken to preserve and protect this resource.

Whatever the trends in American cultural attitudes toward children, the family situation in which they find themselves and the work situation for which they must be prepared will continue to change. It is these factors that will set the limits and the possibilities of public policy for the young, the old, and those in between.

Notes

This chapter previously appeared in a slightly different form in "Age and Dependency: Children and the Aged in American Social Policy," *Milbank Memorial Fund Quarterly/Health and Society* 63 (4) (Fall 1985): 648–70. We wish to thank the *Quarterly* and its editor, David P. Willis, for permission to use this material.

1. Edward Shorter, *The Making of the Modern Family* (London: Collins, 1976); Peter Laslett, *The World We Have Lost*, rev. ed. (London: Methuen, 1971).

2. Lutz Berkner, "The Stem Family and the Developmental Cycle of the Peasant Household: An Eighteenth-Century Austrian Example," *American Historical Review* 77 (1972): 403.

3. Conrad Arensburg and S. T. Kimball, *The Family and Community in Ireland* (Cambridge, Mass.: Harvard University Press, 1941).

4. Phillip J. Greven, Jr., *Four Generations: Population, Land, and Family in Colonial Andover, Massachusetts* (Ithaca, N.Y.: Cornell University Press, 1970), 98.

5. Richard Easterlin, "Factors in the Decline of Farm Fertility in the United States: Some Preliminary Research Results," *Journal of American History* 63 (1976): 600–14.

6. David Hackett Fischer, *Growing Old in America* (New York: Oxford University Press, 1977).

7. Ibid., 224

8. John Caldwell, "A Theory of Fertility: From High Plateau to Destabilization," *Population and Development Review* 4 (4) (December 1978): 509.

9. Mark J. Stern, *Society and Family Strategy: Erie County, New York 1850–1920* (Albany: State University of New York Press, 1987), 47–115.

10. Ibid.

11. Steven Dubnoff, "The Life-Cycle and Economic Welfare: Historical Change in the Economic Constraints on Working Class Family Life 1860–1974," unpublished manuscript, 1978.

12. Glen Elder, Jr., *Children of the Great Depression: Social Change in Life Experience* (Chicago: University of Chicago Press, 1974); Carol Stack, *All Our Kin: Strategies for Survival in a Black Community* (New York: Harper & Row, 1974).

13. Fischer, *Growing Old*, 225; Carole Haber, *Beyond Sixty-Five: The Dilemma of Old Age in America's Past* (Cambridge: Cambridge University Press, 1983), 37; Michael B. Katz, *Poverty and Policy in American History* (New York: Academic Press, 1983).

14. Robert S. Lynd and Helen M. Lynd, *Middletown: A Study in Contemporary American Culture* (New York: Harcourt, Brace, 1929), 35–36.

15. Fischer, *Growing Old*.

16. Paul Douglas, "Foreword," in *The Quest for Security*, edited by Isaac M. Rubinow (New York: Holt, 1934).

17. I. M. Rubinow, ed., *The Care of the Aged* (Chicago: University of Chicago Press, 1931), 654.

18. United States, *Report of the Advisory Council on Economic Security* (Washington, D.C.: Government Printing Office, 1935).

19. Viviana A. Zelizer, *Pricing the Priceless Child: The Changing Value of Children* (New York: Basic Books, 1985), 11.

20. June Axinn and Herman Levin, "The Century of the Child," in *The Century of the Child*, edited by Axinn and Levin (Philadelphia: University of Pennsylvania School of Social Work, 1973), 1–4.

21. Theda Skocpol and John Ikenberry, "The Political Formation of the American Welfare State," paper presented at the annual meetings of the American

Sociological Association, San Francisco, September 1982; June Axinn and Herman Levin, *Social Welfare: A History of the American Response to Need,* 2nd ed. (New York: Longman, 1982).

22. Paul Boyer, *Urban Masses and Moral Order in America, 1820–1920* (Cambridge, Mass.: Harvard University Press, 1978); David J. Rothman, *Conscience and Convenience: The Asylum and Its Alternatives in Progressive America* (Boston: Little, Brown, 1980).

23. Quoted in Axinn and Levin, *Social Welfare,* 164–68.

24. M. F. Bogue, *Administration of Mother's Aid in Ten Localities: With Special Reference to Health, Housing, Education, and Recreation,* Children's Bureau Publication No. 184 (Washington, D.C.: Government Printing Office, 1928), 5.

25. Alexander Keyssar, *Out of Work: The First Century of Unemployment in Massachusetts* (Cambridge: Cambridge University Press, 1986), 94.

26. J. Leiby, *A History of Social Welfare and Social Work in the United States, 1815–1972* (New York: Columbia University Press, 1978), 214.

27. Fischer, *Growing Old,* 182.

28. A. J. Altmeyer, *The Formative Years of Social Security* (Madison: University of Wisconsin Press, 1981), 263.

29. V. J. Burke and V. Burke, *Nixon's Good Deed: Welfare Reform* (New York: Columbia University Press, 1974), 302.

30. U.S. Congress, House of Representatives, *Background Material and Data on Major Programs within the Jurisdiction of the Committee on Ways and Means* (Washington, D.C.: Government Printing Office, 1983).

31. George Hoshino, "The Responsibility of Children for the Support of Needy Parents" (D.S.W. diss., University of Pennsylvania, 1960).

32. Samuel H. Preston, "Children and the Elderly: Divergent Paths for America's Dependents," *Demography* 21 (1984): 435–57.

33. Marvin Lazerson and W. Norton Grubbs, *Broken Promises: How Americans Fail Their Children* (New York: Basic Books, 1982).

34. Zelizer, *Pricing the Priceless Child,* 221–22.

5
Changing Contours of Poverty

This book has been exploring the implications of changes in the U.S. social structure for dependency and poverty. It has argued that three major shifts—the aging of the population, changes in family structure, and the move to a "postindustrial" economy—are having a major effect on the problems with which social policy must cope. For some groups increasing poverty appears to be the direct result of government neglect—particularly the declining effectiveness of Unemployment Insurance and AFDC. Finally, all of these new problems must be seen in the context of a historical structure of gender and racial equality.

This chapter disaggregates these various influences by examining how the contours of poverty have changed over the past fifteen years. The first part of the chapter addresses the underlying assumptions and implications of the official definition of poverty. It analyzes the value bases of alternative ways of defining and counting who is poor in the United States. The second section then uses the distinction between the official definition of *poverty* and *pretransfer poverty* to examine the unique contribution of government income-transfer policy to the well-being of Americans.

Explorations of the Concept of Poverty

The federal government's official measure of poverty, as developed by the Social Security Administration, counts only cash as income available to a family. A poverty threshold is calculated by first pricing the cost of the economy food plan of the Department of Agriculture (based on a 1955 dietary study). Because typically in 1955 Americans were spending one-third of the family budget on food, the poverty threshold (or minimum required income) is calculated at three times the cost of the economy food plan, with some adjustments for family size and a few other variables. If the pretax, posttransfer cash income of a family is below the poverty threshold for its category, the family is defined as poor.

A relatively large literature has developed around the complexities of the poverty definition.[1] The two most troublesome issues involved here are the inability of the current definition to take into account noncash benefits on the one hand and to keep up with increases in the median income of the population on the other. The first error, by ignoring serious aspects of family income, understates resources and thus overstates the number of poor people; the second, by assuming a world without economic growth or changes in consumer budget patterns, underestimates budget needs and thus gives poverty thresholds further and further away from any notion of a normal income.

In 1964, when the official poverty measure was developed, most means-tested programs were cash programs, but the intervening years have seen a huge growth in noncash or inkind benefits. By 1970 the market value of means-tested inkind benefits provided by the federal government reached $22.1 billion compared to $19.8 billion in means-tested cash assistance. Fifteen years later the balance had swung overwhelmingly to inkind programs: food stamps, medical care programs, and housing subsidies. Cash help for the poor was no longer in favor. In 1985 federal means-tested cash assistance was $30.2 billion; inkind benefits were almost twice that—$56.2 billion. Of this total, $36.7 was federal Medicaid payments, $10.7 billion food stamps, $6.2 billion housing assistance, and $2.7 billion free and reduced-price school lunches.[2] The United States Bureau of the Census estimates that annually, since 1979, over two-thirds of all poor families have received food benefits, over half medical benefits, and about 15 to 20 percent housing assistance. Nevertheless, there has been no change in the definition of poverty threshold. Clearly an income measure that excludes such a meaningful part of income distorts both the total poverty figures and their structure.

The Census Bureau has offered an array of poverty estimates that include different benefits as income and measure these benefits by various criteria. An estimate of the number of poor people in the United States in 1985 might be 14 percent, 9.1 percent, 12.8 percent, 11.6 percent, or some other figure in between depending on which noncash benefits are included and how they are valued (see table 5–1).

Should medical care benefits be included at all? To do so would reduce poverty for the aged from the 12.6 percent of the official measure to as little as 2.9 percent if market prices are used to measure their income contribution. Note that this approach has the classical advantage of valuing inkind benefits at their private sector purchasing power. It assumes that average market price is a reflection of value for all income classes and groups—that the values of the lowest economic class are identical with those of the entire consumer class. Although this eliminates the task of making separate personal judg-

Table 5–1
Percentage of Persons in Poverty, by Valuation Technique and Type of Noncash Benefit Included, 1985

Type of Measure	Persons Included					
	All	Under 6 Years	65 years and Over	White	Black	Spanish Origin
Official definition	14.0%	23.0%	12.6%	11.4%	31.3%	29.0%
Market value approach:						
Including food and housing only	12.5	20.8	10.7	10.2	27.5	25.5
Including food, housing, and all medical care	9.1	16.2	2.9	7.7	18.7	18.9
Recipient value approach:						
Including food and housing only	12.8	21.4	11.1	10.5	28.6	26.2
Including food, housing, and all medical care	11.8	20.6	7.4	9.7	26.4	24.5
Poverty budget share value:						
Including food and housing only	12.6	20.9	10.7	10.3	27.9	25.7
Including food, housing, and all medical care	11.6	19.8	7.6	9.5	25.7	23.9

Source: U.S. Bureau of the Census, *Estimates of Poverty Including the Value of Noncash Benefits*, Technical Paper 56 (Washington, D.C.: Government Printing Office 1986), 5–6.

ments as to what is an appropriate price, it has numerous difficulties. On this measure, the more often a person becomes ill, the richer she would become! Difficulties are presented not only by including medical benefits but also by the valuation technique.

Market value techniques for counting inkind benefits are philosophically awkward when applied to any noncash benefit unless it is argued that people are just as pleased to receive food stamps as cash—that they place no value on the right to allocate their own dollars. Valuing benefits at market prices reduces poverty for 1985 by over one-third—from 14 percent to 9.1 percent.

At an other extreme is a valuation technique that would put a strict ceiling on the total value for any inkind commodity. That ceiling would be determined by the proportional share the item normally assumed in a poverty budget. This "poverty budget share-value" approach takes the view that in setting the cash poverty line at a fixed multiple of the economy food plan, a minimum level of other basic necessities was implied. Thus, it would be argued that no value should be assigned to any component (such as medical care) that would usurp the role of the other elements. Food, health care, and housing would not be allowed to be treated as substitutes for each other; presumably panels of experts would determine the appropriate values. In contrast to the first method, this poverty budget share-approach offers a much smaller reduction in poverty figures. Using this measure for 1985, and counting all means-tested benefits to all persons both in and out of institutions, poverty would fall by 17 percent—from 14 percent to 11.6 percent.

Philosophically between these two approaches is the "recipient or cash equivalent value" approach. This approach attempts to value the noncash offering as the recipient would. It presumes that most people prefer cash to inkind benefits and estimates the amount of money that would make the recipient as well off as the noncash transfer value. This does not really assess individual values but some average recipient value. Once again a total group valuation is taken to be that of an individual. To the extent that a poverty group exhibits homogeneous behavior and that the public accepts this judgment, this approach might be theoretically possible. Accepting this approach for 1985 would reduce poverty by 16 percent—from 14 percent to 11.8 percent.

There remains a still more basic question. Why should some noncash benefits be included in the definition of income and not others? If Medicaid, why not Medicare, why not employer paid health and dental insurance? If housing rent subsidies, why not tax deductions for mortgage payments? If free school lunches are part of the income of the poor, is free tuition for faculty children part of the income of the professoriate? In counting some things as income and not others, the assumption is that a poverty concept is an absolute, not a relative, one.

The official U.S. poverty measure was developed in 1964, almost twenty-five years ago, as a market basket index. A fixed food budget was priced and then assumed to be invariant except for price changes. Two major changes have occurred since then: average incomes have grown, and food has become a smaller part of the average budget. In 1955, when food was one-third of the average consumer budget before taxes, people were spending 16.9 percent of after-tax income on food. In 1984 only 10.8 percent of after-tax income was being spent on food at home, and another 4.3 percent on food away from home, suggesting a multiplier of 6.6—not 3—and a much higher poverty threshold.[3]

The years since 1964 have been years of major growth in personal family incomes. One result of using a fixed measure of poverty has been that the gap between poverty and median income has widened dramatically during the period. In 1959, the first year for which an official poverty line is available, a family of four was considered poor if it had less than $2,973; median family income that same year was $5,417. The poverty line was 55 percent of median family income. By 1985 median family income had risen to $27,735, and at $10,989 the poverty line for a family of four stood at less than 40 percent of median income. Economic distance between the poor and the average family has widened steadily.

It should be pointed out that the definition of poverty has a political component. When the staff of the Social Security Administration under the leadership of Mollie Orshansky defined poverty during the 1960s, its initial method produced a figure that was judged too high for political reasons. The staff went back to its calculations and derived a formula that gave a more palatable figure.[4]

There should be no illusions that the official poverty statistics are a measure of scientific or even disinterested origins. Their virtues lie in clarity and consistency over the past twenty-five years. They provide a standard against which relative changes in the well-being of the population and of specific subgroups can be judged.

The use of the poverty line, however, has been muddied in recent years by a debate over its inclusiveness. The poverty level is based on pretax, postsocial welfare cash transfers. Many other variations could be spelled out. The statistical world of poverty is different if food stamps are counted but Medicaid is not, if people in institutions are counted or excluded, if one set of values is placed on vouchers rather than another. Despite these varying definitions of poverty, there is a fairly large poverty population and one with a marked age, race, and gender structure.

The Poverty Data

Another aspect of the official definition of poverty is its inability to differentiate the impact of government income-transfer policy from other influences on poverty. A variety of events can lead a family into or out of poverty. Changes in cash income are the most important. These can range from getting or losing a job, being declared eligible or ineligible for social insurance or public assistance, receiving insurance or annuity payments, or winning a lottery. This chapter is concerned with the role that changes in government programs have played in altering the face of economic need during the past fifteen years.

Trends in Official Poverty

Tables 5–2 and 5–3 present the official trends in poverty for the past fifteen years. The poverty figures can be examined using three indexes of change: changes in the total number of poor (compositional changes), changes in the poverty rate (incidence changes), and contributions to the total change in the poverty population. For all races, the number of poor increased by 10.1 million between 1973 and 1985, a rise of 43.9 percent. If the population is examined by family and age status, the biggest proportional increases were among householders (49.6 percent) and family members other than children or householders (50.1 percent). The number of poor children increased by less—32.0 percent, yet from a different perspective children were the big losers between 1973 and 1985. Because of declines in fertility, the child poverty rate increased from 14.2 to 20.1 percent during these years, an increase of 42 percent. Thus, of the 10.1 million new poor, three in ten were children under the age of eighteen.

The biggest winners were the aged. They are the only major group to enjoy a decrease in their poverty rate. Because of the increased proportion of the population that was aged, however, the decline in their poverty rate did not mean that there were fewer poor aged; their numbers increased by 3.0 percent. Although the chances of an older American being poor fell quite dramatically during this period, the actual number of poor aged remained about the same.

Most groups experienced increased poverty during the period, but the status of black Americans remained stable. The black poverty rate fell by 2 percent between 1973 and 1985; the white rate increased by 36 percent. This pattern held across family status and age groups. White poverty remained between a half and a third of black rates, but increases in the white rates exceeded those for blacks among householders, children under eighteen, and other family members. Only among unrelated individuals and the aged (two overlapping categories) did the gap between black and white poverty widen over the eleven years.

The slight convergence of black and white poverty was particularly striking among female-headed families. Female-headed families are more common among blacks than whites, and the risk of poverty among black

Table 5–2
Number and Percentage of Population in Poverty, by Family Status and Race, Total Population, 1973–1985
(in thousands)

Group	1973			1985			Percentage Growth in		
	N	Poverty Rate	% of Poor	N	Poverty Rate	% of Poor	N	Poverty Rate	% of Total Increase
All races:									
All persons	22,973	11.1%	100.0%	33,064	14.0%	100.0%	43.9%	26.1%	100.0%
In families	18,299	9.9	79.7	25,798	12.6	77.8	43.9	26.1	73.6
Householders	4,828	8.8	21.0	7,223	11.4	21.8	49.6	29.5	23.7
Children < 18	9,453	14.2	41.1	12,483	20.1	37.8	32.0	41.5	30.0
Other family	4,018	5.9	17.4	6,032	7.7	18.2	50.1	30.5	20.0
Unrelated individuals	4,674	25.6	20.3	6,725	21.5	20.3	43.9	-16.0	20.3
Over 65	3,354	16.3	14.5	3,456	12.6	10.5	3.0	-22.7	1.0
Whites:									
All persons	15,142	8.4	65.9	22,860	11.4	69.1	51.0	35.7	76.4
In families	11,412	6.9	49.7	17,125	9.9	51.8	50.1	43.4	56.6
Householders	3,219	6.6	14.0	4,983	9.1	15.1	54.8	37.9	17.5
Children < 18	5,462	9.7	23.8	7,838	15.6	23.7	44.4	60.8	23.5
Other family	2,731	4.5	11.9	4,304	6.4	13.0	57.6	42.2	15.6
Unrelated individuals	3,730	23.7	16.2	5,299	19.6	16.0	42.0	-17.3	15.5
Over 65	2,698	14.4	11.7	2,698	11.0	8.2	0	-23.6	0
Blacks:									
All persons	7,388	31.4	32.1	8,926	31.3	27.0	20.8	-2.4	15.2
In families	6,560	30.8	28.6	7,504	30.5	22.7	14.3	-0.1	9.3
Householders	1,527	28.6	6.6	1,983	28.7	6.0	29.9	0.3	4.5
Children < 18	3,822	40.6	16.6	4,057	43.1	12.3	6.1	6.2	2.3
Other family	1,211	18.7	5.3	1,464	17.7	4.4	20.9	-5.3	2.5
Unrelated individuals	828	37.9	3.6	1,264	34.7	3.8	52.7	-8.4	4.3
Over 65	620	37.1	2.7	717	31.5	2.2	15.5	-15.1	1.0

Source: Calculated from U.S. Bureau of the Census, Current Population Reports Series P-60, Money Income and Poverty Status of Families and Persons in the United States (Washington, D.C.: Government Printing Office, selected years).

Table 5–3
Number and Percentage of Population in Poverty, by Family Status and Race, Female-Headed Households, 1973–1985
(*in thousands*)

Group	1973			1985			Percentage Growth in		
	N	Poverty Rate	% of Poor	N	Poverty Rate	% of Poor	N	Poverty Rate	% of Total Increase
All races:									
All persons	11,357	34.9%	49.4%	16,365	33.5%	49.5%	44.1	−4.0%	49.6%
Householders	2,193	32.2	9.5	3,474	34.0	10.5	58.4	5.6	12.7
Children	5,171	52.1	22.5	6,716	53.6	20.3	29.9	2.9	15.3
Whites:									
All persons	6,642	27.9	28.9	9,778	27.3	29.6	47.2	−2.2	31.0
Householders	1,190	24.5	5.2	1,878	27.4	5.9	63.9	11.2	7.5
Children	2,461	42.1	10.7	3,372	45.2	10.2	37.0	7.3	9.0
Black									
All persons	4,564	55.4	19.9	6,215	51.8	18.8	36.2	−6.5	16.4
Householders	974	52.7	4.2	1,452	50.5	4.4	49.1	−4.2	4.7
Children	2,635	67.2	11.5	3,181	66.9	9.6	20.7	−0.4	5.4

Source: Calculated from the U.S. Bureau of the Census, Current Population Reports, Series P-60, *Money Income and Poverty Status of Families and Persons in the United States* (Washington, D.C.: Government Printing Office, selected years).

female householders continues to be greater than that of whites. Still, by a number of indexes, the gap between their statuses narrowed over the twelve years.

The number of female-headed families exploded between 1970 and 1984. The percentage of families with a female householder increased by 41 percent among whites (9.0 to 12.7 percent) and by 54 percent among blacks (28.3 to 43.7 percent). Given the high risk of poverty among these families, female-headed families constituted almost half of the 10.1 million new poor—between 1973 and 1985. The largest percentage increases were among white female householders and their children: their rate grew by 11 and 7 percent, respectively, and the poverty rate of black female householders and their children fell by 4 and 0.4 percent, respectively.

Blacks continued to suffer from much higher poverty rates than whites in 1985. During the previous twelve years, however, the gap between the two races narrowed; black poverty remained relatively stable, while the economic status of whites declined. The closing of the gap between blacks and whites during these years did not result from "leveling up"—black economic status rising relative to that of whites—but from "leveling down"—white economic status falling relative to that of blacks.

The Declining Efficiency of Government Programs

Because the official poverty definition includes transfer payments, it is impossible to use this concept alone to estimate the unique role played by these payments in helping people out of poverty or keeping them in it. Using the concept of *pretransfer poverty*—defined as a pretransfer, pretax cash income—can avoid this problem. The same calculation technique is used here as is used to calculate official poverty, but public cash income transfers, such as social insurance, veterans' payments, and public assistance (AFDC, SSI, and general assistance) are excluded. The difference between official and pretransfer poverty, then, is the number of families who escape poverty as a result of these cash payments.[5]

One further caution should be kept in mind before the data are examined. Many of the conservative outcomes of U.S. social policy have been the result of the ideological blinder that has been imposed on any investigation. By differentiating pretransfer as preceding "official" poverty we are falling victim to the myth of the autonomous market. Pre–social welfare poverty has a number of causes, ranging from changes in technology to government monetary and fiscal policy. Indeed, a better measure of government poverty policy would include both economic and social policy, a point made recently by Skocpol.[6] Thus, it must be kept in mind that this chapter examines only government policy toward the consumption behavior of the poor.

The data for this investigation are derived from the *Current Population Survey*'s March annual demographic files for 1974, 1984, and 1986. They are concerned with changes in the profile of poverty in calendar years 1973, 1983, and 1985. Each file includes information on householders, families, and primary unrelated individuals in each year.[7] The unit of analysis here is the family (with householder/unrelated individuals defined as one-person families). For this reason, poverty rates will be different from those for individuals.

The choice of 1973 and 1983 as comparison years was deliberate: 1973 was the year in which the poverty rate hit its all-time low of 11.1 percent of the population, and 1983 marks the year in which the recent rise of poverty peaked at 15.2 percent. This comparison has strengths and weaknesses. On the one hand, it provides the clearest comparison of the recent explosion in poverty from trough to peak. On the other hand, it is less well suited for examining long-term trends because it includes the cyclical impact of the 1981–82 recession on poverty. The data for 1985 is included to examine the extent to which the recent recovery modifies our conclusions.[8]

Table 5–4 presents Danziger, Haveman, and Plotnick's data for 1964–83. These data provide the essential context in which the current analysis must be placed. Before 1969 the decline in official poverty mirrored the decline in pretransfer poverty, the result primarily of economic growth and the rise in wages. Beginning in 1970, however, the trend in pretransfer poverty was reversed; it began a steady rise that, while related to recessions, continued even during years of recovery. For example, during the recoveries of 1970–73 and 1975–79, pretransfer poverty never reached earlier lows.

By contrast, official poverty continued to fall through most of the early 1970s. Even as pretransfer poverty rose from 19.2 percent to 20.5 percent between 1972 and 1979, official poverty actually fell by 0.2 percentage points. During the 1970s public cash assistance served to widen the gap between official and pretransfer poverty. Between 1965 and 1969 the average gap between the two was 5.1 percent; the gap between 1970 and 1974 was 7.5 percent and between 1975 and 1979, 9.2 percent. Throughout the 1970s it took larger and larger government cash transfer payments to maintain official poverty at a stable rate, but for a decade social welfare was able to stave off social forces that would lead to rising official poverty rates.

During the 1980s government policy no longer played this compensating role. Although pretransfer poverty continued to rise between 1980 and 1983, official poverty rose even faster, from 13.0 to 15.2 percent. The gap between the two fell to an average of 9.0 percent.

Another way of examining these data is to ask what percentage of the pretransfer poor were removed from poverty by public transfers. These

Table 5–4
Percentage of Population in Poverty, 1964–1983

Year	Official Measure	Pretransfer Poverty
1964	19.0%	—
1965	17.3	21.3%
1966	14.7	—
1967	14.2	19.4
1968	12.8	18.2
1969	12.1	17.7
1970	12.6	18.8
1971	12.5	19.6
1972	11.9	19.2
1973	11.1	19.0
1974	11.2	20.3
1975	12.3	22.0
1976	11.8	21.0
1977	11.6	21.0
1978	11.4	20.2
1979	11.7	20.5
1980	13.0	21.9
1981	14.0	23.1
1982	15.0	24.0
1983	15.2	24.2

Source: Sheldon H. Danziger, Robert H. Haveman, and Robert D. Plotnick, "Antipoverty Policy: Effects on the Poor and the Nonpoor," in *Fighting Poverty: What Works and What Doesn't*, edited by Sheldon H. Danziger and Daniel H. Weinberg (Cambridge, Mass.: Harvard University Press, 1986), 54.

figures again underline the declining impact of government policy.[9] In 1968, 46 percent of the pre–social welfare poor were removed from poverty; by 1976 this had risen to 68 percent. The primary contributor to the removal of the pretransfer poor from poverty was social insurance; the percentage removed rose from 25 percent in 1968 to 37 percent in 1979 and then fell to 34 percent in 1983. Public assistance played a smaller and smaller role. In 1972, 6.3 percent of the pretransfer poor were removed by public assistance; by 1983 only 3.4 percent were.

In a recent study, the Center on Budget and Policy Priorities expanded Danziger, Haveman, and Plotnick's method to include the impact of noncash benefits on antipoverty program effectiveness.[10] The center documented the declining effectiveness of cash programs, including a 50 percent decline in effectiveness of cash programs other than Social Security (families removed from poverty declined from 9.6 percent to 1979 to 4.0 percent in 1983 and then rose to 4.7 percent in 1985). When noncash benefits are included, the results are equally stark. Excluding Social Security, the rate of removal from poverty for families fell from 30.6 percent in 1979 to a low of 16.4 percent in 1983, before rising slightly in the last two years of the study.

The center found that female-headed families were particularly hard hit by these changes. Overall, the rate of removal from poverty as a result of cash programs for these families fell from 18.6 percent in 1979 to 10.1 percent in 1984. When cash and noncash benefits (excluding Social Security) are examined, the rate of removal fell from 35.2 percent to 20.2 percent between 1979 and 1985.

These studies paint a fairly clear portrait of trends in pretransfer and official poverty for the entire population. During the 1970s there was a steady drift upwards in pretransfer poverty, but this trend was arrested to a great extent by the increase in transfer payments, especially Social Security. During the 1980s the increases in pre–social welfare poverty have continued. Rather than being mitigated, however, cutbacks in government transfer policy have given them impetus by reducing the effectiveness of most antipoverty programs (see tables 5–5, 5–6, and 5–7).

This analysis is consistent with these findings. Between 1973 and 1983 the official poverty rate of householders rose from 12.0 percent to 14.7 percent, a rise of almost 23 percent. The rise of pretransfer poverty also was substantial, although smaller than for official poverty. It rose from 24.1 percent in 1973 to 25.9 percent in 1983, an increase of slightly over 7 percent. As a result, the percentage of householders and their families who were poor but rose from poverty after transfers declined from 50 percent in 1973 to only 43 percent in 1983.

Generally, the rise in pretransfer poverty and official poverty affected all groups in the population: workers and nonworkers, young and old, black and white, men and women. Still, some clear patterns emerge as race, gender, and age are examined in more detail.

The decade after 1973 was marked by several dramatic changes in the relationship of poverty to gender, race, and age and by some disturbing continuities. At both the beginning and end of the period, the race and gender structure of official poverty and pretransfer poverty remained intact. Male householders consistently had lower poverty rates than women, whites lower than blacks. For example, in 1973 white males' official and pretransfer poverty rates were 5.4 and 14.4 percent, respectively, compared to the 17.1 and 26.8 percent rates for black men and 24.2 and 48.6 percent rates for white women householders. Black women suffered the double-jeopardy of race and sex: their rates were 50.4 and 66.1 percent, respectively.

Although blacks and women had higher poverty rates, it was white men who had the highest rate of escape from poverty, thanks to government programs. In 1973, 63 percent of the pretransfer white male poor were removed from poverty by public cash programs. The rates for black men, white women, and black women, were 36, 50, and 24 percent, respectively.

The same pattern persisted until 1983, but there were some important changes over the decade. The poverty rate of both female householder groups fell—by 15 percent for whites and 2 percent for blacks. The rates for both

Table 5-5
Poverty, Pretransfer Poverty, and Effectiveness Rate, by Race and Gender of Householder, 1973, 1983, and 1985

Category	1973			1983			1985		
	Official Rate	*Pretransfer Rate*	*Effective Rate*	*Official Rate*	*Pretransfer Rate*	*Effective Rate*	*Official Rate*	*Pretransfer Rate*	*Effective Rate*
White male	5.7%	14.4%	63%	8.1%	16.7%	54%	6.7%	14.7%	54%
Black male	17.6	26.8	34	19.0	28.9	34	16.4	26.9	39
Spanish male	13.1	18.5	29	18.8	26.0	28	17.7	23.7	25
White female	24.2	48.6	50	20.6	39.3	48	19.5	37.9	49
Black female	50.4	66.1	24	49.2	59.2	17	44.1	54.6	19
Spanish female	48.4	67.6	28	44.3	54.8	19	43.7	53.9	19

Source: Calculated from U.S. Bureau of the Census, Current Population Reports, Series P-60, *Money Income and Poverty Status of Families & Persons in the United States* (Washington, D.C.: Government Printing Office, selected years).

Table 5–6
Poverty, Pretransfer Poverty, and Effectiveness Rate, by Age of Householder, 1973, 1983, and 1985

Category	1973			1983			1985		
	Official Rate	*Pretransfer Rate*	*Effective Rate*	*Official Rate*	*Pretransfer Rate*	*Effective Rate*	*Official Rate*	*Pretransfer Rate*	*Effective Rate*
Under 30	13.3%	15.6%	15%	20.8%	23.0%	10%	19.8%	21.4%	7%
30–44	8.9	11.6	23	12.6	15.1	17	11.4	13.5	16
45–54	7.7	11.8	35	10.4	13.8	25	9.7	12.8	24
55–61	10.0	15.6	36	12.6	18.1	30	11.7	17.1	32
62–64	14.0	29.0	52	13.8	29.2	53	13.8	29.4	53
65–74	17.0	56.9	70	13.9	48.4	71	13.0	47.3	73
Over 75	24.1	73.9	67	20.4	65.0	69	18.9	62.2	70

Source: Calculated from U.S. Bureau of the Census, Current Population Survey data tapes (Washington, D.C.; March, selected years).

Poverty, Pretransfer Poverty, and Effectiveness Rate, by Age, Race and Gender of Householder, 1973, 1983, and 1985

Category	1973			1983			1985		
	Official Rate	Pretransfer Rate	Effective Rate	Official Rate	Pretransfer Rate	Effective Rate	Official Rate	Pretransfer Rate	Effective Rate
White males:									
Under 30	5.9%	7.3%	19%	11.2%	13.4%	16%	9.8%	11.0%	11%
Under 30–44	3.6	7.3	23	6.8	8.7	22	5.8	7.2	19
45–54	3.7	6.3	41	5.7	8.1	30	5.4	7.7	30
55–61	4.8	8.9	46	6.7	10.9	39	6.7	10.4	36
62–64	6.4	18.4	65	7.6	21.0	64	7.3	19.0	62
65–74	8.7	46.4	81	5.7	38.2	85	5.6	36.1	84
Over 75	12.9	67.5	81	11.5	55.8	79	7.5	51.5	85
Black males:									
Under 30	13.2	14.3	11	19.8	22.0	10	16.1	20.1	20
30–44	12.4	14.3	13	16.3	19.3	16	12.8	15.4	17
45–54	16.7	22.0	24	13.5	16.8	20	11.9	15.3	22
55–61	20.8	26.3	22	21.2	28.6	26	18.7	25.3	26
62–64	29.3	42.9	32	19.9	37.6	47	26.1	47.2	45
65–74	30.1	68.4	56	21.8	58.5	63	23.9	66.7	64
Over 75	34.0	87.1	61	38.8	85.2	54	31.5	80.4	61
White women:									
Under 30	29.8	34.4	13	28.1	30.1	7	27.3	29.2	7
30–44	21.6	30.6	29	17.3	21.3	19	15.6	19.1	18
45–54	16.0	25.7	38	15.7	20.3	23	13.0	18.4	29
55–61	18.2	27.9	35	19.2	27.3	30	17.6	26.7	34
62–64	22.8	45.3	50	20.8	40.0	48	19.7	42.6	54
65–74	24.8	69.5	64	22.3	57.7	66	18.1	57.5	69
Over 75	31.3	78.0	60	22.3	68.4	67	23.7	67.2	65
Black women:									
Under 30	60.0	67.3	12	61.2	64.1	5	61.9	63.9	3
30–44	49.9	62.7	20	43.7	47.9	9	39.7	43.8	9
45–54	38.2	49.4	23	40.4	49.3	18	33.7	38.6	13
55–61	45.6	58.3	22	43.5	52.1	17	38.7	48.6	20
62–64	48.1	67.2	28	44.0	59.1	26	40.2	57.5	30
65–74	48.2	86.1	44	52.7	81.7	35	39.2	75.3	48
Over 75	61.6	86.2	29	56.1	86.7	35	50.2	83.3	40

Source: Calculated from U.S. Bureau of the Census, Current Population Survey data tapes (Washington, D.C.: March, selected years).

male groups, by contrast, rose: white male householders' poverty increased by 39 percent, from 5.4 to 7.5 percent, while that of blacks rose 7 percent, to 19.0 percent.

The same trends were present in the pretransfer poverty data. The female householders' rates fell—by 19 percent for whites and 10 percent for blacks—while the male householders' rates rose, by 8 percent for blacks and 13 percent for whites. The percentage of the pretransfer poor that were removed from poverty by government programs dropped for every group, except black males (from 33.9 to 34.5 percent removed). The largest declines in the rate of escape were among black women (from 24 to 17 percent) and white men (from 63 to 54 percent).

Householders of Spanish origin paralleled that of other ethnic groups: male-headed families' poverty rose, while that of female-headed families fell. The official and pretransfer poverty rates for Spanish men rose from 13.1 to 18.8 percent (44 percent) and from 18.5 to 26.0 percent (40 percent). Among Spanish women, official poverty fell 8 percent (from 48.4 to 44.3 percent) and pretransfer poverty by 18 percent (from 67.6 to 54.8 percent). As a result, the proportion of the pretransfer poor removed from poverty by public programs fell from 29 to 28 percent for Spanish men and from 28 to 19 percent for Spanish women householders.

In 1973 the poverty rates of householders under age thirty and over age sixty-two were higher than average, but rates for those between these ages were significantly below the average for the population as a whole. For both official and pretransfer poverty, this pattern shifted markedly by 1983. All groups below age sixty-two had significantly higher poverty rates, and all groups above age sixty-two had significantly lower poverty rates by 1983. At the same time, the percentage of the pretransfer poor who escaped poverty through public programs fell sharply for the young and middle aged and held steady for the aged. For example, among householders below age thirty, the percentage escaping fell from 14 to 10 percent, while among those sixty-five to seventy-four, the percentage escaping edged up from 70 to 71 percent.

The decline of poverty among the aged has been one of the few bright spots in social welfare over the past decade. It often is portrayed simply as a result of government action, specifically the rise in Social Security payments, but although Social Security was important, these data suggest that not enough attention has been paid to the role of private income in the improved status of the aged. Not only did official poverty fall, but pretransfer poverty fell as well. In other words, Social Security and other government programs continued to remove the same share of the aged from pretransfer poverty; it was the size of this pool that changed. Forces other than transfer payments played a major role in the sharp decline of poverty among the elderly.

Not every gender, racial, or age group experienced the same shifts in poverty patterns. The contours of both official and pretransfer poverty have shifted unequally with widely varying results. Among white males, for example, pretransfer poverty rose 16 percent (from 14.4 to 16.7 percent) from 1973 to 1983 but only 2 percent from 1973 to 1985. The rise was distributed unequally by age groups. For white males under age thirty, pretransfer poverty rose 52 percent from 1973 to 1985 (7.3 to 11.0; for ages forty-five to fifty-four, pretransfer poverty rose 22 percent those same years; it rose 17 percent for white males aged fifty-five to sixty-one; and it was up 3 percent for the age group sixty-two to sixty-four. For all other white male age groups, pretransfer poverty fell during the interval by percentages ranging from 1 percent for the thirty-to forty-four-year-old group to 24 percent for those over age seventy-five.

Black males, by contrast, did not suffer as much among younger men or benefit as much among the aging. Their pretransfer poverty rates increased by less than that of the entire population for all groups under age sixty-two (indeed, among men forty-five to fifty-four, their pretransfer poverty rate actually fell), while the declines in poverty were smaller for those between sixty-five and seventy-four. Spanish men, too, did not share fully in the decline of pretransfer poverty among those over sixty-five, but they also suffered worse than average increases in the pretransfer poverty of the young. The market poverty rate rose for those under thirty by 65 percent compared to the population figure of 56 percent, and for those between the ages of thirty- and forty-four (64 percent compared to the population figure of 41 percent).

Among women, the general decline in market poverty was reflected across the life cycle. Pretransfer poverty fell in every age cohort for white and Spanish-origin female householders. Among black women, those of working age experienced important declines in poverty, but women over the age of sixty-five had smaller declines in pretransfer poverty than did the population as a whole.

The shifts in pretransfer poverty did not translate directly into changes in the official poverty rate. The major changes in income maintenance policy over the decade had predictable—and in most cases negative—effects on a variety of racial and age groups. The major changes during the decade were (1) the increase in payment levels of Old-Age, Survivors', and Disability Insurance; (2) the weakening of Unemployment Insurance; (3) declines in the eligibility for Supplemental Security Income and Disability Insurance; (4) very large declines in real payment levels under AFDC; and (5) a general retreat by the states in General Assistance. Taken together, these changes meant that specific age, gender, and racial groups suffered disporportionately.

These shifts in government policy affected midlife white males more profoundly than those who were younger or older. Although the rate of escape from pretransfer poverty for men over age sixty-five moved up slightly and that for men under forty-five moved down slightly, the declines among those between these ages were more profound. During the decade the rate of escape from pretransfer poverty fell from 46 to 39 percent among those between the ages of fifty-five and sixty-one from 1973 to 1983 and all the way to 36 percent by 1985. This resulted in a rise of 40 percent in the official poverty rates of this group in the twelve years.

The reasons for the decline in the effectiveness of transfer payments stem primarily from the decline in unemployment benefits during this period. The rate of exhaustion of benefits hit an all-time high during the period and the percentage of the labor force covered dropped significantly. Further changes in the system, including the restriction of extended benefits to a state-by-state basis, also added to the ineffectiveness of Unemployment Insurance as an antipoverty measure.

It should be noted that even with these reductions in the effectiveness of transfer payments for white men, they were still a privileged group. Their poverty rates (5.7 and 6.7 percent for this cohort) remained about half of the average for the population. Still, changes in their effectiveness rate indicate a significant deterioration of the social insurance part of the safety net.

At the other extreme, black women householders suffered from the deterioration of public assistance, particularly from the decline in AFDC eligibility and payment levels. Recall that pretransfer poverty declined for black women across the life cycle, due in large part to their increased labor force participation and work experience. These real economic gains did not translate into major declines in poverty, however. Among women aged thirty to sixty-four, poverty did decline, but not nearly as quickly as did pretransfer poverty. The official poverty of the other age groups actually increased in spite of the decline in pretransfer poverty.

This resulted from a decline in the effectiveness rate for all age groups under sixty-two years of age. The most severe declines were among those women most likely to have young children—among those under thirty and between the ages of thirty and forty-four. Among older women—more likely to be widows and to qualify for survivors insurance—there were some gains from 1983–85.

Among black men, the story was less consistent. Among younger householders, the increases in pretransfer poverty were translated into equivalent increases in official poverty. Thus, the 36 percent rise in pretransfer poverty among black householders under the age of thirty led to a 22 percent increase in their official poverty. Among older men, however, the news was better. Particularly among men between fifty-five and sixty-five years of age, official poverty actually fell at a faster rate than did pretransfer poverty. The effectiveness rate increased from 22 to 26 percent for men fifty-five to sixty-one years of age, from 32 to 45 percent for those sixty-two to sixty-five, and from 56 to 64 percent for those sixty-five to seventy-four.

These data suggest that government programs had a contradictory impact on black male householders. On the one hand, the expansion of Social Security benefits and the use of a benefits formula that favors low-income workers improved the lot of "young-old" black workers. Among younger householders, for blacks as for whites, the increase in pretransfer poverty was not addressed by public income maintenance policy; there were few dramatic changes in the effectiveness rate as the increase in pretransfer poverty was echoed in official poverty.

Finally, among white and Spanish female householders, the impact of the dramatic declines in pretransfer poverty (a product of increased work experience) was muffled by changes in public transfers. The effectiveness rate dropped for all age groups under age sixty-two, with extremely large declines being registered by women under the age of fifty-five. For example, while pretransfer poverty was declining by 28 percent among white women householders, age forty-five to fifty-four, this was not translated into as large a reduction in poverty, which only fell by 19 percent. Similarly, among women of Spanish origin, a decline of 16 percent in pretransfer poverty among those fifty-five to sixty-one did not translate into a significant decrease in official poverty. Aged white and Hispanic women did well over the decade, particularly those over age seventy-five, but the trend in transfer payments cancelled the gains that women had made in the labor market (see table 5–8).

The data on income source pinpoint the declining effectiveness of public income transfers. Among those householders and their families dependent on public assistance, the effectiveness rate plummeted. Those whose only source of income was public assistance saw their effectiveness rate fall from 14 percent to 6 percent, while those who received both assistance and social insurance witnessed a decline from 52 to 32 percent in the rate at which they escaped pretransfer poverty. The same was true among those who both had earnings and public assistance; their effectiveness rate fell from 29 to 15 percent.

Effectiveness rates fell as well among those who received social insurance, although these groups were much more likely to escape poverty than were public assistance recipients. Effectiveness rates fell from 52 to 49 percent among those solely dependent on social insurance and from 86 to 79 percent among those who combined earnings, social insurance, and other income. Finally, the effectiveness rate fell from 63 to 54 percent among those whose income sources were only earnings and social insurance.

Among those with no public transfer payments, the rise in pretransfer poverty was translated into stark rises in official poverty. Among those with only earnings, poverty rose from 7.8 percent to 15.9 percent; among those with earnings and other income, the increases were still significant, from 2.8 to 3.7 percent. These trends were duplicated across race and gender groups.

Table 5–8
Official and Pretransfer Poverty, by Source of Income, Family Households, 1973, 1983, and 1985

Source of Income	1973			1983			1985		
	Official Poverty	Pretransfer Rate	Effective Rate	Official Poverty	Pretransfer Poverty	Effective Rate	Official Poverty	Pretransfer Poverty	Effective Rate
Earnings only	7.8%	7.8%	0%	16.7%	16.7%	0%	15.9%	15.9%	0%
Earnings/insurance	9.8	26.9	64	16.3	34.6	53	14.4	31.5	54
Earnings/assistance	48.8	69.1	29	66.1	78.2	15	65.4	77.0	15
Earnings/other	2.8	2.8	0	4.2	4.2	0	3.7	3.7	0
Earnings/insurance/other	2.0	14.6	86	3.6	12.6	71	2.5	11.7	79
Insurance only	48.0	—	52	52.6	—	47	50.7	—	49
Assistance only	86.0	—	14	92.8	—	7	93.8	—	6
Insurance/assistance	48.4	—	52	70.9	—	29	68.3	—	32
Other combination	21.8	69.1	68	21.5	58.8	63	20.2	56.6	64

Source: Calculated from the U.S. Bureau of the Census, Current Population Survey data tapes (Washington, D.C., March, selected years).

Overall, these data testify to the increasing pressure of pretransfer poverty and the inability of government payments to counter it.

The retreat of government aid was most striking among those who were "helping themselves" by working as well as receiving assistance or social insurance. For all race and gender groups, pretransfer poverty increased and the effectiveness rate fell. For example, among white men receiving social insurance (unemployment, workers' compensation, or disability) and earned income, the pretransfer poverty rate rose from 20.1 to 29.3 while the effectiveness rate fell from 73 to 55 percent. The decline of the effectiveness of working female householders receiving public assistance (usually AFDC) was even more striking. White female householders had their pretransfer poverty move up slightly, but their effectiveness rate plummeted, resulting in a rise in their official poverty from 54.9 to 73.0 percent. The same was true of black women: the pretransfer poverty rate remained fairly constant, but the decline of their effectiveness rate led to a rise in their poverty.

Among those totally dependent on social insurance or public assistance, similar trends emerge. The effectiveness rate of social insurance remained about the same, although black women suffered a decline. Among public assistance recipients, however, effectiveness rates fell across the board: the declining value of public aid translated directly into sky rocketing poverty rates.

In summary, the source of income data allow some of these trends in poverty to be confirmed. Among men, rises in pretransfer poverty were the chief source of increased poverty. Government aid did not increase among men, but it was the labor market that was the chief source of their economic woes. For women, by contrast, it was government policy that was the chief culprit. Among those with earnings, the decline in effectiveness rates meant increasing poverty even as pretransfer poverty declined. For those with no earnings, the receipt of a government check was almost a guarantee of continued poverty.

Chapter 6 turns to a closer examination of the role of race, gender, and work in pretransfer poverty—specifically, changes in personal behavior and changes in market behavior as they affect poverty rates.

Notes

1. See for example, June Axinn, "Value Choices in the Definition of Poverty," in *Rechtstheorie, Beiheft 10, Reason and Experience in Contemporary Legal Thought,* edited by Torstein Eckhoff, Lawrence M. Friedman, and Jyrki Uusitalo (Berlin: Duncker & Humblot, 1986), 363–69; Victor Fuchs, "Toward a Theory of Poverty," in *The Concept of Poverty,* edited by Carl H. Madden (Washington, D.C.: United States Chamber of Commerce, 1965); Mollie Orshansky, "How Poverty Is

Measured," *Monthly Labor Review* 92 (2) (February 1969): 76; U.S. Bureau of the Census, Technical Paper 56, *Estimates of Poverty Including the Value of Noncash Benefits: 1985* (Washington, D.C.: Government Printing Office, 1986).

2. U.S. Bureau of the Census, *Estimates of Poverty* 3–8.

3. "Share of Income Spent for Food," *Family Economics Review,* 3 (1986): 8.

4. See Harrell R. Rodgers, Jr., *The Cost of Human Neglect: America's Welfare Failure,* (Armonk, N.Y.: Sharpe Inc., 1982) for a fuller version of this story.

5. This conceptualization is not new. It has been used by researchers at the Institute for Research on Poverty for over a decade, most recently by Sheldon Danzinger, Robert Havemen, and Robert Plotnick, "Antipoverty Policy: Effects on the Poor and the Nonpoor," in *Fighting Poverty: What Works and What Doesn't,* edited by Sheldon Danzinger and Daniel H. Weinberg (Cambridge, Mass.: Harvard University Press, 1986), 50–77. The authors' concept of pretransfer poverty appears to be identical to our concept of presocial welfare poverty. They go further in differentiating pretransfer from prewelfare poverty, the second taking into account social insurance and veterans' payments. In this chapter, we have used the "income source" variable included in the CPS as a means of investigating the relative contribution of different income sources to one's poverty status.

6. Margaret Weir, Ann Orloff, and Theda Skocpol, "Understanding American Social Politics," paper presented at PARSS Seminar on Work and Welfare, University of Pennsylvania, October 30, 1986.

7. Only the families of householders were included in this file. This included "one-person families" and unrelated individuals if they were defined as a householder. Subfamilies both related and unrelated were excluded from the file because their definition changed over the period and their inclusion would have caused inordinate headaches in data handling. For each family or unrelated individual, household and family characteristics and data on the householder were included.

8. There are some obvious problems in preparing a clean design for this study. We could use a conventional definition of the business cycle (recessions in 1974–75, 1980, 1981–82), but the path of unemployment seems a better index for economic cycles for the poverty rate. Here the persistence of unemployment at near-recession levels (at least by pre-1974 standards) makes it difficult to reach a clearcut distinction between a peak and a trough.

9. Danzinger, Haveman, and Plotnick, "Antipoverty Policy," Table 3.5, 65.

10. Center on Budget and Policy Priorities, "The Decreasing Effectiveness of Anti-Poverty Programs" (Washington, D.C.: Center on Budget and Policy Priorities, 1986).

6
Race, Gender, and Work Experience

The welfare dependency of black Americans has reemerged as a major social concern during the past five years. After nearly a decade of benign neglect, the problems of poor blacks and the ability of the U.S. economy or social policy to ameliorate them have again captured widespread national attention.

Time, for example, noted in February 1987 that the welfare "system is a monstrous mess: it breaks up families, traps the poor in degrading idleness and breeds a self-perpetuating cycle of illegitimacy, poverty, and government dependency." It was cheered to find that a new consensus was emerging on welfare reform "across the political spectrum, from Ronald Reagan to Daniel Patrick Moynihan to Ted Kennedy." As a result, the "political climate is . . . propitious for overhauling the welfare system." Similar sentiments have been trumpeted by most molders of public opinion.[1]

The reasons for the resurfacing of the issue of black poverty are many. The sharp rise of poverty (examined in chapter 5) has focused public attention on the extremely high incidence of poverty among female-headed families, while social critics—both black and white—have attributed the rise in poverty to the problems of teenage mothers and the deterioriation of the black family. At the same time, a number of conservative scholars—most notably Charles Murray—have argued that the welfare system itself is responsible for blacks "losing ground."[2] Finally, Congress—led most vocally by Senator Daniel Patrick Moynihan—and President Reagan have called for a reexamination of the "spider's web of dependency" and how the welfare system can foster self-sufficiency and a strong family structure.

For veterans of the social debates of the 1960s, the recent discussion comes as *déjà vu*. Many of the recent policy issues echo those of an earlier era, and the new concern for the psychological and cultural life of the "underclass" is strikingly similar to the culture of poverty debate of that era. The spectre of a class apart—cut off from opportunities and the cultural guidance of the middle class—has become increasingly menacing.

In many respects, the return of the fear of the able-bodied dependent should come as no surprise. It echoes a set of concerns that have been recurrent in Western society for at least the past two centuries. For example, in his study of Victorian London, Gareth Stedman Jones found that the shadow of a demoralized class of paupers was a major motivation of social reformers of that era. With the improvement of the standard of living of the mass of the English working class in the late nineteenth century, the notion of poverty as inevitable gave way to an optimistic view of the human condition exemplified by the neoclassical economics of Alfred Marshall. "Pitted against the dominant climate of moral and material improvement," Stedman Jones observes, "was a minority of the still unregenerate poor." In explaining the existence of this "residuum the subject psychological defects of individuals bulked even larger than before . . . The problem was not structural but moral, the evil to be combated was not poverty but pauperism . . . with its attendant vices, drunkenness, improvidence, mendicancy, bad language, filthy habits, gambling, low amusements, and ignorance."[3]

American observers were quick to follow the British business class in drawing a clear distinction between thrifty workers and the lumpen pauper class to attribute the problems of the latter to psychological and moral defects. Michael Katz has noted that one of the major themes in the history of welfare policy in the United States has been

> The division of the working class into two groups. These have been called the worthy and the unworthy poor, the working and the non-working poor, or the working class and the lumpen proletariat. The result is the same, whatever the terms: to set off people who receive welfare as outside the working class, as, in fact . . . [a] drain upon those who work, and, hence, to divert working-class sympathy away from welfare measures.[4]

The distinction between the undeserving pauper and the unfortunate dependent became institutionalized in the sharp distinction in the American welfare state between social insurance and public assistance. The current dichotomy is nothing new.

One result of the intellectual tradition has been to insulate the welfare debate from an examination of the structure of the economy and labor market. If the poverty of the pauper or the "underclass" was primarily a result of moral or psychological failings, then the answer to their problem lay in individual rehabilitation. Whether the reform took a punitive or humanistic path (and there are abundant examples of each in American history) was beside the point: the crucial issue was that "welfare reform" had no implications for the rest of the population: it meant reform of the dependent individual, not reform of the economy.

It is striking that much of the recent debate over race and welfare dependency has repeated these tendencies. Although certain statistical concepts have been used repeatedly—the feminization of poverty, the rising incidence of poverty among children—these ideas have rarely received a balanced explanation. The image of a deviant group—not a fundamental stratum of the labor market—has dominated the current debate.

This chapter argues that in postindustrial America once again basic economic changes, not personal behavior or morality, are at the source of the new poverty. The rise in poverty and dependency is related to a number of factors, including the changing age and family structure of the U.S. population already examined, but it is most intimately connected to the restructuring of the labor market and the increase of low-wage, irregular work. Because of this connection, welfare reform faces some severe limits. As long as the market demand for the working poor continues to expand, the welfare system for those able to work will probably have to remain inadequate. The "welfare mess" is ultimately a distorted reflection of the "labor market mess."

In pursuing this argument, this chapter undertakes two tasks. First, it examines the emergence of the recent debate over the "underclass" and traces its centrality to social policy thinking. Then it examines recent trends in work experience and their connection to race, gender, and poverty.

The Rise of the Underclass

The War on Poverty of the 1960s was the last intellectual effort to establish the poor as a class apart. The image of "poverty amid affluence" and (in Michael Harrington's phrase) the "other America" were the dominant themes of the War on Poverty and its accompanying programs. Harrington, for example, called attention to the "vicious cycle" of poverty that cut off the new poor of the 1960s from older traditions of poverty. To grow up in the resulting "culture" of poverty meant to be "an internal alien." Like Harrington, Oscar Lewis used the "culture of poverty" in a careful and specific way: to refer to a group of characteristics that affected some of the poor. Both Lewis and Harrington emphasized the structural realities that generated poverty and the small proportion of the poor who were actually caught in this culture. Lewis, for example estimated that only about a fifth of the poor were part of what he considered the culture of poverty.[5]

As the War on Poverty began in 1963, these intellectual niceties were dispensed with. The image of the poor as apathetic and fatalistic became the touchstone for much of the social policy of the era. The entire concept of "community action" was directed at the psychological rejuvenation of the poor as much as it was aimed at giving them new resources. Indeed, for both intellectual and practical reasons the culture of poverty was a useful construct for policy makers. As Peter Marris and Martin Rein noted, the community action "programmes had not only to provide opportunities, but regenerate a will to respond to them. In part, then, community organization was a form of treatment for collective depression."[6] In assessing the actual experience of community action, they concluded that "the preoccupation with apathy seems misguided." Indeed, rather than working hard to shake the poor from their apathy, community activists found themselves overwhelmed by demanding and often confrontative poor people.[7]

The generalization of the culture of poverty and its association after 1965 with Moynihan's critique of the "matriarchal" black family structure led quickly to its loss of intellectual legitimacy, particularly among advocates of social reform. Indeed, by the late 1960s both the culture of poverty and the critique of the black family had become solely the intellectual property of the right.

The recent concern over the "underclass" is in many ways reproducing this cycle. The use of the concept began among those advocating expanded poverty programs, but over the past few years it has been embraced increasingly by proponents of more punitive policies. In *The Underclass*, Ken Auletta admits that he first used the term "gingerly, fearful that it was somehow racist" and would "present a distorted picture of the American poor." After finding that "among students of poverty" there was "little disagreement that a fairly distinct black and white underclass does exist," Auletta embraced the term.[8]

Auletta, like Lewis and Harrington in the 1960s, was careful to emphasize that the "underclass" was not the same as the poor. Indeed, he approvingly reports an estimate that the size of the underclass is about 2 million, less than 1 percent of the population and less than 7 percent of the 29 million poor Americans in 1980.[9] In addition, when he turns to solutions to the problem, Auletta, although critical of both liberal and conservative conventional wisdom, emphasized the complexity of the problem and the need for expanded community organization, education, and manpower development efforts to address it.

The concern for poverty and the underclass has led to some careful studies of the structural realities of poor blacks. William J. Wilson and John Kasarda, for example, have focused on the centrality of the economic and geographical restructuring of the U.S. city.[10]

Wilson in particular has focused on the role of work opportunities in defining the underclass. Wilson chronicles the "tangle of pathology" that plagues the inner city: violent crime, family dissolution, and welfare dependency. Unlike the new culture of poverty theorists, Wilson finds that neither "racial discrimination or . . . a culture of poverty" can explain these problems. Rather, for Wilson they are due "far more to shifts in the American economy from manufacturing to service industries, which have produced extraordinary rates of joblessness in the inner city and exacerbated conditions generated by the historic flow of migrants, and to changes in the urban minority age structure and consequent population changes in the central city."[11]

In spite of the evidence linking the black underclass to fundamental changes in the economy, the appeal of cultural explanations has continued to grow. Nicholas Lemann's essay "The Origins of the Underclass" marks the reemergence of the cultural explanation of American poverty.[12] Lemann's argument is similar to those made by Lewis and Harrington twenty-five years ago. It emphasizes the isolation of poor blacks, their lack of opportunities, the failure of social institutions, and the development of norms of family and personal behavior that are at odds with those of the dominant society. "The underclass flourished when in the seventies it was completely disengaged from the rest of society," he notes. As a result, the ghetto's "distinctive culture is now the greatest barrier to progress by the black underclass, rather than either unemployment or welfare."[13] Lemann's essay is important for a number of reasons. It marks the return of respectability to the "culture of poverty." He argues quite baldly that black culture (much of it imported wholesale from the rural South) is the primary impediment to black progress. Lemann does not shy away from the policy implications of this position: "The negative power of the ghetto all but guarantees that any attempt to solve the problems of the underclass *in the ghetto* won't work."[14] Thus, Lemann's "solution" to the problems of the underclass envisions "the imposition of a different, and more disciplined, culture." Although this solution includes advocacy of a WPA-like work program, Lemann focuses more on its role in diciplining labor rather than providing the poor with economic opportunity.[15]

Lemann's characterization of the underclass gained a hearing as well among some liberals. Mickey Kaus, writing in the *New Republic*, accepted the culture of poverty as a given. As he noted,

> Right and left now recognize that neither robust economic growth nor massive government transfers can . . . transform a "community" where 90 percent of the children are born into fatherless families, where over 60 percent of the population is on welfare, where the work ethic has evaporated and the entrepreneurial drive is channeled into gangs and drug-pushing.[16]

For Kaus, this reality made workfare too humane of a solution to the problem. Rather, only the elimination of the public assistance, the institution of a required work program paying subminimum wages, and the removal of children from parents who will not submit to these jobs will provide the cultural change that will eliminate the underclass.

The emergence of the theory of the underclass and its accompanying political agenda is marked by more than a little irony. Although the argument that the poor were cut off from "mainstream" prosperity had at least a surface plausibility during the halycon days of the 1960s, this position is much weaker today. During the 1960s the poverty of black Americans stood in sharp contrast to the steady improvement of the rest of the population; today, the rise in black poverty is wholly consistent with the high poverty, unemployment, and displacement that has been experienced by all sectors of the population. Lemann sees the ghetto's "isolation" as a problem, but the real problem may be that the black underclass is *too* much a part of American society.

Before this issue can be judged, however, a fuller sense of the origins of black poverty is needed. Rather than looking again at the statistics on illegitimacy, female-headed families, and crime, though, the focus in this chapter is on the element of black, white, and Hispanic behavior that is most related to financial well-being: work experience.

Poverty and Work Experience

As already has been shown, family and demographic variables have contributed to the increase of poverty since the early 1970s. The general rise in poverty was particularly clear among householders and children. Among racial groups, white poverty increased faster than black poverty. At the same time, the poverty rate of female-headed families increased more slowly than that of other families. Thus, although female-headed households accounted for nearly half of the "new" poor between 1973 and 1985, this was primarily the result of the expansion of the size of this group, not their increased risk of poverty. Indeed, even among female-headed families, poverty increased more rapidly among whites than among blacks.

These trends were affected as well by changes in the regional and metropolitan distribution of poverty. Historically, the South has lagged behind other regions in poverty because of its low degree of economic development and because of its restricted welfare policy. By the same token, residents of central cities, in particular those in the Northeast, have had lower rates of work opportunities—even when they are located near areas of job growth (see table 6–1).

When the data on family households are examined, they show that the general rise in official poverty was echoed within each region and practically every division of the nation. Only New England, whose poverty rate dropped from 10.1 to 9.9, and the West South Central, whose rate fell from 18.9 to 16.8, recorded any decline between 1973 and 1983. The Middle Atlantic states (9.8 to 14.9) and the North Central region (10.0 to 14.3) were the biggest losers in poverty trends.

As in the nation as a whole, this rise in poverty was a result of increased

Table 6–1
Poverty, Pretransfer Poverty, and Effectiveness Rate, by Region, District, and Metropolitan Location, 1973 and 1983

	1973			1983		
Category	Official Rate	Pretransfer Rate	Effective Rate	Official Rate	Pretransfer Rate	Effective Rate
Northeast	9.9%	23.1%	57%	13.6%	26.5%	49%
New England	10.1	23.7	57	9.9	20.9	53
Mid-Atlantic	9.8	22.8	57	14.9	28.4	48
North Central	10.0	21.5	53	14.3	26.0	45
East North Central	9.6	20.5	53	14.0	25.9	46
West North Central	11.0	24.1	54	15.0	26.3	43
South	16.0	27.3	41	16.6	26.6	38
South Atlantic	13.2	24.2	45	14.7	25.0	41
East South Central	18.1	30.3	40	21.1	33.3	37
West South Central	18.9	29.9	37	16.8	25.1	33
West	11.1	23.7	53	12.8	22.8	44
Mountain	12.2	23.9	49	13.8	23.1	40
Pacific	10.7	23.6	55	12.4	22.8	46
Metropolitan location:						
Central city	14.0	27.5	49	18.4	29.9	38
Other SMSA	7.3	17.2	58	9.5	18.9	50
Non-SMSA	15.5	28.6	46	17.9	30.9	42

Source: Calculated from U.S. Bureau of the Census, Current Population Survey, data tapes (Washington, D.C., March, selected years).

pretransfer poverty and declining effectiveness rates. For example, in the North Central region pretransfer poverty increased by 21 percent (21.5 to 26.0), while the rate of removal from pretransfer poverty fell from 53 to 45 percent. Only the West South Central and the West deviated from the pattern of higher pretransfer poverty and lower effectiveness rates. In West South Central the pretransfer poverty rate actually fell over the decade from 29.9 to 25.1 percent; the rise of poverty there was the result of the declining role of public transfers. The West, too, benefitted from Sunbelt prosperity; pretransfer poverty declined by 4 percent (23.7 to 22.8 percent), while the effectiveness rate fell from 53 to 44 percent.

By 1983 the traditional excess poverty of the South had been reduced. Before public transfers, its poverty rate was within one percentage point of the Northeast and North Central regions. Only the West stood out with a distinctly lower rate of pretransfer poverty. The South continued, however, to have a much lower effectiveness rate. Thus, the declining difference between Southern households and those in the rest of the United States was not fully reflected in the official poverty rates. Social welfare transfers did less to reduce poverty in the South than anywhere else in the nation.

Metropolitian location also reflected national trends. In both 1973 and

1983 offical poverty was higher in central cities and nonmetropolitan areas than in metropolitan areas outside central cities. Over the decade, however, central cities edged ahead of rural areas in poverty rate; their poverty rate increased 31 percent, while that of rural areas rose by only 15 percent. Pretransfer poverty, too, was lower in suburbs than in cities or rural areas. Over the decade, these differentials did not change substantially; pretransfer poverty rose by 9 percent in central cities, 10 percent in suburbs, and 8 percent in rural areas.

The effectiveness rate did change in important ways between 1973 and 1983. In central cities, the effectiveness rate fell by 22 percent (from 49 to 38 percent), while in suburban and rural areas the decline was only 14 and 9 percent, respectively. Thus, the explosion of central city poverty was much more the result of declining program effectiveness than economic breakdown. If the effectiveness rate had remained stable for central cities, their poverty rate would have risen to about 15.2 percent.

These trends again raise some question about the role of the "urban underclass," in the increase in urban poverty. If this increase really were the result of a spreading culture of poverty that was sapping individual motivation, one would expect that the explosion of urban poverty to be a result of the individual actions of inner city residents. The data tell a very different story. The pretransfer poverty rate of central city residents rose by only slightly more than that for the entire population and less than the suburban rate. Most of the rise in poverty was the result of the decreasing ability of government cash support programs to lift these citizens above the poverty level. Public neglect and not "underclass culture" appears to explain more fully the rising poverty of the nation's cities.

While these demographic and family trends were affecting both blacks and whites, both groups were also experiencing dramatic changes in their work patterns. To examine the relationship of work experience to poverty, total poverty is disaggregated into two constituents: the *compositional* effects (that is, the number of individuals in a specific population group) and the *incidence* effect (that is, the poverty rate of each group). A rise in poverty can occur either from the growth of the number of individuals in a high-risk group (composition) or from an increase in the risk of poverty for a group (incidence). Did the rise in black and white poverty result from a shift into work-experience groups with traditionally high risks of poverty or was it the result of increasing risk across all groups?

Between 1973 and 1984 adult poverty increased among all races and genders. The poverty population was swelled by 2.3 million white men, 2.7 million white women, 517,000 black males, and 769,000 black females. As a result, the poverty rate for each group increased dramatically; among whites, male and female poverty increased 39 and 23 percent, respectively. Among blacks the increases were 8 percent and 2 percent.

These trends resulted from a complex interplay of compositional and incidence effects. White men saw both their incidence and composition effects move in the direction of greater poverty, while white and black women moved into lower risk groups but suffered from increases in their risk of poverty. Finally, for black men, the incidence effect moved to reduce poverty but was more than offset by their move into high-risk groups (see table 6–2).

White men's position in the labor force declined significantly between 1973 and 1984. The number who worked during the year declined from 82 to 79 percent of the population, including declines among those who worked full time for the full year and part time for the full year. By 1984 more white men did not work because they could not find employment (0.3 to 1.1 percent) or because they were retired (7.0 to 11.1) percent).

Among black men, declines in work experience were even more important. There was an across-the-board reduction in full-time employment; the percentage working full time for the full year declined by 12 percent. At the same time, the percentage of black males who did not work at all during the year increased by 28 percent, including increases for those who could not find work (1.1 to 5.6 percent) and those who were retired (4.4 to 7.5 percent). Overall, only 66 percent of black males worked during 1984, down from 73 percent in 1973.

Among women, just the opposite was the case; among both blacks and whites there were dramatic moves from high- to low-risk work-experience groups. Overall, the percentage of the adult female population that worked increased by 13 percent among whites and 8 percent among blacks. The percentage of the population that did not work because it was keeping house declined by 33 percent among whites (33 to 22 percent) and by 28 percent among blacks (22 to 16 percent). The percentage of white and black women who worked full time for the entire year increased by 36 percent and 29 percent, respectively. This positive shift was muted only by big increases among those who did not work because they could not find work; this group increased by 150 percent among white women and 115 percent among black women. The percentage of women retired also increased by 191 percent among whites and 194 percent among blacks (see table 6–3).

While the composition of the adult population by work experience was shifting, so too was the risk of poverty within work-experience categories. Among those who worked full time—historically the least vulnerable category—blacks recorded major declines in the poverty rate (7 percent for men, 20 percent for women). Among whites, however, the poverty rate of full-time workers increased, by 45 percent among men and 9 percent among women. Full-time workers' poverty rate remained much below that of other groups, but among white men full-time workers' edge declined substantially.

A similar trend was present among part-time workers. Among blacks, the poverty rate was stable among men (32.2 to 32.5 percent) and fell sharply for

Table 6–2
Work Experience, by Race and Gender, Population over Fifteen Years of Age, 1973–1984

	White Males			White Females			Black Males			Black Females		
	1973	1984	% change	1973	1984	% change	1973	1984	% change	1973	1984	% change
Total population	100.0%	100.0%	—	100.0%	100.0%	—	100.0%	100.0%	—	100.0%	100.0%	—
Worked	81.8	78.7	-3.8	52.0	58.7	12.9	73.3	65.8	-10.2	52.0	55.9	7.5
Full time	70.0	67.8	-3.1	34.5	38.9	13.4	62.1	54.0	-13.0	38.0	41.2	8.4
50–52 weeks	54.8	52.5	-4.2	21.1	27.5	30.3	43.5	38.4	-11.7	23.1	29.9	29.4
Part time	11.8	10.9	-7.6	17.8	19.8	11.2	11.2	11.8	5.4	14.0	14.7	5.0
Did not work	18.2	21.3	17.0	48.0	41.3	-14.0	26.7	34.2	28.1	48.0	44.1	-8.1
By reason:												
Ill, disabled	3.8	3.8	—	4.4	4.3	-2.3	8.1	8.5	4.9	9.4	8.8	-6.4
Keeping house	—	0.2	—	32.6	21.7	-33.4	—	0.4	—	21.8	15.6	-28.4
At school	6.6	4.6	-30.3	6.9	4.4	-36.2	12.3	10.7	-13.0	12.7	9.3	-26.8
Can't find work	0.3	1.1	266.7	0.4	1.0	150.0	1.1	5.6	409.1	2.0	4.3	115.0
Retired	7.0	11.1	58.6	3.2	9.3	190.6	4.4	7.5	70.4	1.7	5.0	194.1

Source: Calculated from U.S. Bureau of the Census, Current Population Survey data tapes (Washington, D.C., March, selected years).

Table 6–3
Poverty Rate and Work Experience, by Race and Gender, Population Over Fifteen Years of Age, 1973–1984

	White Males			White Females			Black Males			Black Females		
	1973	1984	% change	1973	1984	% change	1973	1984	% change	1973	1984	% change
Total population	6.1%	8.5%	39.3	9.3%	11.5%	23.7	21.5%	23.2%	7.9	31.8%	32.3%	1.6
Worked	4.2	6.1	45.2	5.4	5.8	25.9	14.5	14.5	—	20.8	17.0	-18.2
Full time	3.5	5.1	45.7	4.5	4.9	8.9	11.3	10.5	-7.1	14.7	11.8	-19.7
50–52 weeks	2.1	2.9	38.1	1.6	2.3	43.1	6.8	4.5	-33.8	8.5	5.9	-30.6
Part time	8.5	12.3	44.7	7.3	10.5	43.1	32.2	32.5	0.9	37.3	31.6	-15.3
Did not work	14.5	17.3	19.3	13.4	18.2	35.8	41.0	40.0	-2.2	43.8	51.7	18.0
By reason:												
Ill, disabled	26.0	26.4	1.5	26.7	29.7	11.2	48.1	45.7	5.0	52.5	54.5	3.8
Keeping house	—	35.2	—	11.7	15.4	40.1	—	60.5	—	42.4	59.4	40.1
At school	10.6	19.9	87.7	10.5	19.0	80.9	38.8	36.3	6.4	40.8	37.4	-8.3
Can't find work	30.3	50.7	67.3	21.1	43.7	107.1	62.2	56.7	-8.8	45.8	66.6	45.4
Retired	11.0	8.4	-23.5	17.6	13.4	-23.9	27.0	22.5	-16.7	30.1	32.9	9.3

Source: Calculated from U.S. Bureau of the Census, Current Population Survey data tapes (Washington, D.C., March, selected years).

women (37 to 32 percent). Among whites, again, there were large increases, with the women's rate rising from 7 to 11 percent and the men's from 9 to 12 percent.

Among those who did not work, the biggest changes occurred among women. Although many women were leaving this category, those who remained faced an increased risk of poverty. Among whites, the poverty rate increased 36 percent (13 to 18 percent) because of large jumps among those who kept house (40 percent), went to school (81 percent), or could find no work (107 percent). Black poverty rose from 44 to 52 percent based on increases among housekeepers (40 percent) and those who could find no work (45 percent).

White men who did not work faced some increase in the risk of poverty (15 to 17 percent), particularly those who were in school and who could find no work. Among black men, however, nonworkers' poverty rates actually declined by some 2 percent. Even the risk among those who could find no work was lower in 1984 (57 percent) than it was eleven years earlier (62 percent).

To clarify these trends, we ran a series of simulations based on "counterfactual" or "what-if" asssumptions. First, we asked what would the poverty experience of these groups have been if there had been no change in their composition by work experience category. Then, we estimated what their poverty pattern would have been if the risk of poverty (the incidence effect) had remained stable (see table 6–4).

The answer to each of these questions differs by race/gender groups. Black and white women recorded similar results. Their shift into the labor force served to reduce the compositional component of poverty substantially. If their overall pattern of work experience had remained the same, there would have been a million more white women and 338,000 more black women in poverty. These increases would have resulted from the combination of large increases among those keeping house and declines among those unable to find work and those who were retired.

The positive influence of increased female labor force participation was negated by the increase in the incidence effect. If the poverty rates within work experience groups had not changed, there would have been 2 million fewer poor white women, including nearly a million women workers, 824,000 housekeepers, and 178,000 who could find no work. Among black women, a stable incidence pattern would have led to 300,000 fewer poor; there would be 86,000 more part-time workers in poverty, but this would be offset by the 295,000 fewer homemakers and 98,000 fewer women who could find no work.

Female householders shared in these general trends. If there had been no change in composition, there would have been an increase of 363,000 in the number of poor white female householders, while among blacks, the shift

Table 6–4
Compositional and Incidence Effects of Changes in Poverty, by Work Experience, Race, and Gender, 1973–1984 (in thousands)

	White Males		White Females		Black Males		Black Females	
	Model I[a]	Model II[b]	Model I	Model II	Model I	Model II	Model I	Model II
Total population	-174	-1,526	1,036	-2,094	-245	95	338	-299
Worked	114	-1,107	52	-960	67	28	97	115
Full time	20	-791	176	-435	82	34	111	29
50–52 weeks	41	-323	-111	-148	19	78	-46	85
Part time	94	-316	-123	-525	-14	-6	-14	86
Did not work	-288	-419	983	-1,133	-312	67	241	-414
By reason:								
Ill, disabled	-9	-13	16	-106	-16	18	37	-20
Keeping house	—	—	1,470	-324	—	—	405	-295
At school	291	-323	384	-307	52	24	141	35
Can't find work	-311	-171	-202	-178	-232	28	-167	-98
Retired	-256	219	-665	314	-64	30	-121	-15

Source: Calculated from U.S. Bureau of the Census, Current Population Survey data tapes (Washington, D.C., March, selected years).

[a] Model I (compositional effect) should be read "If the composition of the population by work experience had not changed between 1973 and 1984, there would have been 174,000 fewer poor white males."

[b] Model II (incidence effect) should be read: If the poverty rate of work experience groups had not changed, there would have been 1,526,000 fewer poor white males."

would have been 98,000. For both races, the shift out of homemaking would have been the biggest contributor. For both races, however, if there had been no change in the incidence of poverty by work experience, poverty would have decreased by 450,000 among whites and 45,000 among blacks. Here again, those keeping house were the most affected group, accounting for 224,000 of the decrease among whites and 40,000 of the decrease among blacks.

Among black men, incidence and compositional effects balanced each other, but their directions were reversed. If there had been no change in composition, there would have been 245,000 fewer poor black men, primarily as a result of 232,000 fewer job-seekers who could find no work. If there had been no change in poverty rates by work experience, poverty would have increased however, with the biggest increase among those working full time for the full year.

Finally, among white men, compositional and incidence effects reinforced one another. If there had been no change in the composition of the population, there would have been 174,000 fewer poor; if the incidence by work experience had remained stable, there would be 1.5 million fewer poor. The compositional change was primarily attributable to changes in those who could not find work ($-311,000$) and those who were retired. This was partially balanced by increases among those in school and those who worked part time.

The impact of changes in incidence were much stronger. If the poverty rate pattern had remained stable, there would have been 1.1 million fewer white males among the working poor, including 791,000 full-time workers and 316,000 part-time workers. In addition, if there had been no change in poverty rates there would have been 323,000 fewer poor students and 171,000 fewer poor who could not find work. Practically whevever they were in the work structure, white males had a higher risk of poverty (see table 6–5).

The net impact of these changes can be expressed in terms of how they affect the total poverty rate of each group. Among white males, constant composition would have lowered the poverty rate in 1984 from 8.5 to 8.3 percent; if the same risk of poverty by work experience had existed as in 1973, the poverty rate would have been much lower: 6.5 percent. Among white women, a stable composition of the population would have raised the poverty rate from 11.5 to 12.8, while stable incidence would have lowered it to 8.9 percent. If no change had occurred in the composition of the population, black women's poverty, too, would have been higher—35.4 percent compared with the actual figure of 32.3 percent. Stability in the incidence effect, however, would have resulted in a decline in the rate to 29.6 percent. Black males would have had the opposite experience; a stable composition would have lowered poverty from 23.2 percent to 20.5 percent, while stable incidence would have increased it to 24.3 percent.

Table 6–5
Poverty Rate of the Population, Actual and Model, Population over the
Age of Fifteen, by Race and Gender, 1973–1984

	White Males	White Females	Black Males	Black Females
Actual:				
1973	6.1%	9.3%	21.5%	31.8%
1984	8.5	11.5	23.2	32.3
Modeled (1984):				
Model I	8.3	12.8	20.5	35.4
Model II	6.5	8.9	24.3	29.6

Female householders, no husband present

	Whites	Blacks
Actual:		
1973	24.5	52.7
1984	27.1	51.7
Modeled (1984):		
Model I	32.3	55.0
Model II	20.5	50.2

Source: Calculated from U.S. Bureau of the Census, Current Population Survey data tapes (Washington, D.C., March, selected years).
Note: For explanation of models, see table 6–4. Figures exclude those in the military.

Even among those most affected by the shift in family structure—female householders—the changes in work experience had a strong effect on poverty. If these women had not moved into the labor force as quickly as they did, their poverty rate would have increased even more dramatically. Instead of rising from 25 to 27 percent among whites and falling from 53 to 52 percent among blacks, the poverty rates would have soared to 32 percent and 55 percent among white and black female householders. Unfortunately, changes in the risk of poverty had the opposite effect; if no change had occurred, the poverty rate for white female householders would have been 20.5 percent (lower than the actual figures in both 1973 and 1984). Among black female householders, there would have been a smaller effect; their poverty rate would have been 50.2, slightly below the actual figures in 1973 and 1984.

Work and lack of work continue to have a powerful impact on the economic well-being of individuals, regardless of family status. The economic changes of the past years—the increase in low-paying service employment, the growth in part-time work, increases in unemployment, and the effect of job displacement—have served to reshape traditional notions of the structure of poverty. Although blacks continue to have higher poverty rates than whites and women a higher rate than men, changes in work experience have reduced these gaps. As these trends continue to shake the economy and social structure this convergence may be expected to continue.

Trends in Pretransfer Poverty and the Effectiveness of Public Transfers

The changing relationship of race, gender, and poverty reflects a number of social forces: changes in the labor market, shifts in the economy, and changes in governmental programs. In order to disaggregate these influences more fully, we return now to the family household data used earlier to examine changes in pretransfer poverty and the effectiveness rate of government programs (see table 6–6).

Although these data are restricted only to the work experience of family households, the changes in the official poverty rate between 1973 and 1983 are similar to those seen in data on the entire population. Generally speaking, poverty increased among those in the labor force, fell among the aged, and rose among those who were ill, kept house, or could not find a job. Thus, the official poverty rate among family householders who worked full time for the full year increased from 2.8 to 3.6 percent between 1973 and 1983. Increases in the official rate were smaller among other working groups, with the exception of part-time workers who worked under twenty-six weeks during the year whose poverty rate increased from 33.0 to 41.2 percent during these years. Poverty fell among the aged from 15.6 to 13.6 percent but rose among other nonworking groups. Increases were largest among those who kept house and those who could not find work.

During the most recent recovery, some of these trends have been reversed while others have continued. Among full-time, full-year workers, for example, the official poverty rate fell between 1983 and 1985 (3.6 to 3.1 percent) as it did among those who worked part time for the entire year (17.5 to 16.6 percent). Among those who worked for only part of the year, however, the recovery has not translated readily into low poverty. For example, among those who worked full time between twenty-six and forty-eight weeks, the poverty rate rose slightly, as it did among those who worked full time for less than half the year.

Among those without work experience, the recovery had less impact. Indeed, poverty remained stable or increased among all of these subgroups. The aged did not lose ground between 1983 and 1985; their poverty rate remained stable at 13.6 percent. The biggest increases in poverty were among those groups whose transfer programs lagged behind most seriously, those going to school (46.1 to 54.7 percent) and those who were jobless (68.5 to 74.9 percent). The poverty rates of the ill and disabled and housekeepers crept up during the year.

To what extent did these trends in official poverty reflect actual changes in the market economy? This question can be examined by comparing the official data with trends in pretransfer poverty. Here, the data suggest that the increase in the poverty of full-time workers was a reflection of trends in the

Table 6–6
Poverty, Pretransfer Poverty, and Effectiveness Rate, by Work Experience, 1973, 1983, and 1985

Category	1973			1983			1985		
	Official Rate	Pretransfer Rate	Effective Rate	Official Rate	Pretransfer Rate	Effective Rate	Official Rate	Pretransfer Rate	Effective Rate
Full time, full year	2.8%	3.5%	20%	3.6%	4.0%	10%	3.1%	3.5%	11%
27–48 weeks	10.2	13.1	22	11.3	14.3	21	11.6	14.8	22
Under 27 weeks	27.8	40.6	32	31.1	42.7	27	32.7	42.3	23
Part time, full year	17.0	37.5	55	17.5	27.1	35	16.6	27.1	39
27–48 weeks	33.0	62.2	47	41.2	57.4	28	26.8	36.7	27
Under 27 weeks	33.0	62.2	47	41.2	57.4	28	39.5	55.6	29
Did not work, by reason:									
Ill, disabled	39.5	78.1	49	40.0	73.6	46	40.6	75.2	46
Keeping house	44.8	80.7	44	48.4	72.7	33	50.0	71.4	30
At school	48.5	62.6	23	46.1	54.1	15	54.7	60.1	9
Can't find job	52.0	74.9	31	68.5	80.9	15	74.9	84.4	11
Retired	15.5	67.2	77	13.6	52.7	74	13.6	51.3	73
Other	39.1	78.5	48	47.2	63.9	26	52.7	69.8	24

Source: Calculated from U.S. Bureau of the Census, Current Population Survey data tapes (Washington, D.C., March, selected years).

market economy, while the experience of part-time workers and those not in the labor force was not. For example, the pretransfer poverty of every full-time work experience group rose quite dramatically between 1973 and 1983, regardless of how many weeks they worked. By contrast, although part-time workers recorded increases in their official poverty during these years, their pretransfer rates declined. Part-time, full-year workers, for example, recorded a decline of 28 percent in their pretransfer poverty rate, while the declines among other part-time groups were also quite substantial.

The experience of those outside the workforce was similar. Although most of these groups recorded increases in official poverty rate, they all experienced declines in their pretransfer poverty rates. Among those keeping house, for example, pretransfer poverty fell from 80.7 to 72.7 percent, even as official poverty rose from 44.8 to 48.4 percent. Those without work were the exception to this generalization; both their official and pretransfer poverty rates increased between 1973 and 1983.

Between 1983 and 1985, pretransfer poverty did not fit into a clear pattern. It generally fell among most groups but rose among those who worked for only twenty-seven to forty-eight weeks even though full time, those who were ill or disabled, those in school, and those who could not find a job.

As might be expected, trends in govenment transfers were not as tied to the economic cycle as was pretransfer poverty. Thus, the effectiveness rate of public transfers exhibited some steady trends during the period. Among workers, declines in the effectiveness of unemployment insurance were translated into declines in effectiveness rates. For example, the rate at which the pretransfer poor among full-time, full-year workers escaped from poverty because of public transfers fell from 20 percent in 1973 to only 10 percent in 1983 and then rose slightly to 11 percent in 1985. Among part-time and part-year workers, cuts in public programs led to a steadier decline in effectiveness rates. Full-time workers for less than twenty-six weeks, for example, saw their effectiveness rates decline from 32 percent in 1973 to 27 percent in 1983 and then fall further, to 23 percent in 1985.

Among those not in the labor market, there was a sharp split in effectiveness rates between the retired, ill, and disabled and those keeping house, going to school, or unable to find work. Among the former, effectiveness rates declined slightly over the period: from 49 to 46 percent for the disabled and ill, from 77 percent to 73 percent for the retired. The other groups experienced sharp declines in their level of protection. Among those keeping house, for example, the effectiveness rate declined from 44 percent in 1973 to 33 percent in 1983 and then further to 30 percent in 1985. There was an even sharper decline among those who could not find work; the efficiency rate fell from 31 percent in 1973 to 15 percent in 1983 and then to a low of 11 percent in 1985. A similar trend was evident among those in school as well.

These trends in poverty and the impact of cash transfers were not consistent across the population; race and family structure had a clear impact on them. These data are analyzed by the ethnicity and gender of the householder (see table 6–7).

Among households headed by men, there were some sharp differences between whites, blacks, and Hispanics.[17] Among full-time, full-year male householders, there were three distinct trends. Whites suffered a sharp increase in their poverty rate between 1973 and 1983. Their pretransfer rate rose from 2.4 to 3.3 percent and their official rate from 1.9 to 3.0 percent. During the recovery, both of these rates improved but did not return to their 1973 rate. By contrast, black male householders who worked full time for the full year actually improved their economic status throughout the period. In 1973 their pretransfer and official rates were 8.0 and 7.2 percent, respectively. Both of these improved in 1983 and then again in 1985. Thus, by 1985 the pretransfer and official poverty rates for black male householders were roughly half what they had been in 1973.

Whereas in 1973 the black pretransfer poverty rate was more than three times the white rate, by 1985 it was one and a half times as high. Among those able to secure work for the full year there was a clear convergence between whites and blacks. Still, the convergence was caused as much by the declining economic status of whites as by the improved circumstances of blacks.

Hispanic men suffered the most profound decline in their economic situation. In 1973 the pretransfer poverty rate of full-year, full-time workers was half way between those of whites and blacks. By 1985 it was more than twice the black rate, 8.9 percent. The same was true of the Hispanic official poverty rate, which rose from 4.9 to 8.8 percent between 1973 and 1983 and then fell slightly to 8.2 percent in 1985. Still, in that year, one in twelve Hispanic male householders who worked the entire year full time was poor—three and a half times the white rate.

Among female householders, the ethnic and racial poverty rates did not converge between 1973 and 1985. Full-time, full-year female householders' pretransfer poverty fell from 4.4 to 2.6 percent among whites, from 21.1 to 10.7 among blacks and from 11.9 to 9.9 percent among Hispanics. Similarly, the poverty rates among all full-year part-time workers also declined over the period, from 41.3 to 28.9 percent among whites, from 66.2 to 54.2 among blacks, and from 65.2 to 37.6 percent among Hispanics.

In 1973, then, there were profound differences in the pretransfer poverty rates of full-year workers. The rate of black female householders who worked full time was more than seven times that of the lowest poverty-risk group, white males. By 1985 sharp differences remained, but a clear convergence had occurred. The rate for black women in that year was three and a half

Table 6–7

Pretransfer Poverty Rate, by Ethnicity and Gender of Householder, and Work Experience, Family Householders, 1973, 1983, and 1985

Work Experience	White Male	Black Male	Spanish Male	White Female	Black Female	Spanish Female
Full time:						
Full year:						
1973	2.4%	8.0%	5.4%	4.4%	21.1%	11.9%
1983	3.3	5.4	9.5	3.1	10.6	9.7
1985	2.9	4.3	8.9	2.6	10.7	9.9
27–48 weeks:						
1973	7.8	19.1	27.0	21.1	45.4	45.0
1983	10.4	15.0	30.4	18.9	36.5	30.2
1985	11.2	15.3	23.0	17.6	30.5	30.8
Under 27 weeks:						
1973	28.1	50.6	37.2	55.9	80.8	71.3
1983	33.3	46.2	53.7	54.1	80.6	66.5
1985	33.3	48.0	48.4	49.4	83.0	65.4
Part time:						
Full-year:						
1973	30.8	43.1	14.1	41.3	66.2	65.2
1983	19.0	45.6	34.6	26.4	59.0	34.7
1985	18.8	40.8	38.2	28.9	54.2	37.6
27–48 weeks:						
1973	31.1	36.8	28.5	55.5	60.4	81.1
1983	25.6	40.1	33.2	39.4	64.7	52.1
1985	25.5	48.0	51.0	39.6	69.1	58.4
Under 27 weeks:						
1973	50.0	69.5	51.8	72.0	95.0	88.5
1983	44.9	66.8	63.8	62.3	93.0	78.7
1985	39.5	60.8	66.9	61.9	89.9	73.4
Did not work, by reason:						
Disabled:						
1973	69.9	85.6	86.7	83.2	88.9	94.6
1983	62.5	79.5	76.2	79.2	89.3	83.0
1985	65.4	80.3	79.2	79.3	90.6	87.0
At home:						
1973	—	—	—	77.5	93.9	91.9
1983	54.3	65.1	94.5	65.9	90.2	88.0
1985	59.6	81.8	82.3	63.9	89.4	84.7
At school:						
1973	47.0	69.5	72.4	79.8	90.7	86.0
1983	47.7	72.1	47.3	74.9	94.2	71.8
1985	45.6	31.4	60.9	71.1	90.7	86.0
Can't find work:						
1973	59.9	69.8	100.0	82.6	100.0	100.0
1983	75.2	77.4	84.2	81.0	92.3	89.8
1985	73.7	89.7	85.1	87.6	92.2	93.2
Retired:						
1973	63.3	79.3	71.3	78.4	90.6	86.9
1983	44.8	62.8	67.1	61.8	80.2	80.3
1985	41.4	72.1	55.8	61.9	74.6	77.2

Source: Calculated from U.S. Bureau of the Census, Current Population Survey data tapes (Washington, D.C., March, selected years).

times that of white men. Equally notable, white women had displaced white men as the group with the lowest pretransfer poverty rate.

Changes in pretransfer poverty were only partly reflected in official poverty rates; changes in the effectiveness of public transfers also played a role. As with the entire population, effectiveness rates generally fell across ethnicity and gender as well as work experience groups. Among full-time full-year workers, the declines in effectiveness were more significant among white male householders than among other men. Their effectiveness rate fell from 21 to 9 percent between 1973 and 1983 before rising to 14 percent in 1985, but the declines for black and Spanish-speaking male householders were slight. Among female householders, declines in effectiveness were larger. Again, among full-time full-year workers, there were substantial declines among Spanish-speaking female householders and a lesser decline among white and black female householders (see table 6–8).

Among full-time workers who had worked less than twenty-six weeks during the year, the groups that suffered the most rapid declines in effectiveness were at the two extremes of the economic hierarchy. White men saw their effectiveness rate decline from 41 to 25 percent, while black women saw theirs fall from 23 to 7 percent. Other groups experienced small declines, or in the case of black males, a fairly substantial rise.

The aged and disabled, protected by Social Security, did not generally suffer from lowered effectiveness rates. Here the exceptions were Hispanic male and female householders. Although white males who were too ill to work experienced a stable effectiveness rate, Hispanic males' rate fell from 40 to 33 percent between 1973 and 1985. Similarly, the white female rate edged up from 44 to 45 percent during these years, but Spanish-speaking women's rate fell from 56 to 24 percent. Thus although Hispanic female householders' pretransfer poverty actually fell during these years, the actual poverty rate increased from 41.3 to 66.0 percent.

Among those who could find no work or kept house, all race and gender groups suffered considerable declines in public transfer effectiveness. Among white male householders, the effectiveness rate fell from 43 to 15 percent among those unable to find work. The figure was still higher than that for any group but white female householders. By 1985 the effectiveness rate for those who could not find a job had fallen to 6 percent or below for black and Hispanic men and black women who headed households.

The three notable trends in this analysis—the declining advantage of white men, the deterioration of the position of Hispanics, and the declining effectiveness of public transfers—are summarized by looking at race and gender differences controlled for the sources of family income. Looking at those dependent solely on earnings, the pretransfer poverty rate of white men rose by two and a half times (4.7 to 11.8 percent), while that of Hispanic men nearly doubled (from 11.1 to 21.8 percent). At the same time, the rates for

Table 6–8
Effectiveness Rate, by Ethnicity and Gender of Householder and Work
Experience, Family Householders, 1973, 1983 and 1985

Work Experience	White Male	Black Male	Spanish Male	White Female	Black Female	Spanish Female
Full time:						
Full year:						
1973	21%	10%	9%	32%	20%	39%
1983	9	13	7	13	25	10
1985	14	9	8	23	16	7
27–48 weeks:						
1973	18	10	20	28	36	26
1983	26	7	21	20	9	17
1985	27	18	13	22	24	10
Under 27 weeks:						
1973	41	28	23	29	23	13
1983	35	23	21	22	17	18
1985	25	38	24	23	7	16
Part time:						
Full-year:						
1973	68	30	33	55	30	38
1983	44	44	23	32	28	33
1985	48	46	29	40	18	15
27–40 weeks:						
1973	54	55	34	54	34	36
1983	39	28	15	35	17	14
1985	33	17	13	29	19	24
Under 27 weeks:						
1973	63	32	18	46	17	20
1983	40	25	24	28	9	11
1985	42	11	22	32	13	\15
Did not work, by reason:						
Disabled:						
1973	63	39	40	44	25	56
1983	62	38	45	44	21	29
1985	62	40	44	45	23	24
At home:						
1973	—	—	—	52	19	23
1983	35	61	8	47	10	13
1985	53	57	28	41	13	12
At school:						
1973	39	25	11	18	0	12
1983	26	16	20	9	0	12
1985	8	75	0	11	8	0
Can't find work:						
1973	43	7	25	36	15	53
1983	20	14	14	20	6	6
1985	15	6	3	17	6	13
Retired:						
1973	83	68	62	66	54	55
1983	83	57	66	70	40	65
1985	83	64	66	69	45	56

Table 6–9
Pretransfer Poverty Rate, by Ethnicity and Gender of Householder, Family
Householders Dependent Solely on Earnings, 1973, 1983 and 1985

Ethnicity and Gender	1973	1983	1985
White males	4.7%	12.6%	11.8%
Black males	12.2	16.3	15.9
Spanish males	11.1	24.0	21.8
White females	16.0	20.9	18.9
Black females	27.1	25.6	25.4
Spanish females	29.5	27.6	29.1

Source: Calculated from U.S. Bureau of the Census, Current Population Survey data tapes
(Washington, D.C., March, selected years).

other race and gender groups either rose marginally or—in the case of black
and Hispanic female householders—actually fell a little (see table 6–9).

The effectiveness of public transfers fell across the board. However, as
with the population as a whole, the most startling declines were among those
dependent either fully or in part on public assistance. Here the impact of cuts
on programs for women and their children, especially AFDC, had the biggest
impact. Whereas a white woman dependent on earnings and assistance in
1973 had a 32 percent chance of escaping from poverty, by 1985 that chance
had declined to 14 percent. The same was true for blacks and Hispanics (see
table 6–10).

The story was even more devastating among those solely dependent on
public assistance. The effectiveness rate of public programs for white women
declined by three-quarters, from 17 to 4 percent. By 1985 blacks and
Hispanics too had effectiveness rates of 4 or 5 percent. By 1985 public
assistance had virtually ceased to remove women from poverty.

Conclusion

The recent emergence for concern about the status of the black poor is long
overdue. Although in many respects the economic position of black
Americans has improved, their poverty rates have remained intolerably high
and the gap between these rates and those of whites is still too large. In
addition, the worries about the black underclass have a firm foundation.
The increase in one-parent families among blacks does spell disaster in an
economy in which two incomes are generally necessary to maintain the
family's standard of living. The results of joblessness—criminality, teenage
pregnancy, and welfare dependency—remain clearly in evidence in poor
black neighborhoods.

Table 6–10
**Effectiveness Rate, by Ethnicity and Gender of Householder, and Income
Source, Family Householders, 1973, 1983 and 1985**

Source of Income/ Ethnicity and Gender	1973	1983	1985
Earnings and assistance:			
White males	29%	15%	17%
Black males	18	18	23
Spanish males	51	26	20
White females	32	11	14
Black females	27	12	11
Spanish females	34	23	21
Public assistance only:			
White males	15	7	14
Black males	11	2	7
Spanish males	17	28	12
White females	17	8	4
Black females	9	4	4
Spanish females	21	6	5

Source: Calculated from U.S. Bureau of the Census, Current Population Survey data tapes (Washington, D.C., March, selected years).

As has been shown, the current concern about the black underclass is strikingly myopic. Although black poverty has risen, this is not the result of deviant behavior. Indeed, to the extent that blacks' status has changed compared to that of whites it is for the better. Through their own increased work experience, black women have seen many positive changes in their status, although too often these have been negated by cuts in public programs. It is not deviance—culture of poverty—that is keeping most poor blacks down, but the persistence of unemployment and the spread of low-wage, unsteady employment.

At the same time, the position of Hispanics has taken a turn for the worse. Their poverty rates have risen sharply as public programs are less able to meet their needs and their status in the job market has worsened. The declining economic position of Hispanics—one of the fastest-growing segments of the population—is one of the most ominous social trends in contemporary America.

The myopia spurred by the concern about the black underclass is having an impact on policy. As shall be shown in chapter 8, the focus of the current discussions of welfare reform is restricted almost solely to the supposed apathy, deviance, and negative self-image of the underclass, and, in particular, the black underclass. One can applaud this attention after so many years of neglect, but this new initiative seems terribly misfocused. The fact is that women family heads—black and white—are doing more now to protect themselves and their dependents against poverty than they ever have.

The economy and the government are preventing them (and white males) from realizing this goal. The economy is doing so by producing a plethora of low-wage and part-time jobs. The government is doing so by limiting eligibility and cutting benefits to those wholly dependent on public welfare and those who try to combine work with income transfers. Although the current welfare debate is attempting to redirect the personal habits and attitudes of a small fraction of the population, the real welfare debate will need to examine much broader features of the U.S. economic and political order.

The tendency of welfare reformers to become preoccupied with the individual characteristics of the dependent has a long, if not distinguished, history. In the next decade, Americans will need to decide whether they will follow this tradition, whether they will ignore the transformation of their economy and instead attempt—by incentives or coercion—to change the habits of a small group of public assistance recipients, or whether they will have the insight to address the more fundamental problems they are facing. Ignoring these problems will not make them go away; it simply puts off the day of reckoning.

The future politics of welfare are uncertain, but it may be useful to examine their recent history. The next chapter turns to the Social Security crisis of the past decade to assess the dynamics that have been influencing current political battles and that will shape the limits of the debates about social welfare in the future.

Notes

1. "Fixing Welfare," *Time* (16 February 1987): 18, 21.
2. Charles Murray, *Losing Ground* (New York: Basic Books, 1984).
3. Gareth Stedman Jones, *Outcast London: A Study of the Relationship between Classes in Victorian Society* (New York: Pantheon, 1984), 11.
4. Michael B. Katz, *Poverty and Policy in American History* (New York: Academic Press, 1983), 239–40; see also his *In the Shadow of the Poorhouse: A Social History of Welfare in America* (New York: Basic Books, 1986).
5. Michael Harrington, *The Other America: Poverty in the United States* (New York: Penguin Books, 1981 [originally published in 1962]), 16ff; on Lewis, see Richard Polenberg, *One Nation Divisible: Class, Race, and Ethnicity in the United States since 1938* (New York: Viking Books, 1980), 196.
6. Peter Marris and Martin Rein, *Dilemmas of Social Reform: Poverty and Community Action in the United States* (Chicago: University of Chicago Press, 1982 [1967]), 188.
7. Ibid., 90.
8. Ken Auletta, *The Underclass* (New York: Random House, 1982), xiii.
9. Ibid., 27–30.

10. John D. Kasarda, "Urban Change and Minority Opportunities"; Elijah Anderson, "Race and Neighborhood Transition"; and William J. Wilson, "The Urban Underclass in Advanced Industrial Society," in *The New Urban Reality*, edited by Paul E. Peterson (Washington, D.C.: Brookings Institution, 1985), 33–68, 99–128, and 129–60.

11. Wilson, "The Urban Underclass," 134, 159.

12. Nicholas Lemann, "The Origins of the Underclass," *The Atlantic Monthly* (June 1986): 31–55; and (July, 1986): 54–68.

13. Lemann, "The Origins" (June 1986): 35.

14. Ibid., 36.

15. Lemann, "The Origins" (July 1986): 67–68.

16. Mickey Kaus, "The Work Ethic State," *The New Republic* (7 July 1986): 22.

17. According to the census definitions, Hispanics can be either white or black. For the purpose of this analysis, we treat them as exclusive categories. Therefore, white and black refer to non-Hispanic members of these races.

7
The Rise and Fall of the Social Security Crisis

The social changes that have been examined so far have occurred over a period of decades. The decline of manufacturing, the emergence of postindustrialization, the changing character of family life with its implications for women, and shifts in the role of race and ethnicity in American life have been long-term, stable trends stretching back at least to the Second World War. The magnitude and duration of these changes make them easy to identify.

By contrast, the ebb and flow of the politics of welfare seems puzzling and contradictory. The Fair Deal of the Truman administration and President Johnson's Great Society contained important reform components, and many aspects of the Nixon administration's domestic policy—especially the introduction of Supplemental Security Income—can be classified as reformist. Other elements of the Nixon-Ford administration, as well as the Eisenhower and Carter years, can be accurately characterized as "benign neglect." The Reagan administration represents the only clear attack on the foundations on the welfare state.[1] It is often felt that Republican administrations are always damaging to welfare and that Democratic administrations always advance the interests of low-income populations, an analysis not justified by history. It is particularly dangerous for the advocates of the poor in the social welfare community to believe this occurs. Indeed, while there is little reason to be optimistic about the United States's ability to predict future swings toward reform or conservatism, the issue is too important to ignore.

Today, the successes and failures of the Reagan administration and the challenge it poses to the recent history of social welfare attract attention. Do the policies of the Reagan administration represent a detour from the history of the expansion of the U.S. welfare state, or do they represent a historical watershed, a sharp break with the previous period? This crucial question for policy analysts and social activists is addressed in this chapter.

The analysis here does not allow for an unambiguous answer. The political forces that brought the Reagan administration to power are deeply embedded in American society; the Reagan presidency is no accident. At the same time, there are other tendencies, some related to the rise of the postindustrial economy and others related to older traditions in American politics, that appear to have undercut the ability of the current administration and its allies to carry through their anti–social welfare agenda. As the problems of postindustrial society mount, the current conservative proposals may become more and more irrelevant.

The chapter uses the Social Security crisis of the late 1970s and early 1980s as a case study of the complex forces that have influenced recent welfare politics. It begins with an examination of the expansion of the welfare state from the New Deal to the early 1970s and then delineates those social and political forces that undercut the New Deal coalition and led to the emergence of the anti–social welfare program of the Reagan administration.

The Rise of the Welfare State

The election of Ronald Reagan and the open attack on the federal government's domestic programs sent shock waves through the social welfare community during the 1980s. Not since the Great Society have those involved in human services faced such a tremendous change in the context and prospects of their field. For many in the human services professions, habituated to incremental increases in the social welfare benefits between 1935 and 1980, Reagan's ascendancy appeared to be a deviation from the path of steady progress that has characterized social welfare for most of a half century.

The growth of social welfare in the United States was based on two critical political coalitions that took form in the 1930s and 1940s: an electoral coalition that provided long-term support for the growth of the federal government's role in social welfare, and a coalition within government composed of administrators, legislators, and lobbyists at the federal level that took advantage of the stable electoral situation to expand the system. The electoral coalition was the New Deal consensus; the internal coalition is called in this book *administrative politics*.

During the 1960s and 1970s both of these coalitions fell into disrepair. These breakdowns fueled the attack on the welfare state and set the stage for the Reagan victories of 1980 and 1984. The president has been blocked in his efforts to dismember the social welfare system. The critical question for the future of pro–social welfare forces is whether new electoral and administrative coalitions can emerge that once again will be able to play a successful political role.

The New Deal Consensus

The limits of the U.S. social welfare system were set over fifty years ago by the New Deal. Although the Roosevelt administration altered the role of the federal government, its political support, its ideological justification of government action, and its policy choices imposed definite constraints on the expansion of social welfare. Particularly when compared to the social democratic regimes that laid the foundation of the European welfare states, the limits of the New Deal are severe.

The strength of the Democratic party was its varied base and its adaptability. During the Depression there was a political convergence of the urban working class and the long-time Southern Democrats. New groups joined the coalition, some of unswerving loyalties, like black Americans, and others with shorter-term interests, such as small businessmen and midwestern farmers.

The coalition swept into power during the elections of 1930 and 1932. Its power derived from two sources: the self-interests of the party's various constituencies and the willingness of the public and politicians to experiment in the face of the Depression. Thus, after experimenting with a probusiness strategy during the first New Deal of 1933–34, Roosevelt had the political latitude to endorse a very different set of policies during the second "hundred days" of 1935.

The volatile nature of the New Deal coalition imposed limits on the extent of government action in social welfare. Ever mindful of political realities, even after he comitted himself to Social Security, Roosevelt rejected disability and health insurance. As a result the Social Security Act, the centerpiece of New Deal social policy, was limited by its initial adherence to actuarial principles, its delegation of power to the states, and its restrictions on coverage. In retrospect, Roosevelt's policies seem timid in the face of massive social upheaval and electoral success. By 1938 the coalition of Republicans and conservative Southern Democrats succeeded in bringing the New Deal to an end.

The New Deal had viewed federal social welfare legislation as either a response to an emergency—or in a more sophisticated version, as a corrective to the glaring defects of capitalism caused by market forces. Rather than being based on a social criticism of the market economy, political capitalism assumed that with minor corrections the market "naturally" worked adequately.

Even this restricted view of the interventionist state was not particularly popular with American voters. In bad times, government action could gain public and congressional support because "something" had to be done, but in better times, the appeals of self-reliance, the work ethic, and negative stereotypes of the poor made federal social welfare actions less palatable.

The programs of the New Deal established the basic outlines within which the subsequent growth of the welfare state occurred. Although the programs themselves were ground-breaking, the principles on which they were based were not: a distaste for direct relief, the use of social insurance as a preventive program, and the stress on maintaining the distinction of the worthy and unworthy poor through the mix of social insurance and public assistance were the guiding principles established by the New Deal and preserved during subsequent administrations.

1. The legitimacy of direct income maintenance was never established during the New Deal. Various New Deal programs—the Federal Emergency Relief Administration, the Works Progress Administration, the Public Works Admininistration—were among the most effective tools against the Depression, but Roosevelt always saw cash relief as "a subtle destroyer of the human spirit," to be discontinued as soon as possible. Even work relief was under constant attack; its premature cutback in 1937 contributed to the depression of that year.[2]

2. The passage of the Social Security Act was the culmination of the struggle for social insurance that had been fought by such partisans as I. M. Rubinow and the American Association for Labor Legislation since the early twentieth century.[3] Old-Age insurance and unemployment compensation were expected to eliminate most of the need for cash assistance and therefore gained more attention than the categorical programs for dependent children, and the blind. This belief—that insurance and other preventive measures would eventually eliminate the need for direct relief—has remained a dominant feature of U.S. social welfare, as the current debate over welfare reform makes clear.

3. Finally, the Social Security Act established the distinction between social insurance and public assistance, a division anchored ultimately in the older distinction between the worthy and unworthy poor. As James Patterson has noted: "Other western nations developed a blend of social policies, including family allowances, health services, housing allowances, and assistance, that benefited the poor and nonpoor alike and obscured the distinction between social insurance and welfare. The separation of the two policies in the United States narrowed severely the scope of welfare . . . making the stigma for those who participated all the greater."[4]

The legacy of the New Deal was ambiguous. Although the Social Security Act represented a major expansion of federal responsibility for U.S. social welfare, the New Deal program set severe limits on the political support, philosophical foundations, and programmatic principles of the welfare state. Nevertheless, it did provide a foundation on which later reform was built.

Administrative Politics

The welfare state grew rapidly between 1935 and 1975 in spite of its conservative origins. Part of the explanation for this lies in the social utility and pragmatic popularity of government spending, but there were other causes of this growth. Among the most important of these was the growth of forces *within* the government that independently produced pressure for the expansion of social welfare: administrative politics.

Administrative politics was marked by a strategy of incrementalism, consensus, and depoliticization. By reducing controversy, providing abundant research to support proposals, and closely matching benefits expansion and the revenues to support them, the practitioners of administrative politics were able to transform the welfare state between the late 1930s and 1980. Although the effects were ultimately felt by all parts of the system, it was social insurance that most consistently benefited from this strategy.

Old-Age Insurance was established under the original Social Security Act in 1935 as a retirement program for employees in private industry and commerce. Benefit payment schedules were based on work experience and were intended to provide standards of living that were related to the preretirement labor force position of recipients. To help ensure widespread acceptance, heavy emphasis was placed on the insurance-like aspects of the program and the large reserve fund that was anticipated.

The first movement from the relatively strict insurance concept toward pay-as-you-go funding came in 1939 when survivor's and dependents' benefits were added. That year, the computation base for benefits was shortened to increase pensions for other workers, as well.

During the 1950s and 1960s Congress repeatedly extended coverage and benefits; the proportion of the labor force covered increased from 58 to 90 percent between 1940 and 1972. With each extension of coverage, eligibility requirements were also altered to "blanket in" those new groups. In 1966 a small special benefit was introduced for those over the age of seventy-two financed from general revenue.

Benefits increased over the period, although not at a steady rate. One of the largest and most redistributive increases was enacted in 1950, providing for an average increase of 77 percent (with rises of 100 percent for the lowest benefit group and 50 percent for the highest). Smaller increments followed in 1952, 1954, and 1958. During the 1960s, when most attention was focused on Medicare, old-age benefits increases slowed down, but as poverty among the elderly became more visible, a new round of increases began. Between 1968 and 1973 average benefits rose 69 percent in part to make up for ground lost because of inflation. After 1974 the cost-of-living-adjustment (COLA) went into effect, which pegged benefit increases to the consumer price index.[5]

Several major programs were added to the system. Disability insurance was introduced in 1956, extended to dependents of disabled workers in 1958, and further liberalized in 1960. Early retirement for women was authorized in 1956 and extended to men in 1961. Hospital and Supplementary Medical Insurance (Medicare Parts A and B) were enacted in 1965.

In summary, between 1935 and 1973, Social Security went from a narrowly based, insurance-like program for a small part of the workforce to a redistributive program covering a major share of the population for a variety of risks. To the original insurance against unemployment and retirement, protection for premature death of wage earners, disability, and illness in old age were added. Where initially the program had benefits rather closely tied to contributions, by 1973 it was quite redistributional from small to large familes, from the healthy to the ill, from those able to work to the disabled, from workers to the retired and unemployed, and from upper-income to lower-income families.

The system is financed through a regressive payroll tax that favors those with income above a set tax base. The original legislation provided for the accumulation of a trust account. Tax collections began in 1937, with payments originally to begin in 1942. In the intervening years, several tax increases were to lead to an account that would accumulate sufficient funds to pay for 40 percent of benefits out of the interest on the reserves.

The financing changes that began in 1939 reconceptualized the reserve fund. Not only was the program to expand, but benefits would start earlier and tax increases would come later. The benefit payment date was moved to 1940, and the scheduled tax increase was postponed for three years. The explicit aim was to avoid a build up of the trust fund reserves and to move to a contingency fund basis. Nevertheless, larger than anticipated funds continued to accumulate. During World War Two benefit payments were lower than projected, and tax receipts were higher. For the remainder of the decade, a pattern evolved in which Congress would set tax rates that led to greater increases in reserves and projections of larger future surpluses than they first expected. Congress would then increase benefits and postpone tax increases. In 1950, the tax rate for employers and employees still stood at 1 percent for each.

During the 1950s and 1960s, program expansion was the primary means of keeping down trust fund reserves. In 1950 Congress considered and rejected a "level-premium" contribution rate that would have led to a large retirement fund without tax increases or general revenue financing. Instead they chose a combination of moderate tax increases and substantial benefit increases that led, in time, to the reality of pay-as-you-go financing.

The growth of Social Security during these years was impressive. It grew from less than one-twentieth of 1 percent of gross national product to 5.5 percent of GNP between 1940 and 1973. A policy of incremental change— the slow establishment and expansion of precedents and increase in benefits— remained the dominant feature of policy making.[6]

In part the system was able to expand more or less peaceably because these were years of strong economic growth. As the economy flourished, the program expanded and the funds grew. In those times, no one, including the forecasters of the Social Security Administration, foresaw the end of the baby boom in the late 1960s or the oil crisis and inflation of the 1970s. Most important, no one anticipated that the nation would experience an extended period in which prices would rise faster than wages. All of these factors became the cause for trouble in the Social Security system.

The expansion of the program between 1969 and 1972 marked the culmination of this system of policy-making and set the stage for its undermining. The legislated increase in benefits between 1968 and 1972 was not based on larger-than-expected trust fund accumulations, as earlier increases had been, but on projections of future fund surpluses that were based on what turned out to be extremely optimistic assumptions of economic growth, inflation, and unemployment. At the same time, the careful incrementalism of the system's executives was replaced, at least in the case of the 1972 increases, by the more dramatic political efforts of Democratic leaders, especially the chairman of the House Ways and Means Committee, Wilbur Mills. The price of the benefit increases of those years was a fiscally less secure and more visible Social Security system.

The steady expansion of Social Security through the mid-1970s was matched by other expansions of the social welfare system. Although the public assistance programs languished during the 1950s (with the exception of disability assistance, which was added in 1950), the Public Welfare Amendments of 1962 set the stage for the expansion of federal funding of social services. The addition of Medicare and Medicaid in 1965, the War on Poverty programs, food stamps, and Supplemental Security Income (SSI) were all accomplished using elements of the administrative political strategy. Between 1965 and 1981 alone, the percentage of the federal budget commit ted to income security and health expanded from 23 to 44 percent.[7]

Federal officials in the Department of Health, Education, and Welfare and in the Social Security Administration played a key role in administrative politics. In spite of the unsuccessful effort in 1972 to nationalize Aid to Families with Dependent Children (AFDC), most administrative welfare proposals succeeded. By and large they appeared incremental; HEW and Social Security Administration professionals managed to insulate them from the most intense political debates.

Although it was orchestrated by administrators, two elements were necessary for administrative politics to be put into law: a set of executive-legislative liaisons that tailored proposals to congressional tastes and a congressional leadership willing to work with the program administrators. Leadership in the bureaucracy and in Congress were the foundation of administrative politics.

The role of liaison was personified by Wilbur Cohen, who from his years on the staff of the Committee on Economic Security in 1934 until his retirement as Secretary of HEW in 1969 served as a bridge between the technical professionals in the bureaucracy and Congress. A host of other program executives, including Social Security Commissioners Altmeyer and Robert Ball, also served as advocates and liaisons.[8] These leaders provided an institutional continuity that was unusual for government. Over the years a group of professionals learned to tailor their proposals for an increasingly willing congressional leadership.

Administrative politics were aided during the postwar years by the stability and prerogatives of congressional committee chairmen. In his long tenure as chairman of the House Committee on Ways and Means, Wilbur Mills emerged as the guide and protector of Social Security legislation. By crafting each bill in committee and limiting floor debate and amendments, Mills was able to protect Ways and Means control of the process and outcome.[9]

Special interest groups supported the administrative and legislative advocates of program expansion. During the 1950s and 1960s organized labor was the most consistent supporter. While wielding influence, however, organized labor usually left the specifics of program change to the professionals within government and "left no distinguishing marks on the program."[10] During the 1970s the role of lobbying was increasingly taken over by the aging lobby. In the 1930s "old age lobbies such as the Townsendites had seemed a little zany to younger Americans." but Patterson found that by the late 1960s "old people began to be called senior citizens. Their 'gray lobbies', increasingly well organized and financed, reflected 'senior power.' "[11]

The final element of the coalition for administrative politics was the cooptation of state and local officials. Although initially resistant to greater federal power, their creative use of grant-in-aids, revenue sharing, and block grants eventually turned state and local administrators (often with federal encouragement) into advocates of increased federal spending. For example, the Public Welfare Amendments, which obligated the federal government to pay 75 percent of the cost of social services for those "likely to become" dependent, allowed state and local officials to expand services to both poor and middle-income groups while federal taxes paid for them.

The expansion of social insurance and other welfare programs was a product of these institutional arrangements. By the mid-1970s the United States had a modern, if "incomplete," welfare state in spite of the general apathy and indifference of the voting public. At the same time that social welfare was expanding most quickly, however, there were a variety of forces working to undermine both its political support and the administrative politics that had led to its successes.[12]

The Decline of the New Deal Consensus

The New Deal coalition had resulted from a convergence of a number of historical circumstances. In the four decades that followed the dynamics of American society broke this consensus and produced a set of social problems that the New Deal had not been designed to accommodate. Most important were the changing class and ethnic stratification of American society and the changing role of women in the economy and society.

One of the most cherished ideals of the postwar United States was the notion that social class had become obsolete. *Fortune* declared confidently: "The union has made the worker . . . a middle class member of a middle class society," while historian Eric Goldman believed that, "New Dealism . . . had created a nation of the middle class."[13] Indeed, in the glow of the 1950s it often appeared that there never had been social classes in the United States. By the end of the 1970s, however, the role of social class and ethnic stratification were clear.

During the prosperity of the 1940s and 1950s the combination of low unemployment and rising wages lifted a large portion of the working class out of poverty. Between 1940 and 1960 the poverty rate fell from nearly a third of the population to under a quarter, largely as a result of general economic growth. These "affluent" workers, many of them newly protected by the mass-production labor unions (auto workers, steel workers, rubber workers, mine workers) and the first generation protected by Old Age and Unemployment Insurance, hoped to construct a firm economic foundation for their security and that of their children.

The general improvement of the economy, however, failed to pull many of those in the lowest tier of the working class out of poverty. Although by the mid-1970s the official poverty rate had fallen below 12 percent, much of the improvement of the 1960s and 1970s was a product of the expansion of the welfare state, not the market economy. Whereas economic growth had brought the upper tier of the working class out of poverty in the 1940s and 1950s, the same could not be said for the bottom tier. For those in the unskilled, insecure, and low-paying jobs it was not the economy that changed, but government action that led to the decline in poverty.

Furthermore, this split in the experience of the upper and lower tiers of the working class was reinforced by ethnic divisions. The upper tier was predominantly white, the descendants of immigrants to northern cities from Europe and rural America. The lower tier was increasingly composed of nonwhite groups, including black Americans who had migrated from the South, Puerto Ricans, and Mexicans, and a new wave of immigrants from Latin America and Asia. These groups entered and for the most part remained in the secondary labor market.[14]

The other major group to enter the labor force during these years was women. The motives for women's entry varied according to social class and ethnicity. For black women, wage labor was nothing new; women's work was an essential element of black families' struggle for survival. For women of the business class, entry into the labor force during marriage was a result of increasing education, the attractiveness of extra earnings, and the impact of the feminist movement. For the white working class, women's work was almost totally the result of economic need. As the economy slowed down after 1965, the increasing labor force participation of women became a means of continuing the rise of family income. Because of occupational segregation, women were confined to the lower tier of the labor market—in jobs with low wages and little security.

The different historical experience of the white and black working classes during the postwar era led to overt conflict between these groups in the 1960s and 1970s. The white working class's economic improvement during the 1940s and 1950s was a product of the expansion of the market economy, while among blacks and Hispanics economic improvement was often the result of government action to increase their incomes and open opportunities for them. Thus, whites continued to look to the private sector and their own actions for prosperity, but the nonwhite working class viewed government as the key to their future advancement.

For the white working class the promise of affluence was only partially kept. After 1965 the gains of the immediate postwar period did not continue; increasingly, wage increases were offset by inflation. What increase blue-collar families did experience was a product of increases in the number of two-earner households, as millions of working-class wives entered the workforce. Thus, the better-off blue-collar workers could no longer look forward to automatic increases in their standard of living.

These macroeconomic changes had serious consequences for the families of the white and the black working class. Among whites, the expectations of the postwar period—a full-time housekeeping wife, college for the children, homeownership, and a consistently rising standard of living—receded. For blacks, although absolute income rose, the dependence on uncertain government support did not allow for the shedding of their traditional family strategy, based on extended kin relations, economic reciprocity, and a short economic horizon.[15] The late 1960s and 1970s were a time of frustration and disappointment for both blacks and whites.

Furthermore, these social trends produced a set of social problems unforeseen when social insurance was enacted in 1935. As the number of urban dependents increased, Aid to Families with Dependent Children became the largest assistance program; the increasing number of independent women, coupled with the low level of female wages, threatened to create a new, largely female pauper class. Finally, with the rise of black militancy and anger, the deferential, obsequious behavior that was expected of welfare recipients gave way to the assertion of welfare "rights."[16] This led ultimately to increases in the percentage of those eligible who actually applied for and received public assistance.[17]

The combination of no progress for white workers and partial, government-sponsored increases for nonwhite workers paid for by regressive taxes turned out to be an explosive mixture. The blue-collar revolt against the welfare state was a product of the resentment, frustration, and sense of betrayal felt by these families. As one commentator put it,

> Working-class people had to bear the brunt of the pressures, in ordinary life, caused by the great in-migration of blacks: competition for jobs, the disruptions caused by block-busting and changing neighborhoods, and all the fear that the great change caused. They had to live through these stains at a time when the strongest traditional working class institutions—the family, the parochial school, the labor union, and the political machine— were all either declining or undergoing transformation that made them less able to cope.[18]

These strains in the economy drove a wedge into the New Deal coalition. During the 1950s the labor movement went into a steady decline as a result of economic and political changes.[19] For a time, the declining power of the unions was offset by the increasing militancy and mobilization of the black movement. Although a part of the New Deal coalition, blacks had found their interests subordinated to the need to preserve the segregationist Solid South.[20]

During the 1950s black support declined as a consequence of Adlai Stevenson's refusal to take up the fight for civil rights, but in the wake of John Kennedy's dramatic appeal for Martin Luther King's release from jail during the 1960 election, black votes provided the winning margin in crucial states. Indeed, according to some researchers, President Johnson's initiation of the War on Poverty was motivated in part by the need to retain black political support.[21]

These tensions in the Democratic coalition could not be contained for long. The interests of blacks and southern diehards could not be reconciled. In addition, the acrimony caused by the Vietnam War exacerbated existing divisions within the party. The accumulation of conflict culminated in the 1968 national convention, where conflict on the floor and in the streets signaled the coming end of a successful coalition.

At the same time that the Democratic coalition was weakened, the morphology of American conservatism also changed. In the 1950s the locus of Republican conservatism had been the main streets and Rotary clubs of the Midwest and the boardrooms of New York and Chicago. During the 1960s, however, conservatism diversified. In the growing states of the Sun Belt, conservatism with an antiestablishment ring found its voices in Barry Goldwater and Ronald Reagan, while in the South George Wallace represented a more belligerent attack on liberalism that was able to mobilize surprising support in the industrial North.

The political wild card of the 1970s, however, was "populism." It represented a general revolt against the "establishment" and a reaffirmation of "traditional" social values. Its voices ranged from Wallace on the right to Jimmy Carter in the middle to George McGovern and Fred Harris further to the left. Its constituencies were the southern working class, the northern ethnic voters, and disaffected westerners. It was what Richard Nixon called "middle America." Although this group was not intrinsically conservative, Republicans successfully captured this vote during the 1970s and 1980s.[22]

By the end of the 1970s the political winds had shifted. Watergate had led to Democratic victories in 1974 and 1976, but the New Deal coalition was coming apart. At the same time, conservatism was finding a new political voice and a new strategy for reentering the political mainstream. These changes set the electoral context for the collapse of administrative politics.

The End of Administrative Politics

The most important factor underlying the decline of the old politics of welfare was the performance of the economy during the late 1970s and early 1980s. In rapid succession, the United States experienced recessions in 1969–70, 1974–75, 1980, and 1981–82. Even during the recovery of 1975–80, inflation and the deteriorating U.S. position in the world economy contributed to general dissatisfaction.

The federal budget became one focus of concern. An old theory—that federal spending caused inflation, hurt productivity, and inhibited private investment—gained new legitimacy among supply-side and monetarist economists. At the same time, the tax revolt, symbolized by Proposition 13 in California, prevented legislators from increasing taxes to lower deficits.

The aftermath of the Vietnam War also shaped federal fiscal policy. As war spending declined between 1967 and 1973, defense spending's share of national income fell from 11 to 7 percent. Thus, domestic spending could increase without either new taxes or increased deficits.[23] By the late 1970s this cushion no longer existed; spending on social welfare became more visible.

In addition to the economy, a number of institutional factors hurt administrative politics. Americans' faith in social planning was hurt by the War on Poverty and the Vietnam War. Between 1969 and 1980 the percentage of Americans who felt alienated from the political structure rose from 36 percent to 62 percent.[24] This disillusionment was related to disruptions within the political structure. In electoral politics, the declining identification with party and the deterioration of grassroots political organizations led to a "dealignment" of politics in which stable coalitions appeared to be a thing of the past.[25] Without these stable alignments, it became more difficult to pursue the administrative politics strategy of incrementalism and depoliticization.

Finally, the passing of time led to a breakdown of the set of accommodations on which administrative politics was based. The post-Watergate congressional reforms weakened the power of committee chairmen. It was harder for them to control dissent both inside and outside committee. At the same time, the personnel that ran the system departed. Secretary Cohen and Commissioner Ball retired, and Wilbur Mills, who had dominated Social Security legislation for so long, was forced to resign in the wake of a personal scandal. The people and institutions that had maintained the old system lost their power, and a new era of uncertainty began.

The Coming of the Social Security Crisis

The political crisis of welfare affected a host of programs. Without the secure political support and institutional arrangements of the past, politicians and advocates had to redefine their position and articulate new strategies. Although budget cuts were targeted at practically all welfare programs, it was the future of Social Security that most captured the attention of citizens and politicians during the late 1970s and early 1980s. The history of the Social Security crisis can illuminate the new politics of social welfare during this period.

The 1972 amendments promised a golden age of Social Security that did not materialize. Instead, within a few years, politicians, professional experts, and the mass media were proclaiming a Social Security crisis. For most of the next decade, the image of system collapse was in the public eye.

The crisis represented the interaction of a number of discrete phenomena. For a variety of reasons, the Social Security trust funds encountered some persistent fiscal difficulties during the late 1970s and early 1980s. These problems lay the economic base of the problem, but they alone were not sufficient to cause a major crisis.

The extent of the crisis was exacerbated by two other phenomena. In professional and academic circles, the monopoly on expertise that the Social Security Administration had historically held was broken; a number of new experts drawn from different branches of the federal government and from outside of government emerged to predict a coming "dependency crisis," to evaluate the macroeconomic impact of Social Security, and to examine the supposedly detrimental impact of Social Security on working people. Following the lead of the experts, the mass media gave Social Security major attention. As a result, there was a broad public debate of the issue. Thus, there were really three discrete elements to the crisis—the fiscal crisis, the expert crisis, and the public crisis.[26]

The fiscal difficulties of the system were real enough. They involved some substantial problems with the structure of benefits and taxes. Not only had large benefit increases been enacted in 1972, but the new indexing system was based on a "coupled" formula that linked the benefits of current retirees to the entitlements of future beneficiaries. This system would have worked well enough in the low-inflation, high-wage-growth environment of the 1960s, but in the stagflation of the 1970s it produced some serious problems.[27]

In particular, the 1972 formula resulted in an increase in the "replacement ratio," the percentage of final wages replaced by retirement benefits. It appeared—using one set of calculations by Robert Myers—that after several decades the replacement ratio would actually exceed 100 percent—that is, workers would receive more in monthly benefits from Social Security than they did from their final month at work.[28]

The imperfection of the indexing formula was compounded, moreover, by the adverse economic conditions of the mid-1970s. The Arab oil embargo of 1973–74 sparked a new round of inflation and then the most serious recession since the 1930s. As a result, the trust funds experienced their first annual deficit since 1964, which raised concern in Congress.

The reform package of 1977 did help relieve the internal problems of the system by adopting an indexation formula that stabilized replacement ratios and increasing taxes to replenish the trust funds. However, it could do little about the prevailing economic environment that continued to affect the trust funds adversely. Consumer prices, to which benefits were pegged, increased by 50 percent between 1977 and 1981, while average weekly earnings, to which payroll taxes were related, increased by only 35 percent. Finally, unemployment rose from 6 percent in 1977 to 7.5 percent in 1981 and 9.5 percent in 1982 and 1983. Revenues were adversely affected.[29]

As a result, the reforms of 1977 did not end the drawdown of the trust funds. The combined Old-Age, Survivors', and Disability trust funds had a net deficit of $4.2 billion in 1978, $1.4 billion in 1979, and $3.6 billion in 1980. By the time the National Commission on Social Security Reform (NCSSR) was appointed by President Reagan in 1981, the retirement trust fund had been reduced to reserves for a few months. Interfund borrowing provided some breathing room, but further changes were necessary.[30]

Although the fiscal problems of Social Security were very real, their gravity needs to be kept in proportion. The Old-Age and Survivors' trust funds were out of balance, but the Disability and Medicare funds ran surpluses for most of the time between 1979 and 1982. At the same time, the total requirements of the system to get through the crisis of the 1980s, estimated at between $68 and $200 billion, seems minor compared to the deficit problems of the federal budget.[31]

Trustbusters: Breaking Social Security's Monopoly "Ownership" of Expertise

As Joseph Gusfield has noted, public problems are often "owned"—that is, some groups establish an acknowledged right to display expertise on a specific problem. For example, during the 1950s psychologists took "ownership" of the auto safety issue because of the apparent pathology of "reckless drivers." Several groups may claim ownership, but through a process of competition and negotiation, the parameters of ownership are resolved.[32]

From this perspective, one interesting aspect of the Social Security crisis was the breakdown of the Social Security Administration's ownership of the issue. First, the efficiency of SSA's monopoly faltered, then a variety of competitors—demographers, economists, actuaries, and political scientists—attempted to establish their own claim to expertise. Before there had been a few members involved in constrained debate; after 1973 the scholarly debate over Social Security became wide open.

One of the reasons for the success of Social Security during the 1950s and 1960s was the lack of controversy over professional analysis of the program. The Social Security Administration was the accepted authority and source of data even among government agencies, and this monopoly extended to nongovernmental analysts at universities, think tanks, and the private sector.[33]

The centerpiece of this dominance was the annual trustees' report and its projections of the status of the program. These projections—first in perpetuity and then for seventy-five years—provided the official numbers that other professionals used to evaluate the program and reform proposals. Furthermore, the projections served a political purpose. They allowed members of Congress and presidents to claim that they were expanding benefits while maintaining "fiscal responsibility."

The breakdown of SSA's monopoly resulted in part from the decline of internal expertise within the agency. Robert Myers, the longtime chief actuary, had a sound professional reputation that gave the official projections a credibility they might not otherwise have had in the private insurance industry and among professional actuaries. In the early 1970s he left SSA and became a moderate, but vocal, critic of the program. One of his successors, A. Haeworth Robertson, who served from 1973 to 1978, was less visible in his years of office but produced extremely pessimistic projections after he left

SSA. Those projections became the basis for conservative pronouncements on the future of the system.[34]

At the same time, when Commissioner Robert Ball was removed in 1973, the program executive passed out of the hands of "insiders" for virtually the first time in the system's history. The first projections of a serious long-term deficit problem were made public just months after Ball had departed.

Thus, during the late 1970s the "true" spokespersons for the system were divided in a way that was reminiscent of dynastic battles in medieval Europe. The real "officials" at SSA began to issue increasingly gloomy forecasts and assessments, while the "officials in exile," particularly ex-Commissioner Ball and Wilbur Cohen, attempted to calm fears. By the early 1980s there was a former official of the Social Security Administration to support practically any view.

Even within the federal government, other agencies and Congress began to make their own projections and pronouncements. For example, during the early years of the crisis, the release of a Senate Finance Committee report written by C. L. Hsaio, a Harvard economist and actuary, signaled the breakdown of SSA's monopoly. Other agencies, including HEW and the Treasury Department, also began to take a larger role in policy debates.[35]

At the same time, with a variety of semi-official projections and increasing attention on the system, academic experts took a renewed interest in Social Security. Some of these, like Henry Aaron and Alicia Munnell, carried on the reformist tradition of the old "insiders," but others became more sharply critical in their analyses. The "baby bust" of the 1970s provoked demographers to worry about the "dependency burden" of the next century. Economists, led by Martin Feldstein, began to question the macroeconomic impact of Social Security. Finally, a number of policy analysts questioned the political rationale of the system and called for its radical restructuring. These trends were discrete but often complementary; taken together they provided powerful claims for ownership of the Social Security problem.

As noted, during the late 1970s the rise in the dependency ratio became an object of concern among a number of scholars. In their book *The Graying of Working America* Sheppard and Rix projected an increasing dependency ratio for the twenty-first century based on the assumption of continuing low fertility. Other scholars accepted these assumptions; within a few years the predictions of a dependency crisis had spawned a string of major studies and dire predictions. "If, half a century from now, one in five Americans is old," demographer Judith Treas warned, "the cost of meeting their needs may outstrip the societal carrying capacity for social welfare programs."[36]

The dependency argument ran into a problem; while the number of aged individuals was increasing, the number of children was declining. If one used a "total" dependency ratio (the sum of youth and aged dependency), the common predictions suggested that the dependency ratio would actually be lower during the "dependency crisis" than it had been during the 1960s. Some scholars argued that the cost of supporting the aged was greater than that of supporting the young; these conclusions were true for public expenditures, but they were not correct when private costs were included. Finally, the literature paid practically no attention to rising productivity and its possible impact on the dependency burden.[37]

Although the dependency burden researchers were not particularly successful in supporting their argument, they did gain a wide audience. Their work was widely read and frequently cited, while that of their critics was not. Like Thomas Malthus, two centuries earlier, they left the impression that inevitable demographic realities would shape the future. Biological necessity—not social and political choice—would mold public policy.

Economic critics of Social Security meanwhile attacked the existing program as economically counterproductive. In an influential study, Martin Feldstein, later to become head of the Council of Economic Advisors, argued that retirement benefits were a form of "wealth" that discouraged the savings rate of the American public. He argued that the security of retirement benefits discouraged individuals from providing for their own retirement through personal savings and that this was the primary reason that the United States suffered from a capital scarcity. Feldstein's thesis was supported by a combination of rational expectations theory, anecdotal evidence, and a tenuous string of logic.

The empirical foundation of Feldstein's argument was weak, a fact that Feldstein on occasion admitted. Indeed, much of the impact on savings that he originally reported was discovered to be a result of programming errors; when the study was replicated correcting the errors, the effect of Social Security on savings was found to be insignificant. In a review of the literature, Henry Aaron concluded that equally plausible assumptions could be used to demonstrate a positive, a negative, or no effect of Social Security on savings.[38]

In spite of these contradictory empirical findings, Feldstein's writings tended to overstate his case. For example, in one article he wrote:

> If individuals think of these contributions as equivalent to savings and reduce their own personal savings accordingly, the effect on total savings would be very substantial. In 1974, personal savings were $77 billion, or eight per cent of disposable personal income. If one assumes there was an $89 billion reduction in personal savings induced by social security, this means that personal savings have been cut to less than half of what they would otherwise be. Of course, not all private savings are personal savings. Corporate retained earnings account for nearly half of all private capital accumulation. In 1974, these corporate savings were $53 billion, and added to personal savings, this means that total private savings were $130 billion,

the total potential private savings of $219 billion had been reduced by about 41 per cent. In the long run, this implies that U.S. capital stock is also about 41 per cent less than it would otherwise be.[39]

In one paragraph, Feldstein was forced to rely on three "ifs" and one "implies" to sustain his argument. Despite the tenuous chain of logic, however, four pages later, he informs us that "it is clear that our current pay-as-you-go social security program has certain grave side-effects."[40]

Feldstein advocated a moderate set of changes, designed to increase savings, capital growth, and ultimately productivity. These included an increase in payroll taxes leading to a build up of the trust funds that would become a source of savings and investment. His hope was that this fund would reduce the long-term rise in payroll taxes by earning interest and eventually increase economic growth.

Nathan Keyfitz, in a series of articles, added a demographic and political twist to Feldstein's argument. Where Feldstein with admittedly weak evidence had argued for the desirability of fuller reserves, Keyfitz accepted Feldstein's argument as "authoritative" and asserted that reform was a demographic necessity.

For Keyfitz, Social Security suffered from a form of "original sin": the blanketing-in of the first generation of retirees under the system. Using pay-as-you-go financing to pay for these freeloaders reduced economic growth and punished today's and tomorrow's workers. "That free gift to those blanketed in a generation ago has been and will be paid for by everyone from then on, to the end of time, losing the interest on his money that is a matter of right to the individual savers who provided for themselves outside of the Social Security scheme."[41]

In addition to the demographic burden associated with the current system, Keyfitz developed a populist political critique of Social Security. Because Social Security was a kind of "wealth," Keyfitz claimed that present practice discriminated against working people because unlike private savings it paid no interest.

> The pension is more costly to working people than it would be if, for at least some part of their protection against old age, they could get the benefit of interest. Too little attention has been given to the sheer inequity of working people obtaining no interest on what amounts to a forced loan, while the rich are free to draw all the interest they can get. It is almost as though the liberals promoting social security had wanted to sterilize workers' savings, to keep them out of capital markets.[42]

Keyfitz went on to argue for a mandated, fully funded pension that would work like private group insurance. Such a program would lead in time to a veritable supply-side utopia: "With increased savings more venture capital would be available and the competitiveness of the economy would be increased. New establishments would come into existence in many industries, and existing establishments would have more possibility of expanding into competition with IBM or Dupont."[43]

Carolyn Weaver and Peter Ferrara were representative of the new conservative policy critics of the system. Weaver, an economist at Virginia Tech, authored a study of the political economy of Social Security funded by, among others, the Liberty Fund, the Center for Libertarian Studies, and the Fiscal Policy Council.[44] She then went on to become a staff member of both the Senate Finance Committee and the NCSSR. Her book viewed Social Security as an exercise in coercive special interests and political manuevering that was, more or less, imposed on the American people. She advocated either a fully funded system or, better yet, a voluntary one. As she noted,

> In all, the lessons from history seem abundantly clear: the existing crisis in Social Security is decidedly not financial in nature, it is decidedly not "unexpected," and it rests squarely in the political and economic failures resulting from a loss of individual choice in 1935. The crisis is at base political, lodged in the institutional weaknesses of the program. If nothing else this crucial period in the history of Social Security should foster the development of competing ideas about the crisis, so necessary for rational decision-making in the future.[45]

Peter Ferrara, who served in the White House Office of Policy Development early in the Reagan administration, was the most visible of the new "mainline" critics. In a number of monographs published by the Cato Institute, Ferrara combined a simple economic argument with political attacks on the system.[46]

In a 1984 article, "Social Security: The Crisis Continues," Ferrara adopted what had become the standard supply-side criticism of the welfare state—social welfare hurts the efficient operation of the economy. "Social Security, as presently structured," he writes, "severely retards economic growth by destroying jobs and discouraging investment. . . . By discouraging employers from hiring and employees from working, the Social Security tax leads to less employment and less output."[47]

Social Security is, quite simply, a bad buy; using payroll taxes to buy private insurance would be better. This raw deal continued, in Ferrara's view, because of the coercive monopoly of the federal government, which "deprives . . . [workers] of control over a substantial part of their income." Ferrara went on to argue that Social Security discriminates against the black, the poor, and the single individual. Ferrara used a variety of liberal criticisms of the system, including that of Henry Aaron, to support its replacement by a voluntary plan.[48]

During the 1950s and 1960s expert opinion on Social Security had largely been contained within a narrow range of issues: how fast to raise taxes and benefits, where to expand the system, whether to introduce general-revenue financing. The limits of the discussion had been set by the program's executives and scholars who shared the official perspective of the program. During the 1970s and early 1980s a new set of more fundamental critiques of the system gained a hearing and a new respectability. Although the particulars might vary from Malthusian nightmare to supply-side populism, the message was the same: Social Security was fundamentally unsound and would continue in perpetual crisis.

At the height of the Social Security crisis, in December 1982, the critique of Social Security was extended. Peter Peterson, a former Secretary of Commerce under President Carter, wrote a series of articles for the *New York Review of Books* with the evocative titles "Social Security: The Coming Crash" and "The Salvation of Social Security." Based on the pessimistic estimates of former chief actuary A. Haeworth Robertson, Peterson linked the problems of the retirement and health insurance programs and projected a possible increase of 44 percent in the payroll tax by the middle of the twenty-first century. Although Peterson's analysis and proposals (cuts in benefits, means-testing) were not new, their appearance in the *New York Review of Books,* an accepted "liberal" journal, gave the crisis a credibility that it had not previously enjoyed. Indeed, as William Achenbaum notes, Peterson's analysis was regularly cited by leading newspapers including the *New York Times,* the *Washington Post,* and the *Wall Street Journal.*[49]

The Experts and the Public

Suddenly the public was faced with all the diversity of opinion and alarm of the experts. It was hard for Congress, or indeed anyone else, to guess public reaction. In the past, the public had been supportive of social insurance without having developed any understanding of the basic economic issues. The risks of bankruptcy, the charges of unfair burdens and of impediments to economic growth—all made public reactions less predictable.

The issues involved were complex. Few Americans could calculate their own Social Security entitlement, much less weigh those of their fellow citizens. Still less could they measure the long-term or the macroeconomic effects of current legislation. The public, which had been treated to decades of reassurances and simple insurance metaphors, was suddenly asked to assess a range of scenarios, to master revenue formulas, and to grapple with the impact of declining fertility and rising inflation on their retirement benefits. Under these circumstances, the public debate could hardly help but produce confusion and alarm.

As politicians tried to deal with the fiscal crisis of Social Security, they also had to calculate the political costs and benefits of any given position on reform. Aside from increased concern that "something" should be done, what they found was rejection of almost all possible options. The polls suggested that the public agreed that federal employees should be covered by social insurance, but otherwise they opposed all other solutions, including tax increases, benefit cuts, taxing benefits, raising the retirement age, and any radical surgery.[50]

Politics is not simply a game of support; it is one of allegiance. Although some issues are decided on a rational evaluation of individual cost and benefits, the symbolic meaning of politics is also important. It is difficult to understand blacks' allegiance to the "Party of Lincoln" or rural Protestants' attraction to Prohibition without an understanding of the cultural symbols that mold political attitudes and behavior.[51]

The symbolic aspect of the Social Security crisis was important for a number of reasons. The complexity of the issue and the lack of popular understanding meant that the expressive, dramatic side of the issue would be important; fear, not hard-headed calculation, often influenced decisions. In addition, the "selling" of Social Security over the previous forty years involved connecting social welfare with more standard American beliefs like work, the "American standard of living," and equity. Finally, the crisis occurred during a period when political alignments generally were perceived as uncertain.

As a result, although the rhetoric of the Social Security crisis included debates over benefit schedules and taxing formulas, it also included dramatic appeals to cultural symbols. Those who could identify their position with "mom and apple pie," it was believed, would emerge victorious.

One of the aspects of cultural symbols that made the politics of Social Security treacherous was their "multivocality." Symbols can simultaneously evoke a series of images. Thus, the symbolic battle of Social Security was not only *which* symbols were important but how to interpret them.

Historically, the supporters of Social Security had attempted to identify it with traditional American beliefs. The insurance metaphor that SSA had developed in the early years of the program was the ideal symbol for this purpose because it evoked prudence, financial soundness, and equity. As the crisis developed, the traditional defenders of Social Security attempted to identify the program with American values and to portray its critics as "radical."[52]

For example, Wilbur Cohen noted that the system "has become an accepted part of our way of life" because its emphasis on "the work ethic and individual and social responsibility . . . appeals both to liberal and conservatives and to most labor and employer groups."[53] Lawrence Smedley of the AFL-CIO Department of Social Security used imagery reminiscent of the

Revolutionary era to defend support for the system: "The social security program has succeeded because the founders of the system had the foresight to create the kind of framework that would stand the test of the future. Hopefully, those of us who are now working to improve social security will be as successful in laying the groundwork for the future."[54]

The symbolism of the Social Security "traditionalists," however, could be appropriated by the other side. Those who advocated a voluntary system, for example, turned the insurance metaphor on its head. If "you get what you contributed," why shouldn't we just have mandated private plans? One of the major preoccupations of public debate during the crisis was to calculate one's "return" on Social Security taxes.

If Social Security were simply a system of taxes and benefits, we might ask how the return could be calculated. Would anyone try to calculate the "return" on one's sales or income tax? Although the task of calculating "returns" on Social Security was tricky enough, the remarkable thing was that it was attempted at all.[55]

Indeed, as a means of exploding the insurance imagery, some critics countered with the image of a chain letter. Portraying Social Security as a gigantic chain letter, in which the cost was constantly being absorbed by someone else, did not simply hold up "pay-as-you-go" financing to ridicule; it cast an air of suspicion and illegitimacy over the entire enterprise. One editorial cartoonist captured the essence of this in a cartoon that portrayed a country yokel in an Uncle Sam costume receiving a chain letter from the Social Security Administration.[56]

The mass media, in particular, used evocative symbols as much as reasoned analysis to make their point. Headlines like "Will Social Security Go Broke Soon?" were more influential than the body of the article, which answered no. Similarly, "the Social Security time bomb," "quick fix," "the slow slide," and "fresh scare" became the common vocabulary of the popular press.[57]

Just as powerful as words were the graphics used by the mass media in portraying the story of the crisis. The well-known graphics of the Social Security cards, for example, provided an example of the multivocality of symbols. The card, featuring a Greek facade and pillars, was intended to reflect the solidity of one's entitlements and to identify Social Security with the architecture of financial and governmental institutions.

During the crisis, this imagery was often reversed. *Business Week,* for example, reprinted an Oliphant cartoon of an elderly couple—obviously threatened—standing under the crumbling columns and facade, which were being momentarily held up with a variety of makeshift reinforcements.[58] Another 1980 cartoon portrayed a middle-aged couple using a card as a diving board preparing to jump into an empty swimming pool.[59] In a slightly more hopeful vein, the *New York Review of Books* cast Alan Greenspan as a modern, albeit weary, Sampson between the columns. One might ask if he is there to keep them from caving in or to hasten their demise.[60]

Tables and graphs were also included in the popular press in profusion. According to Edward Tufte, in his modern classic *The Visual Display of Quantitative Information,* there are a number of standards of graphic integrity that are commonly disregarded: the accurate representation of scale, the use of one-dimensional graphs to portray one-dimensional data, and the correction of monetary values for inflation. Tufte proposes a "lie factor," which he defines as the ratio of the size of the actual effect in a graph divided by the size of the actual effect shown in the data.[61]

The graphics of the Social Security crisis would win no awards for integrity from Tufte. The general drift of mass media graphics was to show "soaring costs" through sharply sloping line graphs. As early as 1976, for example, *U.S. News & World Report* featured a graph to represent the rising income and outgo of the OASDI trust funds. Through the use of a squeezed horizontal scale, a cut-off vertical scale, and no correction for inflation, it portrayed a 94 percent real increase in the expenditures as a 900 percent increase, for a lie factor of 9.6.[62]

Another common target of graphic misrepresentation was the dependency ratio. For example, *Newsweek* in January 1983 portrayed the number of beneficiaries per 100 active workers between 1950 and 2030. By using a two-dimensional human figure, the graph portrayed an increase of 800 percent (from 6 to 50) as an increase of 6,600 percent, producing a lie factor of 8.3.[63]

Perhaps the most frequently misrepresented numbers in the debate, however, were the notorious seventy-five-year projections of the trustees' report. As noted, before 1972 these projections had been used as a symbol of virtue; by demonstrating the fiscal soundness of the system, Congress could raise benefits with impunity. With the emergence of deficit projections after 1973, this symbol of virtue became a symbol of vice. In spite of the miserable record for even five-year predictions, the popular press was covered during the late 1970s and early 1980s with data based on delphic pronouncements for the year 2055.

In addition, by the early 1980s these projections had undergone a curious deflation. Because of the consistent overoptimism of SSA projections, the press began to treat the "intermediate" projection as the optimistic one and the "pessimistic" projection as the most likely case. Given the indexation formula, if one projects a long-term decline in real income (wages compared to prices) over a seventy-five-year period, there is no way to avoid a crisis, at least on paper.[64]

Finally, the public was treated to continuous readings of its own confidence in the system. The trends in the polls were confusing enough, but their portrayal in the press added to the perplexity. For example, in 1979 the public was roughly divided in half between those who had complete or a great deal of confidence in Social Security and those who had "only a little" or no confidence in the system. *Business Week*, however, included those with a "great deal" of confidence among those with "doubts" about the system and was able to report that "80% [of workers] have doubts that the system will . . . be able to pay them full benefits that are promised now."[65] On the other side, through a change in wording between 1981 and 1982, the Harris poll was able to show a rise in public confidence, even though other data would suggest that this was not occurring.[66]

During the late 1970s and early 1980s, after four decades in which members of the public were largely excluded from the Social Security debate, a lively contest developed for their hearts and minds. The outcome of this contest was hardly satisfying to any of the participants. The public refused to align itself unambiguously with any of the partisans; the debate rather led to an increase of fear and worry about the system's future and an erosion of public confidence.

Social Security experienced three crises between 1973 and 1983—a fiscal crisis, a crisis of expertise, and a crisis of public opinion. There were close connections among the three, but they were not identical. Their origins, dynamics, and resolutions were quite different. In the first year of the Reagan administration, many in the halls of political power may have believed that the resolution of the crisis would include the fundamental restructuring of the system. They were wrong. Within three years, the Social Security crisis had ended; its solution included the reassertion of the traditional politics of Social Security: incremental change along familiar lines, the slow increase in taxes, and the decline of public debates.[67]

Crisis Resolution

The Social Security crisis evolved from several components: the economic difficulties of the 1970s and 1980s, erroneous assumptions that led to unforeseen trust fund deficits, the breakdown of expert consensus, and the dealignment of public opinion.

In 1972 the Social Security Administration started using dynamic assumptions of future trust fund reserves that were consistently optimistic. Thus, in spite of the multiplication of models—three until 1980, five in 1981, and four in 1982 and 1983, each year the trustees' report was less sanguine than it had been the year before.[68]

In 1977, after the large tax increase of that year, President Carter proclaimed that the legislation would "guarantee that from 1980 to the year 2030, the social security funds will be sound." In 1977, however, as in 1972, congressional actions based on official projections were unable to stem the increasing deficits of the trust funds. Because benefits were tied to inflation, accurate estimates were critical. The failure of wages to keep pace with prices meant trouble. Between November 1982 and June 1983 the Old-Age Insurance fund had to borrow almost $17.5 billion from the Disability Insurance and health funds and would have been in danger of issuing late benefit checks in July 1983 had action not been taken.[69]

The fiscal concerns provided a rationale to attack the redistributive elements of the system. After three decades of increasing the relative protection of low-income, high-risk groups (and the resulting decrease in poverty among the aged), opponents used the crisis to attempt to reverse this trend, to make the system "dedistributional."[70]

In the last two years of his administration, President Carter proposed some initial cuts in the retirement program and more substantial surgery on disability eligibility. They provoked sharp resistance among Democratic traditionalists, leading, for example, to the founding of Save Our Security, a leading liberal lobbying group. Carter's proposals for disability were acted on, but those for the retirement system were defeated.[71]

President Reagan, moved by the trust fund deficits, the realities of the federal budget deficit, and his own philosophy, took the lead in attacking the progressive features of the system. Starting early in 1981 the Reagan administration proposed major cuts in Social Security. His package included reductions in early retirement benefits, elimination of the minimum benefit, and a three-month delay in the COLA.[72]

Reactions to the first package were immediate. Old lobbying groups, like Save Our Security, were revitalized, Reagan's approval ratings declined. In Congress, Democrats assailed the administration and proclaimed the trust-fund situation less serious. They immediately introduced a "sense of the Senate" resolution, reaffirming congressional support of the existing system. In the face of such widespread condemnation, the president withdrew his support of the package. Although two more attempts to cut the program were floated by the administration in the next several months, they also met with rejection.

The fiscal clock, however, was ticking. Democrats refused to cut benefits and Republicans stood firm on tax increases. Both sides recognized that a compromise was needed, but neither was ready to act before the 1982 elections. In an attempt to neutralize the political impact of Social Security, the president endorsed the reinstitution of minimum benefits (which his 1981 budget had eliminated) and established the National Commission on Social Security Reform under the leadership of Alan Greenspan. Appointed by the president, the Democratic Speaker of the House, and the Republican Senate majority leader and including seven members of Congress, the NCSSR, was to review relevant analyses of the current and long-term financial condition of the Social Security trust funds; identify problems that may threaten the long-term solvency of such funds; analyze potential solutions to such problems that will both assure the financial integrity of the Social Security System and the provision of appropriate benefits; and provide appropriate recommendations to the Secretary of Health and Human Services, the President, and the Congress.[73]

The scope of the problem was well known from three previous commissions. The NCSSR's task was to find a politically palatable resolution that would shift the responsibility for the resolution from Congress, the president, or either political party.

The appointment of the NCSSR signaled a defeat for extremists who wished to revamp the entire system. All of its members subscribed to the basic tenets of the Social Security system. Robert Ball, long-time commissioner and vocal critic of the original Reagan plan, had returned to center stage, as had Robert Myers. As Robert Kuttner noted: "Hiring Mr. Myers to dismantle Social Security would be like hiring Admiral Rickover to privatize the Navy."[74]

Although the NCSSR was wedded to the past Social Security consensus, the context of 1982—prolonged recession and congressional elections—was not amenable to easy solutions. In particular, Social Security became a highly visible issue in the campaign; Democrats reminded the public of the president's 1981 proposals, while Republicans, in the notorious "postman" ads, took credit for the automatic July COLA.

After the election, slow progress was made leading in November to agreement about the extent of the problem. In spite of extension of the NCSSR mandates, a solution could not be reached by the entire commission. A subgroup of the NCSSR, the "Gang of Five," spearheaded the search for a final set of recommendations. Again, the range of opinions was restricted as the most extreme Republicans—William Armstrong and William Archer—and Democrats—Claude Pepper and Lane Kirkland—were excluded from negotiations. The final group—Greenspan, Senators Dole and Moynihan, Ball, and Barber Conable—were all long-time participants in the issue who were committed to the reestablishment of consensus.[75]

The first recommendation of the *Report* of the NCSSR—a unanimous one—signaled the return to a narrower consensus over the nature of the program:

Congress . . . should not alter the fundamental structure of the Social Security program or undermine its fundamental principles. The National Commission considered, but rejected, proposals to make the Social Security program a voluntary one, or to transform it into a program under which benefits are a product exclusively of the contributions paid, or to convert it into a fully-funded program, or to change it to a program under which benefits are conditioned on the showing of financial need.[76]

The other recommendations, most of them approved by twelve of the fifteen members of the full commission, included the coverage of nonprofit and federal employees, prohibiting the withdrawal of state and local government employees, partial taxation of higher-income persons' benefits, a permanent six-month delay in the COLA, increases in the tax rate, the elimination of windfall benefits for persons with noncovered employment, and a number of accounting manipulations. The NCSSR also agreed that if the size of the trust fund had not increased sufficiently by 1987, the COLA would be based on the lesser of price and wage inflation and that if the fund increases enough there will be a catch-up raise. These recommendations were accepted by Congress, which added a gradual increase in the retirement age to sixty-seven.

In summary, the cataclysmic crisis of Social Security was resolved through a rather conventional package of tax increases and the delay of benefit increases. Taken together, the changes resulted in a more progressive tax structure; they increased the tax base, allowed for some general revenue financing, and taxed the benefits of higher income groups. Given the fiscal exigencies, the 1983 amendments fit quite nicely into the tradition of incremental change that had dominated Social Security policy before 1972.[77]

The Social Security reforms of 1983 appear to have been a success. From the end of 1983 until the end of 1984, the balance of the Old-age and Survivors' Insurance trust funds grew by $7.4 billion, the largest one-year increase in history. The $27.1 billion was the highest balance in the fund since 1978. According to the 1985 trustees' report, by 1989 the balance in the OASDI trust fund will reach $127 billion, nearly three times the pre-1983 record. Combined with a prolonged economic recovery, the Social Security crisis has ended.

Indeed, the rapid rise of the trust funds will continue for a long time. Based on the intermediate (II-B) assumptions, by the turn of the century the trust fund will surpass $1 trillion and by 2030 will stand at over $12 trillion. The concern for "actuarial soundness" has led to a policy of increasing the trust fund to cover partially the impact of the retirement of baby-boomers.[78]

The Social Security crisis was the result of the problems of the trust fund during the 1980s, the change in expert opinion, and the public concern over the fate of the system. As a result of the crisis, the trust funds are no longer in danger, and at a political level there has been a decisive return to consensus. To the extent that expert opinion has been prominent recently, it has focused on a new concern: the negative impact of trust fund accumulation on the economy.[79]

Given the decline of the forces that provoked the crisis, what are the prospects for the future of Social Security? It may be that Congress and the president will sit by and let the $12 trillion begin to accumulate, but there is little in the history of the system to suggest that this is the most likely scenario.

Conclusion

Considering the pressure of the increasing needs of the U.S. population, it seems likely that the 1990s may become an era of some incremental expansion of the system, paralleling in many ways the 1950s and 1960s. Rather than cope with dedistributional issues, the federal government will again have to consider what to do with a Social Security "surplus." A number of possibilities present themselves. Congress could simply cut taxes, it could increase benefits under existing programs, it could cover a projected deficit in Medicare, or it could provide new programs. If past experience is any guide, tax cuts are unlikely.

The history of Social Security during the Carter and Reagan administrations is complex. On the one hand, it suggests that a number of the institutional protections that the system had in its earlier days have fallen on hard times. At the same time, Social Security has maintained enough internal and electoral political strength to forestall attempts of the current administration to tamper with its fundamental features. Certainly, the exclusion of Social Security from the deficit reduction debate of the last several years (in contrast to the defense budget) is remarkable given its cost.

It is clear, however, that other social programs have not shared Social Security's immunity. Between 1980 and 1984, spending on OASDHI as a percentage of total federal welfare spending rose from 50 to 57 percent. Although Gramm-Rudman protected a number of public assistance programs from automatic cuts, public assistance expenditures have lagged behind inflation for the most part. For example, over $85 billion more was spent on OASDHI in 1984 than 1980, but only $4 billion more on AFDC and SSI. Its advocates successfully protected Social Security, but poor aged, disabled, women, and children have become more vulnerable.

Thus, an evaluation of the politics of welfare in the late 1980s shares neither the incrementalist optimism that characterized the 1960s nor the gloom of the early 1980s. Among the many factors that need to be evaluated in looking toward the future are (1) public perceptions of poverty and welfare; (2) the continued weakness of the Democratic Party on social welfare issues; and (3) the implications of the structural federal budget deficits for social welfare.

Public Perceptions

As noted, there has been a major shift in public perception of problems of welfare and dependency during the 1980s. The support mobilized in defense of Social Security was the first indication of this change. It has since broadened, so that whereas between 1977 and 1980 public support for government action reached historic lows, it has since moved in the opposite direction. For example, in 1977 only 12 percent of respondents to a *New York Times*–CBS poll believed that too little was being spent on welfare; by 1984 this percentage had doubled. Over the same period, the percentage that believed too much was being spent fell from 60 percent to 40 percent and the percentage who believed that about the right amount was being spent rose from 23 to 34 percent. Thus, although public sentiment still runs against "welfare," the huge majority supporting cuts in these programs has vanished since 1980.

Polling results must be approached gingerly, of course. For example, if results on "caring for the poor" instead of "welfare" are examined, a different view of the electorate emerges. A 1984 poll suggested that 68 percent of Americans thought too little was being spent caring for the poor, while only 7 percent thought too much was being spent. These results may be viewed with skepticism, but they still suggest that the public is willing to consider a return to expansion of these programs.[80]

The polling data suggest as well that by the mid-1980s domestic issues were more important to Americans than the Pentagon build-up. Between 1981 and 1984 the percentage in favor of cutting defense rather than aid to cities increased from 41 to 54 percent. Similar positive attitudes were reported for federal health programs, aid to education, and unemployment compensation. Louis Harris discovered as well that in the 1986 elections, liberal Democrats were surprised to find that voters had moved further to the left than the candidates had realized.[81]

The Democratic Party

Although the public has shifted quite decisively away from an antiwelfare position, the drift of Congress and the political parties has been more muted. Indeed, whereas institutional forces worked to keep policy ahead of public opinion during the 1960s, that situation has now been reversed. American politics are working to keep policy behind public opinion. "The roots of the shift to the right," Thomas Edsall has concluded, "are by now deeply imbedded in the political system, severely restricting the scope of choices available to either party."[82]

According to Edsall, a number of factors have produced this result: the increase in the class identification of the Republican and Democratic parties, the increased sophistication of the business community, the decline of the labor movement, and the increased class-skewed patterns of voting. Edsall believes that these factors will prevent the federal government in the future from reflecting the pro-interventionist feeling of the public. His concern is echoed as well by Ferguson and Rodgers in their study of the Democratic Party. The authors also found that the Democrats' rightward drift was a response more to changes in the increased importance of business financial support than of changing public opinion.[83]

The Structural Deficit

A major legacy of the Reagan administration's is the increase in the federal debt. Between FY1980 and FY1986, the cumulative federal debt increased from $900 billion to over $2.1 trillion. The outstanding debt has risen from roughly a third to about a half of GNP. Even if deficit reduction were to continue—and the evidence suggests that it may not—the federal government can look forward to spending over 15 percent of its outlays on interest payments on the debt, twice the amount of the late 1970s.

In this chapter the focus is not on the economic wisdom of deficit reduction or accumulation but rather on its political effect. By spending a trillion and a half more dollars than it received during the Reagan years, the federal government has placed itself in a situation in which policy decisions will be driven by fiscal decisions for the foreseeable future. This "fiscalization" of policy will work to the detriment of social welfare.

In many respects, the 1990s will face just the reverse of the situation of the late 1960s. Then, the deescalation of the Vietnam War provided some room in the budget that allowed for the growth of domestic spending. In the future, even with a rise in taxes, welfare spending will come into direct conflict with other policy choices. The ability of pro-welfare advocates to keep welfare expansion from becoming controversial under these circumstances will be very difficult.

Here, again, Social Security may well be the exception. The anticipated trust fund increases of the next several decades will provide a revenue source for those who wish to expand the system. The outlook is brightest for those who can be covered by a liberalization of the social insurance system.

There are sizable obstacles to the renewed expansion of the welfare state. The institutional transformation of American politics since the 1970s and the spectre of the federal debt will continue to side with those who wish to limit the response to the future needs of the United States.

One political obstacle, however, should not remain. It is important to understand where future needs are emerging and how best to address them. All of the programs cannot be won, so we need to know which programs are most important and most effective and which will lay the foundations for renewed public and political support of social welfare. The next chapter turns to the prospects for social welfare reform and assesses some current proposals for change.

The 1970s and 1980s were marked by grave predictions over the need to restrain the growth of the welfare state, but the Social Security crisis suggests that much of that debate was overblown. Although the contours of need will certainly continue to change, the willingness of the public to support the welfare state appears strong. It may on occasion fall short of our best hopes, but it will rarely meet our worst fears.

Notes

A portion of this chapter appeared in a different form in Mark J. Stern, "The Politics of American Social Welfare," in *Human Services at Risk*, edited by Felice Davidson Perlmutter (Lexington, Mass.: Lexington Books, 1984).

1. James Patterson, *America's Struggle against Poverty, 1900–1980* (Cambridge, Mass.: Harvard University Press, 1982), provides an excellent account of the "unsung" welfare expansion of the Nixon years. See also Michael B. Katz, *In the Shadow of the Poorhouse: A Social History of Welfare in America* (New York: Basic Books, 1986).

2. June Axinn and Herman Levin, *Social Welfare: A History of America's Response to Need*, 2nd ed. (New York: Longman Press, 1982), 194.

3. Roy Lubove, *The Struggle for Social Security* (Cambridge, Mass.: Harvard University Press, 1968).

4. Patterson, *America's Struggle against Poverty*, 76.

5. The bulk of this account comes from Martha Derthick, *Policymaking for Social Security* (Washington, D.C.: Brookings Institution, 1979), 228–50; June Axinn, "Social Security: History and Prospects," *Current History* (August 1973): 52–56; and William Achenbaum, *Social Security: Vision and Revision* (Cambridge: Cambridge University Press, 1986). Data are derived from the *Social Security Bulletin, Annual Statistical Summary* (Washington, D.C.: Government Printing Office, (1986).

6. Equally impressive was the muted public debate that greeted this expansion. As Martha Derthick and others have noted, the skillful cooperation of program executives and congressional leaders led to the marginalization of program critics and the stifling of congressional, executive, and public input into policy formulation. Derthick, *Policymaking for Social Security*; Mark J. Stern, "The Politics of American Social Policy," in *Human Services at Risk*, edited by Felice Perlmutter (Lexington, Mass.: Lexington Books, 1983), 3–23.

7. Martha Derthick, *Uncontrollable Spending for Social Service Grants* (Washington, D.C.: Brookings Institution, 1975); Institute for Research on Poverty, "Poverty in the United States: Where Do We Stand?,"*IRP Focus* 5(2) (Winter 1981–82): 1–10.

8. Derthick, *Policymaking for Social Security*, 17–37.

9. Ibid., 45–46.

10. Ibid., 110.

11. Patterson, *America's Struggle against Poverty*, 167.

12. In 1977, as administrative politics reached their peak, a *New York Times*–CBS poll found that 58 percent of Americans disapproved of "most Government-sponsored welfare programs" and 54 percent thought "most people who received money from welfare could get along without it." Patterson, *America's Struggle against Poverty*, 202.

13. Quoted in Geoffrey Hodgson, *America: In Our Times* (New York: Vintage Books, 1976), 82.

14. Michael J. Piore, *Birds of Passage: Migrant Labor in Industrial Society* (New York and Cambridge: Cambridge University Press, 1979).

15. Carol Stack, *All Our Kin* (New York: Harper & Row, 1974).

16. Frances Fox Piven and Richard A. Cloward, *Poor People's Movements: Why They Succeed and How They Fail* (New York: Random House, 1979).

17. Patterson, *America's Struggle against Poverty*, 179.

18. Hodgson, *America*, 483–84.

19. James Green, *The World of the Worker: Labor in Twentieth Century America* (New York: Hill and Wang, 1979), 198–209; David Brody, *Workers in Industrial America: Essays on the Twentieth Century Struggle* (New York: Oxford University Press, 1980), 224–29.

20. William Leuchtenberg, *Franklin D. Roosevelt and the New Deal, 1932–1940* (New York: Harper & Row, 1963), 186.

21. Piven and Cloward, *Poor People's Movements*.

22. Hodgson, *America*, 421.

23. Morris Janowitz, *Social Control of the Welfare State* (Chicago: University of Chicago Press, 1976), 45.

24. Louis Harris, *Inside America* (New York: Random House, 1987), 33.

25. Walter Dean Burnham, "The 1980 Earthquake: Realignment, Reaction, or What?," in *The Hidden Election: Politics and Economics in the 1980 Presidential Campaign*, edited by Thomas Ferguson and Joel Rodgers (New York: Pantheon Books, 1981).

26. The best account of the politics of the Social Security crisis is Paul Light, *Artful Work: The Politics of Social Security Reform* (New York: Random House, 1985). In this chapter we have ignored what could be considered the fourth aspect of the crisis: the political. Given the attention paid to the politics of Social Security by Derthick, Achenbaum, and Light, we have not provided an extended discussion of how the crisis played itself out in Congress and the executive branch.

27. The problems were not successfully predicted by the economists and actuaries of SSA. Before 1972 they used a static, level-earnings methodology to project trust fund balances and regularly underestimated the build up of reserves. On recommendation of the 1971 Advisory Council, they began to use a model based on a dynamic view of the economy, which required them to make assumptions about a number of economic activities—unemployment, prices, and income wage growth. The new SSA methodology had many difficulties, leading again to major errors of trust fund balances. In 1972 the best assumption of SSA was for 15 percent inflation

and 12 percent real wage growth for the period from 1973–77. In fact, we experienced 41 percent inflation and only 1 percent real wage growth. As the GAO report concluded:

> Before 1972, a conservative methodology led to underestimates of future trust fund balances. After 1972, the methodology changed in a way that required the Trustees to adopt assumptions about future economic activity. ... The unstable economic conditions experienced by the U.S. economy in the mid- and late 1970s rendered both the Trustees' assumptions and SSA's projections highly inaccurate and, more importantly, threatened the financial soundness of Social Security.

U.S. General Accounting Office, *Social Security: Past Projections and Future Financing Concerns* GAO/I IRD-86–22 (Washington, D.C.: Government Printing Office, March 1986), 3, 28–43. See also *Report of the 1971 Advisory Council on Social Security* (Washington, D.C.: Government Printing Office, 1971), 85–87, and Light, *Artful Work,* 45–51.

28. Robert J. Myers, "Social Security: Don't Push the Panic Button," *America* 133 (20 September 1975): 140–42; Myers, "How Best to Keep Social Security Solvent," *Business Horizons* 19 (December 1976): 45–50.

29. U.S. Bureau of the Census, *Statistical Abstract of the United States 1986* (Washington, D.C.: Government Printing Office, 1986), 390, 417, 720.

30. Robert J. Myers, "Financial Status of the Social Security Program," in *Report of the National Commission on Social Security Reform* (Washington, D.C.: Government Printing Office, January 1983), app, J, 9.

31. Ibid. Two additional points should be made about the fiscal crisis. First, although the "coupled" formula that overindexed benefits led to scary projections and set off all sorts of bells and whistles, in fact it never affected actual benefits; the 1977 amendments changed the formula before it went into effect. Second, as Janice Halpern and Paul Light have noted, Social Security consistently presented what turned out to be overly optimistic projections during this period. They were certainly not alone in doing so; the decline in real wages was unprecedented in postwar America. Indeed, when indexation to prices was accepted in 1972 this was considered a conservative decision because prices had consistently lagged behind wages. Light, *Artful Work,* 45–57; Janice H. Halpern, "Why Another Social Security Crisis?," *New England Economic Review* (September/October 1980): 5 19

32. Joseph R. Gusfield, *The Culture of Public Problems: Drinking, Driving and the Symbol Order* (Chicago and London: University of Chicago Press, 1981); see also Robin Wagner-Pacifici, *The Moro Morality Play: A Case of Symbolic Politics* (Chicago: University of Chicago Press, 1987).

33. Derthick, *Policymaking for Social Security.*

34. A. Haeworth Robertson, *The Coming Revolution in Social Security* (Reston, Va.: Reston, 1982).

35. Derthick, *Policymaking for Social Security;* James W. Singer, "Social Security Fund's Problems Take on a New Urgency," *National Journal* 8 (1976 February 14): 198–204.

36. Judith Treas, "The Great American Fertility Debate: Generational Balance and Support of the Aged," *The Gerontologist* 21 (January 1981): 100; H. L. Sheppard and S. Rix, *The Graying of Working America: The Coming Crisis in Retirement-Age*

Policy (New York: Free Press, 1977); R. Clark and J. J. Spengler, "Population Aging and Demography," in *The Economics of Individual and Population Aging* (Cambridge: Cambridge University Press, 1980); William Crown, "Some Thoughts on the Dependency Ratio," *The Gerontologist* (May 1985).

37. Crown, "Some Thoughts"; D. Adamchak and E. Friedmann, "Societal Aging and Generational Dependency Relationships: Problems of Measurement and Conceptualization," *Research on Aging* 5 (1983): 319–38; Yung-Ping Chen and Kwan-wen Chu, "Total Dependency Burden and Social Security Solvency," Report 266 (Los Angeles: Institute of Industrial Relations, UCLA, 1977); Clark and Spengler, "Population Aging and Demography." See also chapter 3 above.

38. Dean R. Leimer and Selig D. Lesnoy, "Social Security and Private Saving: New Time-Series Evidence," *Journal of Political Economy* (June 1982): 606–29; Henry J. Aaron, *Economic Effects of Social Security* (Washington, D.C.: Brookings Institution, 1982), 40–52; Sheldon Danzinger, Robert Havemann, and Robert Plotnick, "How Income Transfer Programs Affect Work, Savings, and the Income Distribution," *Journal of Economic Literature* 19 (September 1981); Paul Starr, "Social Security and the American Public Household," unpublished manuscript.

39. Martin Feldstein, "Toward a Reform of Social Security," *The Public Interest* 40 (Summer 1975): 83.

40. Ibid., 87.

41. Nathan Keyfitz, "Why Social Security Is in Trouble," *The Public Interest* 58 (Winter 1980): 109. See also his "Age, Work, and Social Security," *Society* 20 (July/August 1983): 45–51. It should also be noted Keyfitz was simply wrong to assert that pay-as-you-go financing was SSA policy during the late 1930s and 1940s.

42. Keyfitz, "Why Social Security Is in Trouble," 119.

43. Ibid.

44. Carolyn Weaver, *The Crisis in Social Security* (Durham, N.C.: Duke University Press, 1982.

45. Weaver, *The Crisis in Social Security,* 190.

46. Peter Ferrara, *Social Security: The Inherent Contradiction* (San Francisco: Cato Institute, 1980).

47. Peter Ferrara, "Social Security: The Crisis Continues," *Consumer Research Magazine* 67 (September 1984): 36

48. Ibid., 37.

49. Peter Peterson, "Social Security: The Coming Crash," and "The Salvation of Social Security," *New York Review of Books* (2 and 16 December 1982); Achenbaum, *Social Security,* 239.

50. Light, *Artful Work,* 58–74.

51. Joseph R. Gusfield, *Symbolic Crusade: Status Politics and the American Temperance Movement* (Urbana: University of Illinois Press, 1976); Victor Turner, "Religious Paradigms and Political Action: Thomas Becket at the Council of Northampton," in *Drama, Fields, and Metaphors,* Victor Turner, ed. (Ithaca: Cornell University Press, 1974).

52. On early use of the insurance metaphor, see Jerry Cates, *Insuring Inequality* (Ann Arbor: University of Michigan Press, 1982).

53. Wilbur Cohen, "Social Security: Focusing on the Facts," *American Federationist* (April 1978): 6.

54. Lawrence T. Smedley, "Changing Patterns of Social Security," *American Federationist* (January 1973): 10.

55. "The Social Security Crisis," *Newsweek* (24 January 1983), 19.

56. Keyfitz, "Age, Work, and Social Security"; cartoon by MacNelly reprinted in Light, *Artful Work*, 31.

57. Ibid., "Will Social Security Go Broke Soon?," *U.S. News & World Report* (15 February 1982): 35–36; "Fresh Scare over Social Security," *U.S. News & World Report* (16 February 1976): 68–70.

58. *Business Week* (16 June 1980): 108.

59. Reprinted in Light, *Artful Work*, 87.

60. *New York Review of Books* (17 March 1983): 41. Cartoon by David Levine.

61. Edward R. Tufte, *The Visual Display of Quantitative Information* (Cheshire, Conn.: Graphics Press, 1983), 53–78.

62. *U.S. News & World Report* (16 February 1976): 68.

63. *Newsweek* (24 January 1983): 19.

64. Peterson's articles from the *New York Review of Books* are a fine example of projection deflation. Peterson, "The Salvation of Social Security," 54.

65. "A Growing Disillusionment with Social Security," *Business Week* (12 March 1979): 26.

66. Light, *Artful Work*, 72–73

67. David Stockman, *The Triumph of Politics: The Inside Story of the Reagan Revolution* (New York: Avon Books, 1985) 196–212.

68. On the politics of assumptions, see Light *Artful Work*, 45–57.

69. *New York Times*, 21 December 1977, A19.

70. Light, *Artful Work*, 5, passim. Accounts of actions between 1981 and 1983 are available in Light's book and Achenbaum, *Social Security*, 81–102.

71. Achenbaum, *Social Security*, 68–69, 224–225; *New York Times*, 31 December 1978; Joseph Califano, *Governing America* (New York: Simon and Schuster, 1981), ch. 9.

72. For an example of the animus of the Reagan administration toward Social Security, see Stockman, *The Triumph of Politics*, 194–209.

73. Executive Order 12335, 16 December 1981. Published in *Weekly Compilation of Presidential Documents* 17 (21 December 1981): 1371–94. Reprinted in *Report of the National Commission on Social Security Reform* (January 1983) (Washington, D.C.: Government Printing Office,) app. A.

74. Robert Kuttner, "The Social Security Hysteria," *New Republic* Dec. 27 1982, 19; Light, *Artful Work*, 163–76.

75. Light, *Artful Work*, 181–82.

76. *Report of the National Commission on Social Security Reform*, 2–3.

77. Indeed, it should be noted that even the big "negative" in the amendments from a reformist standpoint—the COLA delay—could be seen as a return to the pre-1972 situation. Congress had historically derived considerable political benefit from its regular voting of benefit increases. The COLA had the politically unfortunate impact of providing no political payoff. Because one delay could lead to another, the

1983 amendments have increased the *discretion* of program executives and Congress in giving COLAs. This was illustrated quite dramatically during the summer of 1986 when the president and Senator Paula Hawkins tried unsuccessfully to derive political benefit from favoring the granting of a COLA in 1987 even if inflation did not warrant it.

78. GAO, *Social Security: Past Projections and Future Financing Concerns*, 49, 52.

79. Alicia Munnell and Lynn Blais, "Do We Want Large Social Security Surpluses?," *New England Economic Review* (September/October 1984); Milton Gwirtzman, "Social Security in Terra Incognita," *The Journal of the Institute for Socioeconomic Studies* 10 (Autumn 1985): 1–12.

80. Fay Lomax Cook, Ernesto Constantino, Rick Adamek, and Susan Popkin, "Catalog of Social Welfare Questions Asked in National Surveys 1935–1984," unpublished manuscript, April 1985.

81. Thomas Ferguson and Joel Rodgers, *Right Turn: The Decline of the Democrats and the Future of American Politics* (New York: Hill and Wang, 1986), 21; Louis Harris, *Inside America* (New York: Vintage Books, 1987), 296–301.

82. Thomas Byrne Edsall, *The New Politics of Inequality* (New York and London: W. W. Norton, 1984), 20–21.

83. Ferguson and Rodgers, *Right Turn*.

8
Conclusion: The Prospects for Change

The social changes discussed in this book have been extensive. The population is aging, which poses profound issues for current conceptualizations of dependency and productivity. Changes in women's work and family arrangements continue to challenge traditional ways of supporting children and organizing essential social services. Finally, the reorganization of the labor market has created new economic risks and placed new pressures on social welfare, changing the demography and severity of poverty and need.

In the face of these profound changes, however, the American welfare state has been relatively immobile for over a decade. Some social programs have been cut, and many have seen their effectiveness reduced. More often, programs have simply failed to change significantly, leaving new needs and demands unanswered. Although the voluntary and private sectors have occasionally picked up the slack, more often they have not had the resources to do so. The gap between social need and social provision has grown too large.

An analysis of the details of policy and program innovation is beyond the scope of this study. Nonetheless, some assessment of the possibilities of improving existing programs and initiating new ones is in order. This is a particularly good time to consider the direction of innovation because many social welfare reforms are currently under discussion, including increases in the minimum wage and the addition of catastrophic health coverage to Medicare.[1]

Welfare reform has received considerable public attention in recent years. Given the increases in poverty and the obvious holes in welfare coverage, one would hope that the prospects of comprehensive welfare reform would call attention to the social changes that have been examined in this study. Unfortunately, rather than addressing these issues, the current debate has been restricted to a more limited number of concerns.

The Welfare Reform Agenda

The welfare reform debates of 1986 and 1987 are incomplete and off target. There has been extended discussion of the growth of female-headed families, the need for job training and work incentives, and a concern for what is seen as a growing black underclass. Absent from the review for the most part is an acknowledgment of the diminishing opportunity structure facing U.S. workers, the growing inadequacy of earned income for all—white men as well as black or Hispanic women—and the increased ineffectiveness of our income-transfer programs. Many of the goals of welfare reform are worthwhile, but it fails to address the central questions facing social welfare in the future. It is not as much bad as misdirected.

In mid-1987 the fate of the current welfare reform movement is unknown. The House of Representatives is moving to pass a plan that requires work or job training for adult recipients whose children are over the age of three, establishes a national education, training, and work program, provides transitional continuation on Medicaid and child care benefits for those who find work, and requires states to provide benefits to two-parent families.[2] Senator Moynihan has recently proposed the Family Security Act of 1987, which stresses increased federal and state enforcement of child support payments. Although less generous in increasing payments than the House plan, Moynihan's bill embraces most of its key provisions. The Reagan administration has continued to voice support for welfare reform but has failed to endorse specific legislation. It has instead continued to support allowing states more flexibility in the use of current funds. Although there is a great deal of support for some change, it is unclear what program, if any, will emerge from the One Hundreth Congress.[3] Both the House and Senate bills address many difficulties with the current program for dependent children. Universal coverage for two-parent families has been long overdue. Increased emphasis on education and job-training is appealing to those across the political spectrum, and work requirements, although they continue to ignite opposition from welfare rights activists, have won increasing acceptance as the proportion of mothers in the labor force has grown.

Most interesting, the welfare reforms currently under consideration are surprisingly humanistic given the proposals that have emerged during the Reagan administration. The president has long advocated national work requirements such as those implemented in California when he was governor and has claimed that his program put 76,000 recipients to work (a claim disputed by state officials).[4]

Early in his presidency, Reagan took his cues on welfare reform from his domestic policy advisor Martin Anderson. Anderson, in his 1978 book, *Welfare,* argued that the welfare reform efforts of the Nixon and Carter administrations had been thinly disguised attempts to implement a guaranteed annual income.[5] The most objectionable feature of these efforts in Anderson's view was the payment of welfare benefits to the working poor. Part of Anderson's objection was his concern that high-income families would be "on welfare" if payments were phased out slowly. In contrast, Anderson advocated a "commitment to the philosophical approach of giving aid only to those who cannot help themselves."[6]

The early proposals of the Reagan administration were in many respects consistent with Anderson's perspective. The most notable feature of the welfare "reform" embodied in the Omnibus Reconciliation Act of 1981 (OBRA) was the deletion of the earned income set-asides for AFDC recipients. By eliminating this incentive for welfare mothers to find part-time or low-paying work, the legislation sought to reemphasize the difference between poorly treated welfare recipients and honorable workers.[7]

During his first term, then, the president's justification for cuts in welfare was negative; other priorities—economic growth, reducing the size of government—rationalized the reduction of welfare. After 1984, however, a positive critique emerged. In developing his welfare reform initiative, President Reagan was clearly influenced by the work of Charles Murray, author of *Losing Ground*.[8] Where Anderson had claimed that the War on Poverty had been won and that "Americans who truly cannot care for themselves are now eligible for generous government aid," Murray claimed that the status of the poor had truly deteriorated since the 1960s.[9] "Basic indicators of well-being took a turn for the worse in the 1960s, most consistently and most drastically for the poor," Murray writes. In explaining this decline in the status of the poor, and in particular the black poor, Murray assigns almost exclusive blame to the welfare system itself. Murray sees the deterioration in the condition of the poor as a "rational" response to the rules of the game defined by the supposedly liberal policy elite of the 1960s and 1970s: "The most compelling explanation for the marked shift in the fortunes of the poor is that they continued to respond, as they always had, to the world as they found it .... The first effect of the new rules was to make it profitable for the poor to behave in the short term in ways that were destructive in the long-term ... [and to] subsidize irretrievable mistakes."[10]

Anderson's program, based on the notion that conditions have really improved since the 1960s, focused primarily on tightening up the welfare system to reduce fraud and to increase the distinction between the deserving and undeserving poor. It anticipated some tinkering to eliminate waste and limit the growth in benefits but did not look to a basic transformation of the system. In contrast, Murray, who believed things had gotten worse, presented a radical plan for fixing welfare: eliminate it. Because Murray believed that any "social transfer increased the net value of being in the condition that prompted the transfer," and that the "less likely it is that the unwanted behavior will change voluntarily, the more likely it is that a program to induce change will cause net harm," he saw federal programs as doomed to fail.[11] The "scrapping [of] the entire federal welfare and income-support structure for working-aged persons, including AFDC, Medicaid, Food Stamps, Unemployment Insurance, Worker's Compensation, subsidized housing, disability insurance, and the rest" would, in Murray's view, provide powerful incentives for the lazy to go to work, for parents to keep their children from becoming teenage mothers, and for localities and voluntary groups to increase their role in maintaining social order.[12]

Without critiquing Murray's use of data or his conclusions (tasks that others have already undertaken),[13] it is clear that the Reagan welfare reform initiative, begun with his 1986 State of the Union address, drew its inspiration from Murray, not Anderson. Indeed, when the president remarked in a radio address that in examining the War on Poverty, "I guess you could say poverty won the war," he was directly repudiating Anderson's position.[14]

The president raised the visibility of welfare reform with his "spider's web of dependency" imagery during the State of the Union address and his call for the "real and lasting emancipation" of the poor from a "welfare culture" that had led to the "breakdown of the family." He was unable, however, to maintain control of the issue. Indeed, the year-long study that Reagan called for amounted to little, producing only recommendations that states be given more flexibility to experiment over the next five years.

The lack of presidential influence over the current welfare debate reflects the shift in public opinion and the political impact of the 1986 congressional elections. More important, however, the state experience with welfare reform provided a powerful impetus for administrative changes in the system nationwide.

The primary motivation for state welfare reform was the OBRA of 1981, which allowed states to experiment with their federally funded welfare programs. Four particular innovations have gained widespread acceptance: (1) work-incentive (WIN) demonstrations, which allowed states to experiment with a single agency to provide training and employment opportunities; (2) community work incentive programs, which provided experience and training for individuals not able to find employment; (3) job search, which allowed states to assist individuals in obtaining regular employment; and (4) work supplementation, which allowed states to use AFDC funds to develop and subsidize work positions instead of paying welfare benefits.[15]

The effect of these innovations was mixed. In some states, including Pennsylvania, AFDC demonstrations took place in a punitive context, including the exclusion of able-bodied recipients from general assistance. Other states, including Massachusetts, Michigan, and California, fit AFDC changes into broader approaches to job training, employment, and welfare. Overall, the General Accounting Office noted that the greatest limit to the state experiments is that expanding them or making them more effective would cost more money, money that would ultimately have to come from the federal government.[16] As a result of the state experiences, public welfare administrators and governors moved into the forefront of the campaign for welfare reform. "With the experiments has come ideological confluence," according to the *National Journal*. "Liberals have given up insisting that 'workfare' and its variants are unfair to welfare recipients. And conservatives . . . have had to acknowledge that single women with children simply must work."[17] Although motivated by the practical concerns of politicians and administrators, the governors' welfare proposals embraced the cultural interpretation of the underclass. In their view, the minority of welfare recipients who stay on the rolls for many years suffer from a set of social ills, including illiteracy, teenaged pregnancy, drug use, and dropping out of school. Even this perspective had a practical turn, however. The theory of the underclass provided the governors with a ready justification for increased federal funds for a broader range of programs—job training, education, and health.

The welfare reform effort of the past two years has been motivated by contradictory forces: the subterranean shift in public opinion, the changing political fortunes of the Democrats and the president, and the practical concerns of governors and public welfare administrators, have made revisions in AFDC appealing. At the same time, the theory of the underclass has provided an ideology that has been embraced by both conservatives and middle-of-the-road advocates and policy makers.

The current welfare reform effort may be as significant for what it ignores as for what it addresses. Although the number of female-headed families in poverty has grown, as a group these householders have entered the labor force and improved their economic status more rapidly than the population as a whole. The rest of the new poor, the product of low-wage jobs and economic disruption, not the culture of the underclass, have been largely ignored by the current debate. For example, in 1985 there were two and a half times more adult workers below the poverty threshold than there were adult AFDC recipients. The welfare system of the future will have to go far beyond the changes in AFDC currently under consideration if it is to meet the needs of this group.

The issue of race and poverty has reemerged as a visible social problem. The continuing plight of poor black women and their children deserves the long-overdue attention, yet their current visibility has been tied closely to the deviant image of the underclass. As in nineteenth-century London, the current debate focuses on a group cut off from the normal behavior of the population.

As has been shown, such a characterization is unjustified. Today's poor blacks and Hispanics are not deviants. The work behavior, income, and poverty status of blacks and whites has converged over the past decade. They are not suffering from individual pathology but from the general growth of low-wage work throughout the economy.

This point is graphically illustrated by Isaac Shapiro in a recent study. Shapiro found that as a result of the stagnation of the minimum wage and the growth of low-wage work, the number of workers below the poverty level increased from 6.5 to 9.1 million between 1979 and 1985, and the number of full-time, full-year workers below the poverty level rose from 1.3 million to 2.0 million. Nearly a quarter of all hourly workers—13.4 million Americans—are earning wages of under $4.50 per hour.[18]

The growth of low-wage work poses two challenges to welfare reform. Most directly, it suggests that the size of the problem of poverty is growing. As long as dependency and poverty could be equated with not working, the solution seemed to be simple: put people to work. The current growth of the working poor suggests that the next war on poverty will need to address both the nonworking and working poor.

Addressing the problem of the nonworking poor will remain difficult. Although the Reagan administration has tried to reinforce the distinction between the worthy and unworthy poor, the realities of the U.S. economy have not been cooperative. If the "underclass" is to be moved off welfare, they need to be provided with opportunities that make the alternative attractive. One way to do this is to assure that the economy has jobs that pay a decent wage. If the growth of low-wage work persists, the opportunity strategy is severely limited. The other option, of course, is to make welfare look less desirable. The cutting of benefits, restriction of eligibility, and the use of punitive sanctions can drive people from the welfare rolls without addressing the broader issues in the economy—but it will do so at a serious social cost.

In summary, the optimism over welfare reform in its current form is short-sighted, even if it does achieve its immediate goals. Either today's initiative will lead to a more general attack on poverty in the economy, which will require broader labor market reform, or it will narrow to a punitive campaign to drive poor people from the benefit rolls and to reduce the cost of welfare. Policy makers and the public must grasp the vital connection between the poor and the functioning of the market economy if they are to pursue the best path.

Postindustrial Work and Social Welfare Policy

Although real welfare reform may be a while in coming, it still makes sense to consider the role of social welfare policy in addressing the problems of dependency and poverty in the decades to come. First, the relationship of work to social welfare under current social programs is examined, then some possible alternative approaches to these problems are explored.

Current Programs

The current social welfare system consists of three sets of cash programs, each with a distinctive set of eligibilities, benefits, and recipients. Because work experience (including reasons for not working) and market income are among the primary eligibility standards for these programs, the shifts in these factors that have been described can be expected to have important effects on the system in the future.

The largest set of programs are the social insurances: Old-Age, Survivors', and Disability Insurance and Unemployment Insurance.[19] Eligibility for these programs is tied to work history, and benefits are based on previous contributions. These programs are funded through payroll taxes and have federal trust funds. In 1983, 24.7 million individuals collected retirement benefits, 3.9 million disability benefits, 7.3 million survivors' benefits, and 2.3 million unemployment benefits.

The second tier of the welfare system is the categorical means-tested programs: Supplemental Security Income and Aid to Families with Dependent Children. SSI is a means-tested program for the aged and disabled. It is federally funded and usually federally administered. Some states provide a supplement to federal payments. In 1983 the federal government spent $8.7 billion and state governments $2.1 billion on benefits for approximately 4 million recipients. AFDC is a state and locally administered program partially funded through a federal grant-in-aid. In 1983 approximately 10.8 million individuals received benefits under this program.

Trends in the benefit levels of SSI and AFDC have diverged in the past decade. SSI is indexed for inflation, which has protected the real value of the benefits. By contrast, by the mid-1980s average AFDC benefits—when corrected for inflation—were 35 percent lower than they had been fifteen years earlier.

The final tier of the cash support system is general assistance. This term refers to a set of state programs for those in financial need who are not covered by other programs. Although thirty-seven states and the District of Columbia have general assistance programs, of the 1.3 million recipients in September 1983, 78 percent came from six states—Illinois, Indiana, Michigan, New York, Ohio, and Pennsylvania.

These programs vary widely in coverage, benefit levels, and effectiveness. For example, in 1984 average monthly benefits under OASDI were over $400, while those under SSI were $219 and those for AFDC recipients were $107. In addition, many states, including Pennsylvania, have programs that exclude the "able-bodied" from the general assistance rolls.

As currently constructed, the social welfare system covers some of the major risks of industrial society—retirement, disability of wage-earners, and unemployment. In addition, other groups that are cut off from the workforce—mothers with dependent children, the disabled, and the aged poor—have programs that provide poverty-level support. The "able-bodied" unemployed and those without eligibility for other programs can turn to state general assistance. The working poor have no substantial cash programs on which to rely.[20]

How will the movement toward a postindustrial economy affect this system? Perhaps the most important impact is on the social insurances. As noted, eligibility and benefit levels of existing social insurance programs are based on an individual's work history. The adequacy of coverage under Old-Age, Survivors', Disability, or Unemployment Insurance is a function of the consistency of one's career. The disruptions experienced by today's workers will therefore be multiplied when they are in need of these benefits.

Retirement benefits, for example, are computed on an indexed average of monthly earnings (AIME) with the five lowest years of earnings disregarded. Work history disruptions that lead to lower annual earnings will reduce benefits at retirement or in case of disability. This impact is multiplied in the case of families because the benefits of survivors and dependents are based on the worker's primary insurance. One particular threat in an unstable economy is to the older worker experiencing job disruption. This was a rapidly increasing share of the population during the 1970s. Between 1970 and 1983, for example, the proportion of men aged 60 to 61 who were out of the labor force increased from 17 to 30 percent, while the increase among those 55 to 59 years of age was from 10 to 20 percent.[21]

Workers in their fifties who lose their jobs and cannot find another face a decline in their AIME and their basic benefits as well as being forced to take early retirement, which reduces benefits by 20 percent. Thus, in one example, a worker who is unemployed at age fifty-nine, receives unemployment benefits for twenty-six weeks, and takes early retirement at age sixty-two will receive between ages sixty and sixty-four less than 30 percent of the income she or he would have had if remaining employed. Furthermore, after age sixty-five, the worker's public income would be more than 20 percent lower than what it would have been without the disruption.[22]

During the 1970s Disability Insurance was used to some extent by those forced to retire prematurely. It became a major support program for those under sixty-two years of age, the number of beneficiaries increasing from 2.6 to 4.8 million between 1970 and 1979. Roughly one in four of the disabled were over age fifty-five. Since 1980, however, a congressionally mandated disability review has resulted in a drop of 20 percent in the number of beneficiaries of this program. If this were to become permanent policy, another protection against the risks of future work patterns has been removed.

Finally, unemployment insurance with its basic twenty-six weeks of coverage is inadequate to deal with the longer periods of unemployment that have become common in American society. During the 1981–82 recession, the benefit-exhaustion rate (38.5 percent) and duration of benefits (17.5 weeks) hit postwar highs, while the percentage of unemployed covered by the system hit an all-time low. Indeed, in 1984, after two years of recovery, the ratio of average weekly benefits to average number of unemployed stood at 25.7 percent, down from 38.6 percent in 1980.

In summary, the social insurances reflect the impact of the increased disruption of the postindustrial economy. On the one hand, as a consequence of job displacement and the increase in part-time or part-year employment, the proportion of the labor force that is eligible for some programs, particularly disability and unemployment insurance, will decline, leaving a large number of workers with no coverage. On the other hand, as a result of less consistent work histories, the level of benefits for some strata of the workforce are likely to decline. For some groups— the aged and disabled— eligibility for SSI will cushion their reduced benefits. For others, including surviving mothers and their children, the impact will be more profound.

The effect of more economic stress on public assistance programs is harder to assess. It is likely that SSI will become an increasingly important part of the income-security system for a variety of reasons. First, declines in eligibility under Old-Age and Disability Insurance will increase the number of disabled and aged for whom SSI is a primary income-support program. Second, because of work-history disruptions, there will be a likely increase in the number of OAI and DI recipients who also are eligible for SSI. Finally, the increase in displaced and unemployed older workers is likely to increase those who seek to establish disability claims as a means of supporting themselves.

The recent history of SSI supports these conclusions. Among the aged, for example, the number of SSI recipients fell from 2.3 million in 1975 to 1.5 million in 1983. However, in the last several years these numbers have stopped declining. Among the disabled, the number of DI recipients has declined from a peak of 2.9 million in 1978 to 2.6 million in 1984, but the number receiving SSI has continued to grow from 1.3 million in 1974 to 2.2 million in 1978 to 2.6 million in December 1985.

Although SSI may face substantial increases in the years to come, AFDC will probably continue to stagnate or decline. The program recorded no increase in number of recipients between 1971 and 1984 and the real value of average benefits has declined substantially. In addition, the number of women between the ages of eighteen to twenty-four will fall from 14 million in 1985 to 12.5 million in 1990 and 11.8 million in 2000. In the absence of major changes in eligibility, it is unlikely that AFDC will see any major increases in the years to come.

If high unemployment persists, the decreasing effectiveness of unemployment compensation will increase the number of "able-bodied" poor. However, given state welfare policies, this increase in demand for general assistance is unlikely to lead to actual expansion of these programs. Rather, the growth of a stratum of adults without homes, incomes, or entitlements is likely to become an important element of the future contours of poverty.

Finally, postindustrial work patterns will lead to the growth of the working poor. The part-time, part-year worker, the low-wage service worker, and the employed female householder all have greater likelihoods of falling into this group. Between 1978 and 1984 alone, the number of prime working-age individuals who worked but were still poor increased by more than 60 percent, reaching 7 million, of whom 2 million worked full time for the full-year, and these trends are likely to continue.

If the social welfare system does not change, the shifts now occurring in the labor force will have major impacts on the well-being of Americans in the years ahead. Although most of those covered by the social insurances will do well, there will be increased poverty among those who have to rely on public assistance and those without any coverage at all. Among men, these trends will be exacerbated by their withdrawal from the labor force; among women, increased labor force participation will partially offset the increase in the risk of poverty. Overall, however, the future prospects are anything but heartening.

The implications of these shifts for race are hard to assess. Blacks and Hispanics are less likely to be covered by social insurance and—when they are covered—collect lower benefits under these programs. As these programs' effectiveness declines for the population as a whole in the years ahead, the effect is likely to be felt disproportionately by blacks and Hispanics. For public assistance the growth of SSI is likely to increase the proportion of recipients who are white, leading to a convergence of the races here. In other words, social insurance is likely to become the preserve of a smaller, better-off, white constituency in the years ahead, while public assistance becomes larger and multiracial.

Alternative Approaches

The preceding section reviewed the impact of likely changes in organization of work on the existing social welfare system. As with the "current-services budget," this assumption provides a useful baseline for assessing the ways in which economic change will affect the major programs of the welfare state.

The welfare reform agenda of the next decades must include programs for those who are currently poorly covered and those who are not covered. Three groups, in particular, warrant increased attention: female householders and their children, the working poor, and the long-term unemployed.

Poor female householders have been the most visible of the new poor in the past few years. Charles Murray has argued that the increase in their number is the result of the welfare system, while Mickey Kaus in a 1986 article claimed, less directly, that the welfare system provides an "umbilical cord" that allows the number of unmarried mothers to grow. The policy goal of Murray and Kaus is clear—to uproot the "culture" of the underclass by reducing cash-payments that render this lifestyle profitable.[23]

The data on these families calls into question the breadth of the "underclass" prescription. Rather than standing out as increasingly deviant, the female householder is becoming more like the nonpoor female householder. She is working more, staying at home less, and generally facing an increasing risk of poverty whatever her work status. Indeed, it seems likely that if AFDC had retained the real value of its benefits and if the set-aside (the provision that enabled workers on AFDC to retain a part of their earnings as a work incentive) had not been reduced, the poverty rate and share of the poor in this group would have declined sharply during the past eleven years.

By 1973 there was a consensus that AFDC was a seriously flawed program. Benefits varied widely by states; it favored family break-ups because of state restrictions on its two-parent component, AFDC-UP; and the high "tax" that it imposed on earnings discouraged work. Since 1973 none of these conditions have gotten better, and in addition, benefits have dropped sharply. Today's welfare reform movement, even though it is little more than the resuscitation of the welfare reform agenda of the early 1970s, would greatly aid this group.

One alternative would be simply to cover women and dependent children under SSI. In one stroke, this would increase benefits, protect against inflation, and ensure uniform standards. This—combined with work incentives, including training and job opportunities—would produce a more humane and effective program than the current one.

The biggest economic impediment to improving public assistance is the increase in the number of poor workers. Cash assistance has always been defined in terms of "less eligibility," the concept that the highest welfare payment should be lower than the wage of the lowest-paid job. The proliferation of low-wage work presents a bigger and bigger block to real welfare reform. Indeed, an early indication of this problem was the failure of President Carter's Better Jobs and Incomes Program; even in the 1970s the cost of supplementing workers' wages to keep them higher than welfare was too great. Today the growth of the working poor and near-poor makes the problem even more intractable.

The solution to the problem of the working poor lies in a combination of labor and welfare policy. Labor policy, including increases in the minimum wage (which is currently at its lowest level since 1955), mandated fringe benefits for low-wage and part-time workers, and easing the task of organizing these groups, would all rely on the private economy to reduce poverty. The positive results of this strategy would be twofold. First, welfare benefits could be raised without creating a severe work disincentive for these workers. Second, the direct costs to government of aiding the working poor would not be greatly increased.[24]

On the negative side, of course, would be the argument that increases in the minimum wage might lead to a decrease in employment. The tradeoff between fewer working poor and fewer jobs is one of the central problems of modern political economy. According to Isaac Shapiro, the evidence that a higher minimum wage actually decreases employment is relatively weak. Although the 1977 Minimum Wage Study Commission estimated that a 10 percent increase in the minimum wage would reduce youth employment opportunities by 1 percent, the effect on adult employment was weaker. Indeed, although some studies do suggest that the minimum wage decreases employment growth, others find no such effect. With the rapid decline in the number of teenagers in the population (the same trend that should reduce the AFDC rolls), the argument in favor of a low minimum wage is losing some of the credibility it has enjoyed in recent years.[25]

Finally, the victims of long-term unemployment and job displacement present the most severe challenge to the social welfare system. These individuals now must face periods of prolonged "resource depletion" as they spend their savings, sell their homes, and give up their possessions before they can qualify for public assistance. The increased incidence of this experience testifies to the lack of adaptation of the current welfare state to a new set of realities.

One solution to the problems of this group is to reform current social insurance programs. There is no magical reason why unemployment insurance should last only twenty-six weeks; lengthening the period of coverage would serve to reduce benefit-exhaustion rates and increase the proportion of the unemployed covered. The long-term impact of unemployment on OASDI benefits could be accommodated by relatively small changes in the current benefit and eligibility formulas. They are presently designed to give a better return on contribution to those with the lowest wages. Minor liberalization of these formulas would prevent severe deterioration in the protection the programs afford to most workers.

The real challenge posed by long-term unemployment is to formulate policies that allow displaced workers to reenter the job market. Among the alternative approaches to this problem are increased job-training programs, increased public employment, and the development of individual training accounts, similar to IRAs, that would allow workers to prepare for the possibility of job disruption.

To conclude, a postindustrial welfare state could develop in a number of directions. The traditional public assistance programs may attract an increasing proportion of the population in the future but would primarily need to have eligibilities extended and benefit-levels increased. To prevent the increased impoverishment of the long-term unemployed, broadened unemployment compensation and new job-training and job-creation programs would be necessary. Finally, the problems of the working poor could be addressed through a combination of labor policy meant to raise their compensation and supplementary programs.

Political Prospects

The proposal for reform and expansion of the welfare system comes at a moment when the public debate is dominated by calls for a restriction of government operations and a diminution of government's role in the economy. From a broader historical standpoint, the possibilities for change may not be as slim as they might appear. First, there is little in this agenda that has not at some point in the past been a politically viable proposal. Second, recent trends in politics suggest that in post-Reagan America the prospects for some welfare expansion will not be slim.

The growth of the welfare state between 1935 and 1980 was the result of two powerful political forces: the New Deal coalition and the development of an administrative bureaucracy with a commitment to steady expansion of welfare programs. After 1968 both of these forces lost much of their power, setting the stage for the reverses of the 1980s. The political and social history of the 1980s, however, suggests that these shifts will be more a deviation than a permanent change of course.

The social welfare setbacks brought about by the Reagan administration were a long time in coming. They were spawned by the economic squeeze experienced by workers, as inflation and taxes took a larger share of their earnings. This was fed by the breakdown in electoral and administrative coalitions that was examined in chapter 7 and the emergence of issues—racial antagonism, the expansion of defense spending, and budget crises—that changed the direction and mood of the politics of welfare.

The past six years suggest that many of the trends that affected welfare politics may have been reversed. First, the drift of public opinion appears to have altered. As Ferguson and Rodgers noted during the 1980s there has been a decline in the support for a defense build-up and increased interest in the expansion of social spending to reduce poverty, increase jobs, and improve education.[26]

Second, the cuts in social welfare spending have been less than expected during the Reagan presidency. Although many programs were cut significantly by the Omnibus Budget Reconciliation Act of 1981, the president has been unable to achieve any major victories in reducing social welfare spending since then. In 1983 the federal government spent $96 billion more on social welfare than it did in 1980. Gramm-Rudman-Hollings and the president's stand on tax increases will put increased pressure on social spending in the next several years, but it is not clear that they will have a long-term effect.

In this respect, it is important to remember that compared to other advanced societies, the United States still spends relatively little on social welfare, even after the expansion of the 1970s. Indeed, by 1984 the United States was spending a smaller proportion of its gross national product on social welfare than in any year since the early 1970s. The evidence from international comparisons supports the view that the United States certainly can afford an expanded welfare state.[27]

Third, there has been a reassertion of internal control over social welfare policy making. During the first two years of the administration, there was a real broadening of the significant players in the social welfare arena, with conservatives grabbing an increased share of attention. However, the resolution of the Social Security crisis in 1982–83 was accompanied by the return to prominence of more traditional constituencies. In 1981 the Social Security debate was highlighted by White House domestic advisor Peter Ferrara's plan to scrap Social Security for voluntary pensions; by 1983, after intensive political fighting, former Social Security Commissioner Robert Ball was leading the move to depoliticize the issue through a modest program of increased taxes and delays in cost-of-living adjustments. The resolution of the Social Security crisis suggests that more orthodox patterns of welfare politics have returned to the federal government.

Finally, and most central to this book, the changing demography of poverty in the United States suggests that the bitter racial and gender divisions that have undermined progressive politics in the past decade may be waning. The image of a well-off and secure white working class and an impoverished black underclass that framed the racial disputes of the late 1970s and early 1980s is giving way. The population in need of assistance— while still disproportionately black, Hispanic and female—is becoming more white and male as the job market changes.

The convergence of the economic status of blacks and whites does not guarantee a convergence in their political perspectives. Indeed, the history of the South suggests that the struggle of poor whites and poor blacks can generate a vicious form of racial antagonism. Nevertheless, the economic trends pose the real possibility of a common agenda of welfare and labor market reforms that would cross race and gender boundaries.

In the coming years, workers will need new forms of protection against the threats of low wages, irregular hours, and job displacement. It is true that the working poor and displaced will remain disproportionately black, Hispanic, and female, but these problems will touch all workers, whatever their race, gender, or family structure. Although these issues have yet to push their way onto the current political agenda, they will not go away.

More than at any time in U.S. history, the problem of poverty is tied to the workplace. Women, including female householders, are working more than they ever have. The reason they are poor stems from an economy that is unable to provide them with enough work and high enough wages to escape poverty. At the same time, men—both black and white—are facing an increasing risk of falling among the working poor and near-poor. The emergence of postindustrialization calls for a new look at the U.S. response to need. The answer lies in the emergence of a set of innovations: reforms of unemployment compensation, a commitment to job training, and an exploration of public employment. The potential recipients of the future are not a narrow stratum of young men and women who have turned to lives of criminality, teenage motherhood, or drugs, but a broad cross-section of the population, experiencing the problems of part-time work, extended periods of unemployment, and the challenge of job dislocation.

In 1980, after years of welfare expansion, high inflation, and slow economic growth, the public was ready to believe that large social welfare expenditures sapped money from "productive" activity and needed to be cut. By the late 1980s Americans have seen that neglect of public welfare can itself be part of the productivity problem. One of the heartening aspects of the current welfare reform debate, indeed, is the recognition that government must take responsibility for allowing all citizens to become productive members of our society.

The current debate has remained too narrow in its definition of productivity, a point that was noted in chapter 3. Although the private economy is a powerful contributor to U.S. national wealth, all labor, not just that in the private labor market, contributes to the well-being of this country. The nurturing of children, caretaking of the elderly, participation in community development, and action to improve the physical and emotional health of one's neighbors all add to well-being in the fullest sense of that term. If the private economy is unable to provide for needs in these areas or to make use of the human resources that are available, the public sector will again be called on to do so.

Notes

1. *New York Times*, 2 August 1987.
2. "House Panel, Badly Split, Clears Welfare Bill," *New York Times*, 11 June 1987.
3. "Child Support at Heart of Welfare Plan," *Philadelphia Inquirer*, 20 July 1987.
4. The *New York Times* reported that the president claimed that his program put 76,000 people into private enterprise jobs. According to a 1976 study, however, the

program did not "achieve any of its impact objectives" and only two-tenths of 1 percent of adult recipients in the thirty-five counties covered by the study participated in the program. *New York Times,* 13 April 1986.

5. Martin Anderson, *Welfare: The Political Economy of Welfare Reform in the United States* (Stanford, Calif.: Hoover Institution, 1978).

6. Ibid., 153.

7. For the impact of OBRA on recipients, see Tom Joe and Cheryl Rodgers, *By the Few, For the Few: The Reagan Welfare Legacy* (Lexington, Mass.: Lexington Books, 1986). Indeed, in an early statement of the administration's social welfare philosophy, Anderson identified five fundamental elements: (1) the primacy of a sound economy; (2) fair, but limited, eligibility standards; (3) reduction in waste and fraud; (4) return of power to states and localities; and (5) strong opposition to a guaranteed income. Martin Anderson, "The Objectives of the Reagan Administration's Social Welfare Policy," in *The Social Contract Revisited: Aims and Outcomes of President Reagan's Social Welfare Policy,* edited by D. Lee Bawden (Washington, D.C.: Urban Institute, 1984), 15–27.

8. Charles Murray, *Losing Ground: American Social Policy 1950–1980* (New York: Basic Books, 1984).

9. Anderson, *Welfare,* 15. It is worth noting that this passage echoed the "truly needy" terminology that dominated the Reagan administration's justification of its early cuts in welfare.

10. Murray, *Losing Ground,* 9.

11. Ibid., 212, 216.

12. Ibid., 227–28.

13. See, for example, Rino Patti *et al.* "Gaining Perspective on *Losing Ground*" (New York: Silberman Foundation, 1987).

14. Julie Kosterlitz, "Reexamining Welfare," *National Journal* 6 December, 1986): 2926.

15. U.S. General Accounting Office, "Work and Welfare: Current AFDC Work Programs and Implications for Federal Policy" (Washington, D.C.: General Accounting Office, 1987).

16. Ibid., 122–23.

17. Neal R. Peirce, "Governors' Breakthrough on Welfare Reform," *National Journal* 14 March 1987): 637.

18. Isaac Shapiro, "No Escape: The Minimum Wage and Poverty" (Washington, D.C.: Center for Budget and Policy Priorities, 1987), 7–10.

19. The health programs, Medicare, Medicaid, and veterans' programs are excluded from this discussion. Although they provide great benefits to recipients and constitute a substantial share of social welfare expenditures (in 1983, of the $399 billion spent by the federal government on social welfare, $57 billion were spent on Medicare, $19 billion on Medicaid, and $8 billion on veterans' health and medical programs), most of these payments went directly to vendors. Given the problems in estimating their "value," they constitute a study in themselves.

20. The working poors' social welfare eligibility is confined to a few inkind programs—food stamps and low-income energy assistance—and the earned-income tax credit for those with families. The new income tax law, by widening the

zero-bracket and increasing the earned-income tax credit, provided additional tax-relief to this group.

21. Virginia P. Reno and Daniel N. Price, "Relationship between Retirement, Disability, and Unemployment Insurance Programs: The U.S. Experience," *Social Security Bulletin* 48 (5) (May 1985): 34–35.

22. For details of example, see Mark J. Stern and June Axinn, "Inequality and the Post-Industrial Welfare State," a paper delivered at the annual meetings of the Society for the Study of Social Problems, August 1986.

23. Mickey Kaus, "The Work-Ethic State," *New Republic* (7 July 1986).

24. According to the Center on Budget and Policy Priorities, in 1978 a family with one wage-earner making the minimum wage fell $1,150 below the poverty line. Seven years later, the gap had widened to more than $4,000. Nor is minimum-wage employment a minor part of the labor force. According to the Labor Department, 4.1 million workers were paid the minimum wage and another 1.8 million (not covered by legislation) were paid less than the minimum wage. "The Working Poor," unpublished factsheet.

25. Shapiro, *No Escape*, 14–16; *Report of the Minimum Wage Study Commission*, vol. 1 (Washington, D.C.: Government Printing Office, 1981), 38; Gary Solon, "The Minimum Wage and Teenage Employment: A Reanalysis with Attention to Serial Correlation and Seasonality," *Journal of Human Resources* (Spring 1985): 292–97; Fred Block, "Rethinking the Political Economy of the Welfare State," unpublished ms. 1986.

26. "On federal aid to cities, those [voters] preferring cuts in military spending to cuts in the programs grew from 41 percent to 54 percent between 1981 and 1984; for federal aid to education, from 60 percent to 71 percent; for federal health programs, from 58 percent to 67 percent. For unemployment compensation, they grew from 46 percent to 70 percent over 1981–82 alone." Thomas Ferguson and Joel Rogers, *Right Turn: The Decline of the Democrats and the Future of American Politics* (New York: Hill and Wang, 1986) 21, see also Fay Lomax Cook, Ernesto Constantino, Rick Adamek, and Susan Popkin, "Catalog of Social Welfare Questions Asked in National Surveys, 1935–1984," unpublished paper, April 1985.

27. "Social Security and the Economy," *Social Security Bulletin, Annual Statistical Bulletin* (1986): 66.

Index

About the Authors

June Axinn is professor of social welfare at the University of Pennsylvania School of Social Work. She received her doctorate in economics from the University of Pennsylvania. The coauthor of *Social Welfare: A History of the American Response to Need* and *The Century of the Child,* her articles on family policy, Social Security, poverty, and aging have appeared in a wide variety of books and journals, including *Social Work, Milbank Memorial Fund Quarterly/Health and Society, The History of Education Quarterly,* and *The Family Coordinator.* She is book review editor of *Administration in Social Work* and on the editorial board of a number of leading journals in the field. During 1987–88 she is a visiting professor of economics at Temple University Japan and is doing research on aging in the Far East.

Mark J. Stern is associate professor of social welfare and history at the University of Pennsylvania School of Social Work. He received his Ph.D. in 1980 from York University. He is author of *Society and Family Strategy: Erie County, New York 1850–1920* and (with Michael B. Katz and Michael J. Doucet) *The Social Organization of Early Industrial Capitalism.* His articles have appeared in *Social Service Review, Social Work, Journal of Social History, American Quarterly,* and many other journals. During the 1987–88 academic year, he is Fulbright lecturer at the American Studies Center, Shanghai International Studies University in the People's Republic of China.